THE ART OF
ROCK
PAINTING

LEARN TO PAINT
FUN DESIGNS AND DOODLES

SCOTT BULLOCK

STERLING INNOVATION
New York

STERLING INNOVATION
New York

An Imprint of Sterling Publishing
1166 Avenue of the Americas
New York, NY 10036

book design by Gavin Motnyk

photo credits:
Paints: © Antonsov85/Shutterstock
Brushes: © Umkehrer/Shutterstock

ISBN 978-1-4351-6011-8

This book is part of *The Art of Rock Painting* kit and is not to be sold separately.

For information about custom editions, special sales, and premium and corporate purchases, please contact Sterling Special Sales at 800-805-5489 or specialsales@sterlingpublishing.com.

Manufactured in China

LOT # 4 6 8 10 9 7 5 3

www.sterlingpublishing.com

CONTENTS

AN INTRODUCTION TO ROCK PAINTING

Welcome to the world of rock painting, an easy and fun way to express yourself creatively. For the first-time painter, it is a simple way to gain an understanding of how to use the various tools and media without the usual pressure associated with traditional approaches. It's also a great way to learn how to let your imagination run free and create something uniquely yours. Unlike most regular painting surfaces, such as paper or canvas, the shape of the rock often lends itself to the image you create. Imagine a rounded, oval rock with a turtle or frog painted on it!

Rock painting can be as simple or complex as you want it to be. You can paint anything on your rocks, such as flowers, bugs, animals, sports themes, interesting patterns, portraits, or words. Paint letters on your rocks and use them to spell out a word or message. You can even use them to create game pieces to play chess, checkers or tic-tac-toe. Stack them in fun ways; place a frog rock on top of another rock painted with a lily pad. If you can imagine it, you can make it real.

It doesn't matter if you've never drawn or painted before. There is no right or wrong way to paint rocks. The best part is, if you make a mistake or don't like what you've created, you can just paint over it and start fresh with a new idea. As with anything, practice makes perfect so the more you do it, the better you'll get. In this book, we'll go over how to set up to paint, tools to use, and review a step-by-step guide for completing a design. You'll be painting like a pro in no time!

Just as you have limitless options of what to paint on your rock, so it is with what you can do with them when they're completed. They make great display decorations. Painted rocks work inside, but also outside in flowerpots or along a garden's edge or path. They also make great gifts. Why not share your art with friends and family?

GETTING STARTED

Let's get started by first familiarizing yourself with your kit. You should have an assortment of rocks, a variety of acrylic paints, and a fine tipped brush.

SUPPLIES

You won't need much to delve into this fun hobby!

Rocks

The rocks in the kit are cleaned and ready for you to begin painting on them. Should you acquire new rocks, be sure they are thoroughly washed (to rid them of dirt and debris) and dried with a towel. They should be completely dry prior to working on the surface.

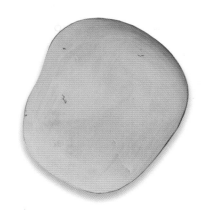

Acrylic Paint

Acrylic paint is an opaque, water-based paint with a quick dry time. It's perfect for painting on rocks and allows for a variety of different approaches. A good palette of colors should have at least the primary colors—red, blue, and yellow—as well as white and black. You can use these to mix almost any color, but a trip to the local arts and crafts store will give you a broader selection of colors without having to mix your own. You may even find fluorescence, glow in the dark, or metallic colors that would be fun to use. One of the best parts of acrylic paint is you only need water to clean your brushes or thin the paint.

Clear Acrylic Glaze

Clear acrylic glaze provides a number of uses. You can add a little color to the clear glaze to make strong, thin washes of color as well as use it to protect your finished works upon completion. In particular, you'll want to do this for all rocks that will be displayed outside as additional protection from the weather. A little glaze goes a long way so experiment to find the amount that best suits your needs.

TOOLS AND TECHNIQUES

Anyone can create beautiful painted rocks using the following tools and techniques.

Acrylic Brushes

There are a variety of types and sizes when it comes to acrylic brushes. Everyone has their own preference, and it will be up to you to experiment and find the ones you like. The brush that comes with your kit is perfect to get started, but if you'd like to add more, we'd recommend a #12 flat or filbert for basing out rocks or covering large areas quickly; #4 and #2 round for filling in smaller areas and general painting; and a #0 or smaller round for fine detail work. You can choose to go with either a natural or synthetic brush fiber.

Find a clear, flat work surface with good light. Before starting, place newspaper or plastic on your surface to protect it from unexpected spills.

Styrofoam Plates

Styrofoam plates or plastic egg cartons are perfect for mixing paints. Avoid using paper plates to mix paints. The paper will absorb the water from the paint and cause it to dry. It could also make it more difficult to smoothly mix colors.

You will need a small plastic cup, plastic food storage container, or a large bowl of clean water to clean brushes or to thin paint. The larger the container the less frequently you'll need to change the water. When the water gets dirty, replace it with clean water so you don't muddy your colors. *Always* wash and dry your brushes thoroughly after working with them. Never leave your brushes soaking in your container when you are finished painting. This will damage the handle and curl the bristles. Good brush maintenance will keep them in shape for years to come.

Paper Towels

Paper towels will come in handy to dry your freshly washed rocks and to dry your brushes after washing them.

Pencil

Keep a pencil on hand to sketch your designs on the rocks but also to jot down ideas and sketches for future projects.

Sketch Pad

Always have a sketchpad or scrap paper on hand so you can work out ideas, refine your designs, or just practice drawing.

Utility Blade

A utility blade is a great tool for scratching out small areas and fine detail from your rocks.

You can use other tools and media beyond what we recommend here to experiment and achieve different effects. Regular household items you can use include toothpicks for fine detail, cellulose or sea sponges for different textured backgrounds, or cloth rags for lifting paint. You can also cut your own stencils.

STEP-BY-STEP INSTRUCTIONS

LEARN TO PAINT A BUTTERFLY

1 Select a rock with a fairly flat surface. Wash and towel dry the rock if it's dirty. Once it's dry, base the rock out in white. It may take several coats for solid coverage. We'd recommend a larger brush for faster coverage, but a small one will work just fine, too.

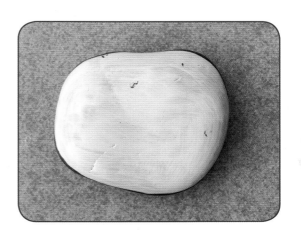

2 Using your pencil, sketch the butterfly on your rock. Try to fill as much of the surface as possible with the image, but leave a little space around the edges for your background color.

3 Paint the background a pale blue. For pale blue, use approximately ten parts white paint, three parts blue, and one part yellow. Take your time and come right up to the edge of your drawing. Several coats may be required and you'll want to use the small brush to ensure that you can get around tight spaces.

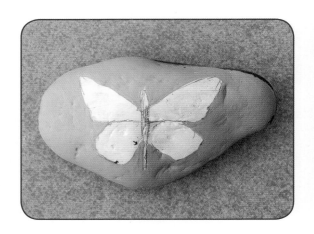

4 To create orange, mix equal parts red and yellow. Start at the top and fill in the wings. Add a little more yellow to the orange as you get closer to the bottom of the wings to give them a nice transition.

5 Add the black line work. By adding a little water to your black, your lines will flow more easily. For line consistency, be sure to frequently recharge your brush with paint. Finish by adding a few white highlights. Let dry and enjoy.

GALLERY OF DESIGN IDEAS

LEAF

For this design, try using spray paint instead of applying the colors with a paintbrush. Use a real leaf as a stencil instead of doing the line work yourself.

TREE

Use two different colors for your base to create a more colorful design. Be sure to blend the colors to avoid hard lines.

BEETLE

Although this design seems difficult, it is possible to re-create if you are patient and build your image slowly by adding one color at a time.

HUMMINGBIRD

Simple line work that varies in thickness can make an image come to life.

MULTI-HUED STONE

Thin your paint so it is almost the consistency of water. Then use an eyedropper to apply and let it drip and drizzle over the rock.

MANDALA

Choose a larger, flat rock and start painting from the center and move outward. Vary straight and curved lines for a more dynamic design.

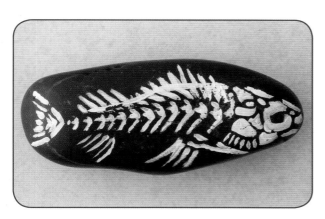

BONE FISH

After your design dries, use a utility knife to slowly and carefully remove excess paint to make some bones thinner.

LOVE

Add a three-dimensional feel to your design by using glue and a fine material—like glitter or fake train grass—that can be sprinkled on top of the rock.

STYLIZED FLOWER

Use "puff paint" to create texture in your design. Practice squeezing the paint out of the tube before applying it to your rock.

FEATHER

Sometimes fine line work can be difficult with a brush. Don't be afraid to use other tools, like a toothpick or pin, to apply your paint.

SQUID

Gold leaf is a difficult material to work with, but with practice and patience you can add luster and richness to your image.

FISH

Rather than using puffy paint over your base, apply the puffy paint and then paint over it to emphasize the texture.

SPIRAL

Use highly contrasting colors in order to emphasize the shape or texture of the rock. Use more than two colors to diminish this effect.

WOODSY OWL

For designs like this one, use a reference picture. Practice drawing your subject with pencil and paper before you start painting.

SIMPLE DAISY

It's okay to use permanent marker to apply the initial line work. Be careful, however, because it is difficult to correct mistakes.

BOTANICAL

Don't be afraid to create complete scenes, like this garden. It's best to keep it simple.

FREEFORM

Once you are feeling more confident with your brush, try painting on the rock without sketching first and let the design emerge as you go. Use your imagination!

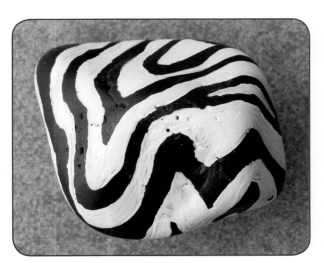

ZEBRA STRIPES

Nature provides ideas for many different textures and patterns. Animal prints are easy, fun, and make for interesting and recognizable designs.

COW SPOTS

Use a fine brush to paint the background instead of painting the shapes. The painting, left, shows white lines are painted on a black background.

HEART

Colors will be more vibrant with a white base instead of black. More than one coat of white will be necessary for a solid background.

WOLF

You can create an image using negative space. Rather than painting the wolf, paint the background and let the figure emerge.

SKULL

Applying a very thin wash of paint over an already completed design can add a weathered or aged feel to your rock.

BIRD

Adding small elements around the main object can balance the design and create a more pleasing image or give the rock some depth.

MULTI-COLOR DESIGN

Finish your rock with a topcoat (like glaze) to make the colors more vibrant and provide a layer of protection.

PRETTY POLKA DOT

This is a simple design, but with multiple rocks and different colors, they make a striking display when arranged together.

BICYCLE

You don't have to fill the entire surface of the rock. Sometimes a small element with a black background can have a greater impact.

ABSTRACT

For something quick and easy, try using gold or silver paint markers. Make sure you shake the pens well before using.

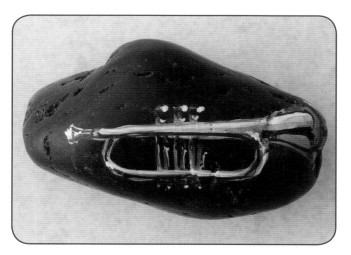

TRUMPET

This works well alone, but it is also fun to paint a different instrument on separate rocks to create your own "band."

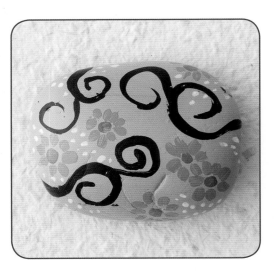

FLORAL SWIRLS

Don't be afraid to mix elements, such as traditional flowers in an otherwise abstract design that includes line work or blocks of color.

YIN AND YANG

Your design can convey a feeling, philosophy, or idea and represent a well-known symbol like this yin and yang.

FLEUR-DE-LIS

You can create an interesting design by layering different techniques and media. Look around your household and experiment!

HAPPY FISH

The shape of the rock can give you an idea for subject matter, or you can look for a rock that fits your idea.

TEXT AS THE IMAGE

It can be fun to use rocks to convey messages to your friends and family. Keep it simple and easy to read.

ROSE

Use different angles on organic subject matter to get creative and add an element of mystery. You don't always have to worry about realism.

DOG

Use a photo to help you create a portrait of your pet.

BEE

To add an extra dimension of depth, create a cast shadow by blending a small amount of black paint to the color of your background.

ABOUT THE ARTIST

Scott Bullock was born in 1967 and grew up in rural South Carolina. As a child, he spent much of his time writing stories and then illustrating them with his own drawings. As a young adult, he moved to Chicago to study art, where he developed a fascination for the play of rich colors, tight detail, and hidden meaning of art. Now living in New Orleans, he playfully creates his art mostly through experimentation. Rather than having a preconceived notion of his creations, he takes an idea, nurtures it as he creates, and allows it to grow until the meaning of the work finds its way out. You can see more of Scott's work at ScottBullock.net.

THE CAVE PAINTINGS
OF BAJA CALIFORNIA

The Great Murals of an Unknown People

Written and Photographed by
HARRY CROSBY

Other Illustrations by
Joanne Haskell Crosby

A COPLEY BOOK

Commissioned by
HELEN K. COPLEY

Edited by
RICHARD F. POURADE

PREVIOUS COPLEY BOOKS

The Explorers, 1960
Time of the Bells, 1961
The Silver Dons, 1963
The Glory Years, 1964
Gold in the Sun, 1965
Ancient Hunters of the Far West, 1966
The Rising Tide, 1967
The Call to California, 1968
Historic Ranchos of San Diego, 1969
Rex Brandt's San Diego, 1969
Marines of the Margarita, 1970
The Sign of the Eagle, 1970
The Colorful Butterfield Overland Stage, 1971
Anza Conquers the Desert, 1971
From Fingers to Finger Bowls, 1972
Our Historic Desert, 1973
The King's Highway in Baja California, 1974

Library of Congress Cataloging in Publication Data

Crosby, Harry, 1926-
 The Cave Paintings of Baja California.

 Sequel to The King's Highway in Baja California.
 Bibliography: p.
 1. Indians of Mexico--Baja California--Antiquities.
2. Rock paintings--Mexico--Baja California. 3. Petro-glyphs--Baja California. 4. Baja California--Antiquities.
I. Title
F1219. 1. B3C76   972'. 2'00497   75-18265
ISBN 0-913938-16-7

DEDICATION

The Cave Paintings of Baja California
is dedicated to man's enduring quest to
give meaning to what he sees and feels.

HELEN K. COPLEY

CONTENTS

THE LAND OF THE CAVES — BOCA DE SAN JULIO

A Foreword

S lowly the curtain is being lifted on the story of man's past in this hemisphere.

The Cave Paintings of Baja California is the first detailed report on a chapter that has long been neglected by historians, archaeologists and artists.

It is a tantalizing disclosure of a sweeping panorama of Great Murals executed by an unknown people in a land which barely has been penetrated by modern man.

Baja California is truly a "last frontier." A new paved road barely touches its hidden areas which still hold the secrets of time.

The Cave Paintings of Baja California is a sequel to The King's Highway in Baja California published by Copley Books in 1974 and represents six years of study and many excursions by muleback into regions hardly known to descendants of the original White settlers of mission times.

In The King's Highway in Baja California, the original El Camino Real — the road of the Jesuit padres of almost three centuries ago — is traced the length of Baja California, and actually traversed for the first time in a hundred years.

The Cave Paintings of Baja California reaches back beyond the natives who were there when the first Europeans arrived, to a people with surprising artistic ability who painted Great Murals on rock walls that match and often excel those which have been found in prehistoric European caves.

The author calls them simply "The Painters."

Most of the paleolithic people of North America engaged in some sort of rock art, creating a vast reservoir of carvings, paintings and engravings.

But the Cave Paintings of Baja California seem to have no relation to other prehistoric art of the Southwest. Neither do they seem to have any relation to the curious rock alignments of intricate design, running hundreds of feet in length, which are found atop gravel mesas in the lower Colorado Desert — pictures only for the gods in the skies.

Perhaps The Painters were a different people. Perhaps they descended from a different migration from Asia. Archaeology is just beginning to grasp how many waves there have been and how far back they reach in time.

The legends of natives occupying the peninsula when the Europeans arrived, and vague reports of ancient burials, refer to them upon occasion as "The Giants." Some cave wall handprints suggest a small people.

That is all that anybody really knows about them as a people. Where they came from, and what happened to them, is lost in antiquity. But this book lifts the curtain on proof of a prolific existence, and the paintings that they have left behind them are becoming a treasure of Mexico.

RICHARD F. POURADE

A Chance Introduction

In the sierras of central Baja California, hidden by a most forbidding terrain, thousands of brilliant paintings survive in caves and shelters. Here a prehistoric people created giant images, assemblages of heroic men and animals. Their time passed, they laid down their brushes and disappeared, their art was lost to sight and their existence was reduced to the breath of a legend. On these pages the Painters reappear. With their own works they make a place in our consciousness. Their isolation in time and space is done and a lost fragment of our being is returned.

ON THE TRAIL OF THE CAVES — LA ANGOSTURA DE SAN JUAN

On a slope about a mile north of Rancho La Candelaria, some twenty-five miles southeast of San Ignacio, is a mammoth boulder which had dislodged from a nearby mountain and rolled to a stop. Where the north side of this fifty-foot monster turns under there is a series of Indian paintings in shades of ochre, brown and red. Several years ago I was guided to the spot. It was my first encounter with rock art in Baja California.

The subjects, as I recall, were various animals and birds. Most of the paintings were rather small and had been damaged by water seepage and rock deterioration. Two, however, caught my eye because of their greater size and the artistic skill with which they had been executed. One was a deer with a full set of antlers and the other a mountain sheep with the characteristically curved and swollen horns. The pair were side by side, done in the same maroon paint and apparently by the same hand; each was about four feet in length. I photographed them and put the matter rather in the back of my mind. There things rested for several years.

Today, as I re-inspect these photographs, I am surprised at my original nonchalance. The paintings are intrinsically beautiful and, to the best of my knowledge, have not to this moment been reported or published. Yet in those days I was consciously exploring; I was making maps and following trails and trying to collect all sorts of data on the country. Why was I so unimpressed by an encounter with prehistoric art?

I suppose the answer is contained in certain constants of human behavior. The more important we hold a thing to be, the more difficult we find the concept that it is not already well studied or well known. I have had a love of paintings all my life. I have studied the history of cave art and in earlier years I visited Lascaux, Altamira and other celebrated paleolithic sites in Europe. I was enthralled by the stories of their discovery

and, I am sure, envious of those who first found these treasures of ancient art. Why then my total failure to comprehend the significance of what I saw at La Candelaria?

During the time of my first interest in Baja California I was surprised and delighted by Erle Stanley Gardner's discovery of giant painted figures in the central part of the peninsula. Photographs showed art works of a scope that could be called murals in every sense of the word, the great murals of prehistoric Baja California. Gardner's story was spectacular; the works were found by the use of helicopters flying into the farthest recesses of the remotest mountains. I envied Gardner his personal Altamira. I had heard also that an archaeologist, Dr. Clement Meighan, had accompanied Gardner and written a thorough study of his findings. Further reading had revealed that at least some of the large rock paintings had been known since mission times. I also learned that a French naturalist named Leon Diguet had visited dozens of such sites in 1894 and written a monograph on the subject. Those bits of knowledge must have conditioned my response. I simply supposed that the world of science had been alerted and that the phenomenon had been well studied. Further, La Candelaria was on a dirt auto road, and a local rancher directed me to the paintings. I assumed that he had showed them to others and that they were widely known.

In the early spring of 1971 I was determined to explore the Sierra de San Francisco north of San Ignacio. Rock art was only one of many things that I had on my mind. Most specifically, I was scouting for data on the isolated and old-fashioned people of the mountains. I planned to photograph significant aspects of their culture and to record folklore, oral history and anecdotes. To this end I hired Eustasio "Tacho" Arce as a guide. The man had been born in the sierra, had a fine personal reputation and was held to know the country better than any other. It was to prove a fateful decision.

The itinerary and details of that trip are not important here. We rode the mountain trails for nearly two weeks and visited a dozen ranches. I got my pictures and a great deal of information. It was a pleasant and rewarding time, and the last ranch on our itinerary seemed to cap the climax.

Rancho San Gregorio lay in an oven of an arroyo on the northeast corner of the sierra, the gulf side. Here, some forty years before, Loreto Arce Aguilar founded a ranch based on a small but permanent spring. Tacho, as a very young man, got his first job from Loreto and he labored at transporting supplies and building materials the forty miles or so from San Ignacio or Santa Rosalía to the ranch. When we rode in, Loreto and his family made us very welcome and I had an especially satisfying time with photography, interviewing, and eavesdropping on conversations between the old friends. The place itself was very compelling, with charming buildings and impressive groves spectacularly set in a narrow gorge. These, as well as the tidy condition in which all was kept, set it apart as the best of the places we had visited. After two nights and a day we sat at breakfast just before we would leave.

Tacho, however, was not quite satisfied to go. He and I had discussed paintings several times. We had even looked at a couple of minor specimens along the way. Here, he remembered, were others and he suggested a short detour to inspect them. Nothing about his manner implied anything out of the ordinary, and the works we had seen previously were certainly not exciting. I weighed the probable loss of half a day and decided, on reflection, not to miss the experience. "After all," I remember thinking, "you will never come back all this way to San Gregorio."

Tacho led up the canyon a few hundred yards and pointed up the steep west bank. There, perhaps two hundred feet above us was an unremarkable cave fairly long but apparently only a few feet high. The rock face over the cave was stained in shades of red-brown and gray. As we toiled up a precipitous trail our view was hampered by the hillside brush and piles of fallen or tumbled rock. As a result we were very close before we got our first real look at the place. Surprise is an inadequate word for my reaction.

Over the slit-like opening of a long shallow cave was a vast expanse of fairly smooth rock surface. On that was painted a tumultuous cavalcade of human and animal figures far greater than life size. All the beasts seemed to press forward in movement from right to left; huge red and black deer and an equally immense red mountain sheep dominated the surge. The figures were all executed in a strange sort of partial superimposition that gave a powerful sense of motion. Each animal seemed to be in mad flight treading on the heels of those ahead and straining to free himself from the crush behind. Scattered among the creatures of this bustling frieze were a variety of strangely static humans. Whereas the hurrying animals moved in profile across the stony canvas, the men faced us, frozen into identical erect postures with their arms upraised.

I was astonished and overwhelmed. The impact of that vast canvas is impossible to describe. Travel in Baja California certainly had conditioned me to expect Indian remains, to study them and appreciate their significance. But until that moment I think it is fair to say that none had had an emotional impact. I admit to viewing *metates* and arrow heads and trails and rock circles as mute and rather sad reminders of what is irrecoverably lost. This flamboyant painted scene at San Gregorio had no such content. Here the work of artists blazed defiantly across the ages as living speech. Nothing I had encountered before so put me in the presence of a supposedly unknowable people. Unconsciously I began to think of them as the Painters in the same spirit that the Basketmakers of the American Southwest were named for their most characteristic artifacts.

I was seized by a particularly powerful impression. The great mural seemed entirely out of place. I realized as I stared up at it that I was carried back to paleolithic Europe. The art simply did not resemble anything I knew from the Americas and it did indeed match in many ways that on the walls of Lascaux. It is true that the large static human figures with their classic proportions have never been found in the Ice Age art, but neither did they match the fantastic or grotesque man-figures common in New World rock art. But the animals; they indeed harked back to ancient times in every way. I found myself entertaining and rejecting wild associations. How could such resemblances be coincidental? How could any influence be felt across such spans of time and space?

The rest of my visit was curiously anticlimactic. Tacho soon pointed out that the entire inner roof of the cave was decorated as well. We got down on our knees and inspected the work. It was all beautifully executed in smaller animal figures. There were marvelous rabbits, birds, deer and a snake as well as indeterminate beasts

and others so overpainted as to be indecipherable. The riches were immense but nothing for the moment could compete with the impact of the first impressions which I had received. I finally stopped pouring over it all and made pictures.

Then followed a dream-like sequence of events. Tacho led the way over a hill to another cave with other marvels. I remember a ten-foot whale and a brace of *borrego* but it was really too much to take in after the other. I walked back to the ranch in a daze.

The morning was gone and Loreto Arce insisted that we stay for lunch. I welcomed the offer as an opportunity to find out more about the paintings. We sat in the shaded porch of San Gregorio and our host threw more dry wood on the flames of my excitement. There were, he assured me, many more such works in the area and no one from the outside, Mexican or American, had ever visited any of them.

Those words rang in my thoughts day and night as we rode back toward San Ignacio. After a day of agonizing I made up my mind not to ride away with so many unanswered questions. If Loreto had reported facts, a gold mine of lost art waited to be found and photographed. If he exaggerated, all I could lose was time. As soon as I told Tacho my decision I felt immensely relieved. We turned back into the sierra and, despite the fatigue of two weeks on the trail, there was a fresh sense of adventure in the air.

That evening I poured out my thoughts to Tacho, and I asked his frank opinion. What did he suppose that we might discover? Tacho was very honest about his knowledge. His experiences in the sierra were largely during the years of his youth. Since, he had married and worked in a number of lowland ranches, some well away from the sierra. He recalled the men who in the time of his youth had known the caves well. Most of them were dead; he was unsure of the knowledge possessed by their sons. From his own memories only a few specific places stood out, one in particular which he had not seen in thirty years. We could go to that and I could evaluate it and thus Tacho's memory and judgment. On that note we set out.

After a rugged crossing of the sierra's heights we began a descent into the upper reaches of Arroyo El Batequi. The *cuesta* had not been used for years and was heavily overgrown. We

SAN GREGORIO I

In 1971 a rancher in a remote part of the Baja California peninsula directed the author to this impressive painted cave and told him that he was the first outsider to see it. At first the exciting discovery seemed only a happy accident, a once-in-a-lifetime stroke of fortune. But there were stories of more unvisited paintings in the mountains and the decision was made to explore the substance of at least one such rumor. The trail led to El Batequi.

6

EL BATEQUI

The author inspects the painting whose discovery set him firmly on the trail of the prehistoric Painters of central Baja California. After making the two major finds illustrated on these pages he became convinced that the Sierra de San Francisco concealed a treasury of primitive art. The hunt was on.

were tired and scratched by the time we finally reached the relative tranquility of the arroyo's rocky bed. We rode gratefully down to the west in the warm sun.

Late in the afternoon we came to the place remembered by Tacho, a large overhung cliff high on the northwest side of the arroyo. After the day we had had, I suppose it would have made sense to wait for morning before climbing up, but I was too keyed up to face a night of uncertainty. Tacho understood. We unloaded our worn out mules and burros and the two of us crossed the wash and started up the steep slope. I will admit that I was tired and the little climb to the cave seemed like a major undertaking, but, by laboriously putting one foot in front of the other, I finally got up to the cave level. Tacho had missed his mark just a little and we were too far north, so we made our way along the top of the slope inspecting the walls above us for signs of paintings. The first string of overhung places was completely blank. Then we came around a corner and found ourselves standing in front of our objective.

The painted place of El Batequi consisted of a vertical back wall, twelve to sixteen feet in height, overhung by a short ceiling with a huge cliff jutting out above. The wall was made of a soft, fine-grained rock in a pale beige tone. Both wall and ceiling were unusually flat and smooth.

My first glance at the back wall revealed that it had been heavily painted. There were vestiges of all sorts of handsomely delineated men and animals. Alas, vestiges, and nothing more. I hurried down the long wall and searched for a truly surviving picture. There was none. Without any resort to exaggerated sentiment, I know that was one of the greatest disappointments I have ever experienced. The daydream that had begun at San Gregorio came crashing down and I stood there dog-tired and bitterly disappointed. All around me was irrefutable evidence of a great center of primitive art; only enough of the substance survived to show the magnitude of the loss. The tragedy far transcended the dashing of my personal hopes.

The cause of the terrible deterioration was not difficult to determine. That beautiful smooth rock, waiting like a ready-stretched canvas, had another and tragic quality. Exposure to normal atmospheric conditions apparently caused the binder in that sandy stone to weaken, and, thus

weakened, it gradually shed its particles a grain at a time. Exposure to rough weather seems to have played a small part in the destruction at El Batequi. The overhang was almost a perfect barrier against rain, even when wildly wind-blown, yet the highest and most sheltered places were nearly as badly deteriorated as those most exposed.

As I wandered around in low spirits, Tacho went ahead around another corner. He returned and said that there was a similar display next door. Around I went, and the wounds were opened all over again. There was an even longer gallery, with an even more inviting wall. On it I made out the familiar sad remains of fantastic men and graceful animals.

I glanced at the ceiling. A miracle! There above me was the most beautiful rock art I had seen in Baja California. In that instant I was overwhelmed with emotions: admiration and thanksgiving. I looked for the cause of the survival. The back wall with its lost art was of the same soft rock as the shelter I had just left, but the ceiling was of another somewhat different stuff. The contact between the two was exactly at the line between wall and ceiling. That ceiling rock was not perfect by any means; it had sloughed off enough fine surface material to weaken the colors painted on it. It also displayed thousands of tiny pits. But the important thing was that that ceiling material had just enough structural integrity to support a great painting and bring it down through time. The gift seemed magnified in a place where so much had been lost.

I stood dazzled, it was several minutes before I looked around. In front of me on my right was a loose pile of large stone chunks. They had fallen from a natural column which divided this gallery from the other. The painted ceiling was about fifteen feet above the floor of the shelter for most of its length, and then, at the far end, curved down to nearly meet the floor. The entire length was covered with an incredible cavalcade of animals and men.

Surprise and delight mounted as I walked the length of the area looking at the work overhead. I went through stages of realizing the quality and significance of what I was seeing. At first I was attracted to the artistry and finesse of a grouping of deer at the right end of the procession. That for me had the air of a highly stylized, sophisticated form of primitive art. Then I was impressed by the power and motion of great dark animals at the left end which were in quite a different style.

At last, after I had examined the mural figure by figure, it dawned on me that unity and composition were its greatest glories. It was clearly not the work of a single artist; that was demonstrated by different styles and techniques. It was certainly the product of many generations. Some of the figures were much, much older, and in places the work displayed four or five layers of superimposed painting. The wonder was that all the artists who contributed the animal figures sensed an urge to preserve the movement of the herd. All but a few trivial exceptions ran from left to right in one long sweep.

The human figures seemed curiously detached. Even though some were deeply entangled in the confused overpainting, they stood apart in spirit: no sense of participation emanated from them. The combined effect of the active and static was powerful. The inexorable force of the galloping beasts was countered by the inertia of the men. This impression was heightened by an unusual device used in depicting several of the human figures. They were painted from the front as usual, but the vertical division was made so that the darker half of each one looked like a man in profile facing the deer. Thus the flow of the herd appeared to be encountered by several men with arms up-raised as if to halt the procession. Whether intended or not, the device undeniably added tension to the scene. All the man-figures so treated seem to be from the hand of one artist. The technique used to create the combined head-on and profile effect is very unusual and may even prove to be unique.

Gradually my first shock from the encounter at El Batequi wore off and was replaced by a proud and proprietorial mood; now I had the acute desire to share the experience. In those moments I knew the loneliness of private art collectors and I understood why so many donate their treasures to society. When the sun was setting and Tacho went down the hill to ready the animals, I was still pacing back and forth under that great cavalcade as if I were trying to commit every detail to memory.

Finally I turned away and stumbled down the slope. We rode quietly in the dusk to Rancho Batequi where there were water and pasture for our animals. That night our camp was under a wide spreading *mezquite*. I placed my sleeping bag in a natural garden of handsome plants with lush green foliage. As the moon rose, large trumpet-shaped flowers of the purest white opened all around me and the air was filled with heavy perfume. It was the wild Datura which the Indians called *toloache* and used as a drug to create the dreams of their rituals. Somehow it seemed ordained to be so. I spent a fitful night haunted by the beauty around me and by what I had seen that day.

Once again, as at San Gregorio, I was overwhelmed by the sense of a people, a living culture, expressing itself to me in powerful terms. In my mind those silent arroyos once again echoed with voices. I pictured the caves alive with people practicing the many skills that put the Great Murals on the walls. I imagined paint making and scaffold building before the artists could begin, and then the processes of sketching and painting. I wondered what special people the actual Painters might have been. Priests? And was the painting or its completion accompanied by ceremony? Were these places visited by all of the tribe, were they chapels in a sense? Or were they hidden places where medicine men worked out the tribal destiny alone with their own magic?

Over and over during that night I opened my eyes and the unblinking moon would bring me back to a quiet and empty arroyo. But not even the light of morning could completely break the spell. All around me at dawn were still the white faces and fragrance of *toloache* and a sense of the powerful reality of what was painted a short distance away.

Despite that climax, the trip continued and, before its momentous three weeks were done, I had visited all the great sites previously reported by Diguet, Gardner and Meighan and more new ones as well. But nothing really changed the conviction and the resolve that gripped me under the Great Mural of El Batequi.

That experience really ends this introduction as it ended a brief phase of my life. I no longer had the slightest doubt about what I was going to do. If Tacho could produce such a place from a thirty-year-old memory, I knew that there must be other men and other memories.

RISTIN CROSBY DECKER

EL BATEQUI

Among the Great Murals this grand cavalcade uniquely gives the sense of being an organized composition. Even the overpainting does minimal damage to the design and helps to create the sense of a herd pressing strongly across the stage of some ancient tableau. The implicit cooperation between successive generations of artists would be impressive in any context but it is astounding among the Painters whose hallmark was the artistically destructive practice of overpainting without regard to the size, color, line or flow of previous works. Most of the Painters' hoofed animals show a curious four-digit pattern which gives their feet almost the appearance of hands. This photograph of the hoof of a peninsular mule deer shows the reason. The Painters not only depicted the cloven hoof but also the dewlap claws splayed to the sides so as to appear in the outline. This spatial rotation of anatomy is consistent with their treatment of human feet and women's breasts.

The First to Find Them

California began as a geographic myth, an insular place on the right hand of the Indies. Then it became the line of misty peaks which scarred the sunsets as the Conquistadors looked west. In the mid-Eighteenth Century, California still meant only the peninsula and many thought of that as an island. Two or three Jesuit missionaries, toiling in this most rocky of vineyards, made surprising finds of ancient art. During two centuries their little-known accomplishment was augmented at long intervals by the efforts of a French chemist and an American writer of detective fiction. This oddly-assorted group carries the flag, beats the drum and sounds the fife for a slowly gathering parade back to the places and times of the Painters.

During the last thirty years of the seventeenth century, the university city of Bologna, Italy, was the seat of a strange little colony of frustrated men. The Jesuit Expulsions of the 1760's had retired most non-Spanish missionaries of that order to their homelands, but Spain and all her possessions were barred to them. Those of Spanish extraction were placed under papal care and were largely concentrated at Bologna. These had recently been the most active of men, the shakers and movers along the frontiers of Catholic Christianity. Their new idleness must have been a trial, coupled as it was with little hope for any return to the labors in which their lives had been immersed. One of the many crosses they had to bear in their banishment was an almost total ignorance among Europeans about the lands in which they had worked. The California group was especially incensed. The only available account of their missionary field was by a Jesuit who had never seen the peninsula. The compiler, Miguel Venegas, had worked from the reports and letters of missionaries who had served on the ground, but he had not been content with an editor's role. Venegas' text was filled with his own narrow judgments and with insertions which were intended to defend and fortify the Jesuit position. The published form of Venegas' already second-hand account was heavily edited and revised on its way into print. This work, now known as *Noticia de la California*, was widely popular and was soon translated into several languages. The resulting spread of misinformation and half-truths distressed the few men who knew California.

The unusual circumstances have proved a boon to peninsular history; under ordinary conditions these people would not have been so aware of the poor material in circulation and its impact, nor would they have had time to reflect and act against it. Now, in exile, such objections were possible. Johann Jakob Baegert and Benno Ducrue published works of reaction in Germany.

At Bologna, another of them, the Spaniard Miguel del Barco, planned an ambitious tome of "corrections and additions" to the Venegas text. This huge work, several hundred handwritten pages, was destined to have a curious history. Another Bologna exile, Francisco Clavijero, a young Mexican who had not served in California, was nevertheless an intimate of that group. He was intelligent and literate, participated in years of discussions and reminiscences and eventually wrote a book, *The Story of California*. His work drew heavily on that of Miguel del Barco but it had the graceful form of a complete text whereas the old missionary's writing was an earnest set of point by point refutations and clarifications. Clavijero was published in 1785 and his work became a standard history for nearly two centuries. Del Barco's manuscript, which never had a public airing, was shelved and virtually lost even to scholarship. Finally in 1972 the Mexican historian, Miguel Leon-Portilla, published an annotated copy as *Historia Natural y Crónica de la Antigua California*. What a treasure it is! Del Barco proves to have been an admirable reporter, thorough, observant, and amazingly unbiased. With one stroke, the reappearance of his text virtually doubles our firsthand knowledge of early historic California. Here are lengthy accounts of missionary labors, Indian languages, legends, customs, dress, and crafts; a virtual ethnography focussing on the mid-peninsula where most of the Bologna expatriates had worked. In it also we find our first concrete references to the Great Murals.

Apparently, during the Bologna years, the Indians' own beliefs and prehistory were discussed and there must have been much interest in a persistent legend about giants on the peninsula. Oddly, it was in this connection that cave painting came into Miguel del Barco's book. For a written account, he turned to one of the group who had been an eyewitness. Joseph Mariano Rothea, the missionary at San Ignacio from late 1759 until the expulsion in 1768, responded to del Barco's request with a few priceless paragraphs. Thanks to the survival of del Barco's manuscript we have Rothea's historic account "copied," as del Barco assures us, "to the letter ... without any alteration."

The propositions that probably argue that there were giants in California can be reduced to three. First, the bones that are encountered in various places. Second, the painted caves, and third, the general belief of the elders.

(Rothea here offers an extended account of digging up giant human bones near the *visita* of San Joaquin, then he returns to the matter of our direct interest.)

... I happened to investigate several painted caves but I will only talk about one which is the most noteworthy. This one would be about 30 to 35 feet long and about 16 feet wide. Its form was like half a vault that rested on a pavement of the same material. From top to bottom it was all painted with various figures of men, women, and animals. The men had loose shirts with sleeves; beyond this a greatcoat and breeches but no shoes. They had their hands open and somewhat raised with extended arms. Among the women was one with loose hair arranged on the head and a dress of a native Mexican type called *huipil*. The paintings of the animals represented all those now known in the land, like deer, jack rabbits, etc., and others now unknown like the wolf and the pig. The colors were the same that are found in the volcanos of the Tres Virgenes: green, black, yellow and flesh-colored. The durability of these colors seemed notable to me; being there on the exposed rock in the inclemencies of sun and water where they are no doubt struck by rain, strong wind or water that filters through these same rocks from the hill above, with all this, after much time, they remain highly visible.

Finally, with these preliminaries, I gathered the oldest Indians of the mission to ascertain what information they had among them relating to this legend about giants. I asked that the same be done at the missions of Guadalupe and Santa Rosalía whose missionaries then were Father Benno Ducrue at the first, and Father Francisco Escalante at the second. And, as I remember, there chanced the coincidence that this said inquiry was made, or one of them at least, on the same day that I carried it out with my people.

All agreed in essence, it was known that from fathers to sons the knowledge had passed that, in very ancient times, there had come from the north a group of men and women of extraordinary stature; they came fleeing from one another. Part of them directed their course along the coast of the Southern Sea, and of these, they told me, are still seen the wraps that they fashioned and that are like those that the present Californians use, but very large by comparison. I was not able to investigate with my own eyes these memories which are the only things that remain of these first people. The other part of them directed their course to the rugged portion of the sierra, and they are the authors of said paintings. In truth, those that I saw are convincing because, without scaffolds or other implements suitable for the purpose, only giant men would have been able to paint at so much height.

They told, lastly, that part of them (the giants) died at each others hands, and part also were killed by the self-same Californians (the tellers' ancestors) who would not tolerate such strange residents in their land.

Joseph Mariano Rothea

Miguel del Barco also gives us a second account in which he relates what was told to him by Padre Francisco Escalante.

The missionary at Santa Rosalía (de Mulegé) says that, among his Indians survives the same knowledge of giants that came from a place in the north, who painted, in the territory of his mission, a cave which the same missionary went to see and which is almost as large as the other of the mission at San Ignacio (i.e., the one described by Rothea above). This one is about 35 feet long, sixteen feet or more wide and sixteen high with little difference (from Rothea's cave); this one is not in the form of a vault but rather of a flat ceiling formed of one (layer of) rock thick and strong enough to support a high mountain. This flat ceiling is painted and full of figures now of animals and now of men armed with bows and arrows representing the hunts of the Indians. These paintings are well preserved, clear and perceivable, not withstanding being on the naked rock without other preparation, and that in wet times and in fogs the air of the cave cannot help but be damp. Apart from this, he says that it is untutored painting, that it is very far from the niceties of this art. Nevertheless, he gives us to understand that its authors had more application, more talent and more understanding than the (present) natives of that country.

Some salient points emerge in these accounts. The Cochimí, the people of the missions involved, had widely known legends which dissociated them and their ancestors from the Painters, and the paintings were already impressively old, at least in the missionaries' opinion. As far as the actual belief in giants was concerned, we can remain skeptical. There is no need to doubt Rothea's discovery of huge bones; such individuals are encountered here and there all over the world. Del Barco, in fact, had his own doubts expressed directly after the Rothea quotation.

Like the rumor, the more it is spread, the more things are magnified. The memory which remained of the stature of these giants, communicated from father to son in the passage of many centuries (though we do not know how many, nor is it possible to ascertain among the Indians), this memory, I say, has grown to the point that the people of this land say that the giants were so large that, when they painted the ceiling of a cave, they lay on the backs on the ground and that even thus they were able to paint the highest part. An enormous fable that, for its verification would necessitate those men to have a height of at least thirty feet, unless we imagine extremely long paint brushes in their hands! Beside, even if they said that, standing on the floor of the cave, they painted the highest parts of it, it seems difficult to believe. It is simpler to persuade oneself that, for this work, they found and conveyed to the cave, or caves, some wood with which to form a scaffold, which, with the little height that it could have, was enough that the giants could have painted comfortably, nor for this did they lack sufficient wood. What is certain is that these pictures represented clothed people and animals that were not found in California. One can well believe that their creators were not natives of that land but came to it from other regions.

Not long after this activity in Bologna, the talented Spanish Viceroy of New Spain, Conde Revilla Gigedo, requested the formation of a thorough collection of documents relative to discoveries and missionary activity in the area for which he was responsible. In 1792 a compilation was ready and it contained a considerable natural history of Baja California which has been traced tentatively to the Jesuit Juan Bautista Mugazábal who died in 1761. If the attribution is correct, this work contains the oldest known reference to rock art on the peninsula, if not to Great Murals specifically.

In all of civilized California, from south to north, and particularly in the caves and smooth cliffs, rustic paintings can be seen. Notwithstanding their disproportion and lack of art, there can be easily distinguished the likenesses of men, fish, bows and arrows, and diversely assembled lines in the fashion of written characters. The colors of these paintings are four: yellow, red, green and black. The majority of the images are painted in very high places, and from this, some infer that there is truth in the constant tradition of giants among the ancient Californians. Be that as it may, at the Mission of Santiago, which is located in the south, there is exposed to view on a very high, smooth cliff a series of stamped red hands. In the tall boulders near the beach, fish of different shapes and sizes, bows and arrows, and some obscure characters can be seen. In other places, there are Indians armed with bows and arrows, and at their feet various species of insects, snakes and mice, with lines and characters of a different form.

It has been impossible to ascertain what these figures, lines and characters mean, despite extensive questioning of the California Indians. The only thing which has been determined from what they say, is that they are from their ancestors, and that they have absolutely no knowledge of their significance. One could infer from the paintings and lines of the Californios that they are symbols and meaningful signals with which they attempted to leave a memory for posterity or of their settlement in that place, or of some wars or other political or natural events. These paintings are not like the (mainland) Mexican ones, but must have been (independently) developed.

Several interesting items emerge from this entry. It is more general geographically than those cited above. It seems to show a knowledge of the Great Murals but it focusses more sharply and accurately on smaller works which are common in the mentioned Santiago area near the cape. Red hands, fish and "diversely assembled lines" are characteristic of that region. The casual reference to the giant legend suggests that its association with rock painting was very widespread among missionaries and presumably among the natives.

After the decade of del Barco, Clavijero and the Revilla Gigedo collection, nearly a century passed without any notice of peninsular rock art. This long dry spell was broken when, in 1882 and 1883, a Dutch physician, Herman Frederik Carel Ten Kate, pursued his interest in anthropology with a long journey through the American Southwest and northern Mexico. He visited the Cape Region of Baja California, dug up ancient burials, collected artifacts and noted a few rock paintings. He soon published several accounts of these activities.

Meanwhile in the mid-peninsula some events occurred which were soon to affect the history of the Great Murals. A citizen of Santa Agueda, José Rosas Villavicencio, discovered copper deposits near what is now Santa Rosalía. After some small scale efforts showed the magnitude of the find, a French corporation financed by Rothschild banking interests acquired all the pertinent mining claims. By negotiated agreement with the Díaz regime of Mexico, the corporation, which was popularly known as El Boleo, also got virtual control of two thousand square miles of adjacent territory and, tacitly at least, the people within it.

By 1889 the concern had installed and manned mines and mills and created the company town of Santa Rosalía. Among the personnel imported for this enterprise was a French industrial chemist named Leon Diguet. Diguet, born in Le Havre in 1859, seems to have taken a broad interest in the region's naturalism. He knew Ten Kate's published papers and they may have served as a basis for his inquiries. At any rate, during his three-year stint with the company, he explored and collected in the area, and on his return to France in 1892 he was able to give extensive collections to the Museum of Natural History and the Museum of Man in Paris.

The quality of these collections and Diguet's enthusiasm attracted attention and shortly afterward he was authorized and financed to lead an expedition to collect and observe in Baja California. This proved to be only the beginning of a series of five such ventures in various parts of Mexico.

The Baja California exploration of 1893-94 appears to have produced most of his contacts with rock art and is the basis of his important paper, "Notes on the Pictographs of Baja California" (1895), which has recently been published in English. Diguet's work and especially this article and its photographs and drawings entitle him to be considered the first student of the Great Murals. Through him the outstanding sites of San Borjitas, San Juan and Cuesta Palmarito were disclosed to the world and, indeed, the whole phenomenon was rediscovered. Despite extended travels, however, it is noteworthy that Diguet managed to visit only a fraction of the sites now known to exist and he missed the greatest concentration altogether, a complex of exquisitely painted caves and shelters in the heart of the Sierra de San Francisco. This first *aficionado* was quite aware of the problems that kept him from even greater discoveries. The final words of his 1895 paper are eloquent to this point and, incidentally, almost as true today as when they were penned. "The inhabitants of the villages and towns often only know them through hearsay, and it is with difficulty that the ranchers of the interior are induced to direct a stranger to them."

After Diguet there was a hiatus of over fifty years before the Great Murals became a topic of remark or study again. In 1951 Barbro Dahlgren and Javier Romero came to San Borjitas cave under the aegis of Mexico's prestigious Instituto Nacional de Antropologia y Historia. Their findings were reported in a paper and illustrated in a 1954 issue of *Artes de Mexico*.

None of the discoveries or publications to that time, and they covered a period of nearly two hundred years, had made any impression on the larger world public. The next adventurer on the Great Mural horizon was to change all that. Beginning in the mid-1940's, Erle Stanley Gardner, the writer of detective stories, had made a hobby of Baja California exploration. His trips were recorded in a series of rambling adventure books and he developed a large coterie of friends and helpers for his elaborately mounted assaults on out-of-the-way terrain. He also met and befriended a number of the people from Baja California's formidable outback. Around 1960, one of them, José Rosas Villavicencio (a relative of the discoverer of the Boleo copper deposits) in-

16

formed Gardner of huge paintings near his childhood home in the Sierra de San Francisco. The mystery novelist was getting on in years but he had the enthusiasm and imagination as well as the financial resources required for an exploration of the sierra. He arranged for the use of helicopters and, with Villavicencio's help he was able in 1962 to visit the *pueblito* of San Francisco and a group of caves between the ranchos of Santa Teresa and San Nicolás in Arroyo San Pablo.

When Gardner saw the size and character of the artwork, he realized that he had uncovered a major archaeological site and that it would create a lot of interest in the outside world. To his everlasting credit, he used his influence and resources not only to publicize his find but also to study it. Very shortly after his first trip to the painted caves he was back with a qualified archaeologist, Dr. Clement Meighan of the University of California at Los Angeles.

The results of these two explorations have been reported by Gardner with a sensational spread in Life Magazine and in his book, *The Hidden Heart of Baja*, the latter in the unstructured, conversational, and highly subjective style of his other Baja California books. He depended on no research whatever and the book abounds in quaint and fanciful observations, interpretations and homemade myths. Dr. Meighan's report was another matter altogether. Appearing as a terse twenty pages in *American Antiquity* in 1966, his article, "Prehistoric Rock Paintings in Baja California," demonstrates admirably what a professional could accomplish on the basis of fieldwork carried out in three days at a site. The sheer volume of his collections and recorded data is exceedingly impressive, and here it is combined with thorough analysis and comparative observations made possible by the author's wide experience with Southwest Indian cultures. This paper and the slightly enlarged version appearing under the somewhat less satisfactory title, *Indian Art and History* in the Dawson Book Shop Travel Series, are the Great Murals' only serious study to date. The accomplishment inevitably invites regret that Dr. Meighan could not have followed with a thorough and definitive study, an effort which almost certainly would have solved many of the mysteries surrounding the Great Murals.

However, in the light of their past, it would almost seem appropriate that knowledge continues to be added in small and grudging increments. The process continues in the pages which follow.

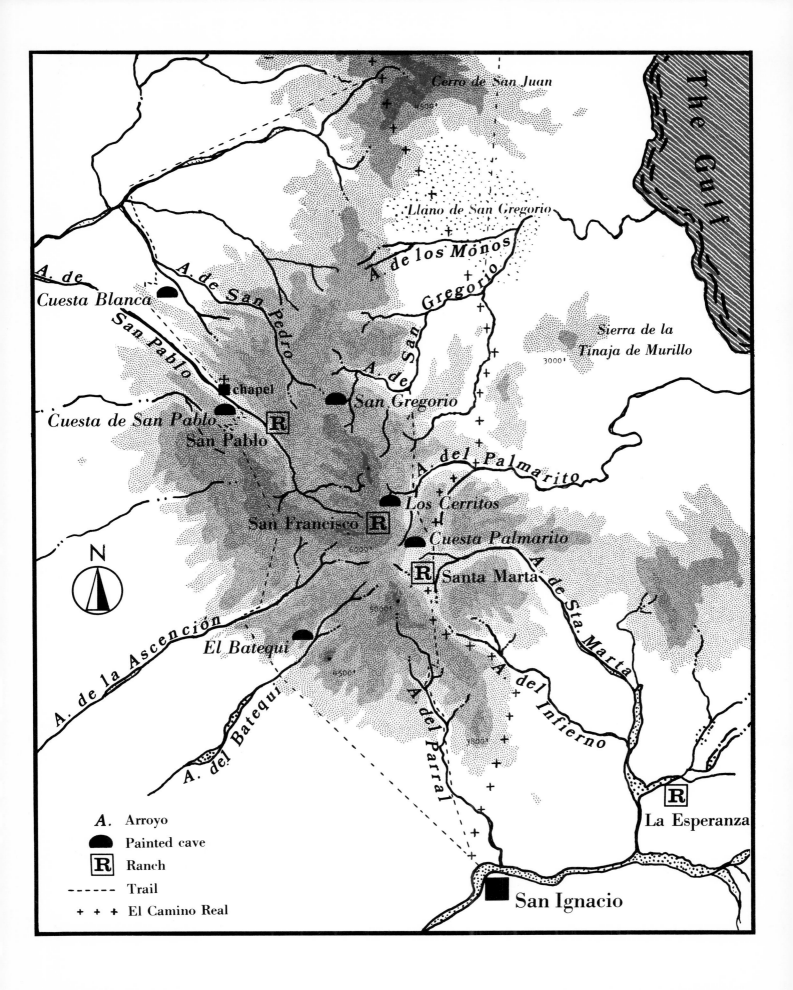

Cerro de San Juan

The Gulf

Llano de San Gregorio

A. de los Monos

A. de San Gregorio

A. de Cuesta Blanca

A. de San Pedro

San Pablo

Sierra de la
Tinaja de Murillo

3000'

chapel

Cuesta de San Pablo

San Pablo

San Gregorio

A. del Palmarito

Los Cerritos

San Francisco R

Cuesta Palmarito

Santa Marta

A. de la Ascención

A. de Sta. Marta

El Batequi

A. del Batequi

A. del Infierno

A. del Parral

La Esperanza

San Ignacio

A.   Arroyo

   Painted cave

R   Ranch

- - - - -   Trail

+ + +   El Camino Real

The Sierra de San Francisco

North of San Ignacio and south of the line which divides Baja California's states lies a mountain wilderness, the deeply eroded remains of large volcanic outpourings. This rugged mass rises from the surrounding desert to heights of more than five thousand feet and covers an area thirty miles from north to south and half of that from east to west. Its uplands command views west to Scammon's Lagoon and the Vizcaino Desert, and east to the abrupt eminences of the Tres Vírgenes volcanoes towering in front of the gulf. The sierra embraces a world that would never be suspected from the low, barren scape without. Groves of palms and pools of water are set between walls of vertical grandeur carved from rich-colored rock. A few ranches built by a simple and hospitable people nestle near the rare water sources. Here also are the grandest remains of the Painters, corridors decorated by their hands and haunted by their spirits.

Two centuries of recorded encounters and my own experiences had indicated that the Sierra de San Francisco was a gallery of ancient art. They also showed that the Painters had contrived to hide that art in a labyrinth that would have gladdened the heart of Minos of Crete. Thus far the efforts to find the lost works had been very haphazard and it stood to reason that the results must have represented only a fragment of the potential. The problems were complex; actually a number of factors quite beyond the actions of the Painters conspired to hide and guard their secrets.

The physical character of the terrain has obviously been the greatest single deterrent to anyone entering and knowing the Painters' realm. Though the area most involved is no more than three or four hundred square miles, the form which that area has taken is amazingly complex. It is not only an involved problem to know the land or find one's way about, but it is also a physically demanding terrain in the simple terms of getting from one place to another. Area is a poor measure of these difficulties. It does no good to think of this sierra as thirty-five miles long unless you are going to fly over it. On the ground the trails are forced into tortured horizontal and vertical courses which multiply the air line miles by some incalculable amount.

There are other matters. Water is scarce or absent in most parts of the sierra. And the complexity of the land form insures that no man approaches the accomplishment of knowing it all; each rancher knows his small part as it suits his needs. Further, these local people have little curiosity as far as Indian remains are concerned;

they are not a part of their cultural heritage. None of the aboriginal people persisted long enough to leave legends or impart a sense of spirits, magic or fervor. For the profoundly practical men of the mountains these works have always been useless artifacts found on every side and, since there has been little demand, the supply is largely uninventoried.

Once the decision was made to find the Painters' work, a system was needed, a *modus operandi* which would take advantage of local knowledge and avoid time-consuming repetition during what would obviously be a number of expeditions.

The key to all this was Tacho Arce. Here in one man was the master of all the trails and water supplies, the lore and skills surrounding the use of animals, and the friend or relative of every sierra family. The last was by far the most critical. In Tacho's company there were no closed doors, he was the key to the people and their memories.

The Arce name is perhaps the oldest in all the Californias. The progenitor here was Juan de Arce, reputed to have been of English birth, and certainly a presidial soldier who came to Loreto in 1698. Tacho's great-great grandfather, Buenaventura Arce, was the benevolent despot of the San Ignacio region, a man who claimed the first ranch titles from independent Mexico and who served from the 1820's to the 1870's as formal or informal *alcalde*, a sort of mayor-judge of the village and its environs.

Tacho was born in 1911 at Rancho San Francisco in the heart of the sierra. As a child he herded goats then grew to the estate of a boy capable of handling the mules and burros taking cheese down from the mountains and returning with supplies. As a young man he left the sierra for a long career as a *vaquero*, or cowboy, and a tenant cattle rancher. In time he helped to support his family by sharpening his considerable skills as a hunter, an asset which led to professional guiding of those who came after the trophy of a *borrego*, or bighorn sheep.

With Tacho's help a plan was evolved which would eventually take us to every corner of the sierra and involve most of its people in our search. We would use his ranch of La Esperanza, fifteen miles northeast of San Ignacio, as a headquarters. He would be notified of impending trips and would be responsible for acquiring an assistant and the needed animals and their gear. Our equipment and supplies were stored at his place and, between trips, he would collect information from his many friends as they passed on their way in and out of the mountains. In practice, his listening station was to provide clues that lay far beyond San Francisco, data that served to lead us to rock art sites as far afield as the regions of San Borja and Mulegé.

But all of this only implemented the basic idea which was to ride into the sierra, question all the ranchers of successive regions and follow up their suggestions. To date that enterprise has consumed parts of three years and has included six different expeditions into the Sierra de San Francisco alone. And while Tacho and his son Ramón have been nearly constant figures as

guides, I have been joined on different trips by various friends and family members. The first of these expeditions will serve to show how it went. For the rest, we will concentrate on the mountains, the caves, the paintings and the shadowy presence of the Painters.

THE ARROYO DEL PARRAL

The largest arroyo on the southern end of the Sierra de San Francisco is called El Parral. It was born on the southern slopes of Cerro Santa Marta, a five-thousand foot peak, and it carries its periodic floods out of the mountains and across the mesas to dump huge and tempestuous volumes into the arroyo of San Ignacio just east of the town. La Muralla, a three-mile long dike of rock and rubble, was erected in Jesuit times to keep the marauding floods of El Parral from devastating the vital fields and orchards of the mission. Since far earlier times this waterway has served as the principal avenue between the oasis of San Ignacio and the seasonal food resources of the uplands.

There was no inhabited ranch in the entire drainage of El Parral, indeed no one may ever have lived there for longer than a season. For information we went instead to San Lino on the north side of Arroyo San Ignacio to see Jorge Espinoza, a man nearing eighty. He and his father and his grandfather before them had run cattle in El Parral. Jorge did know the whereabouts of several paintings and he provided minute directions. His son, José María "Chato" Es-

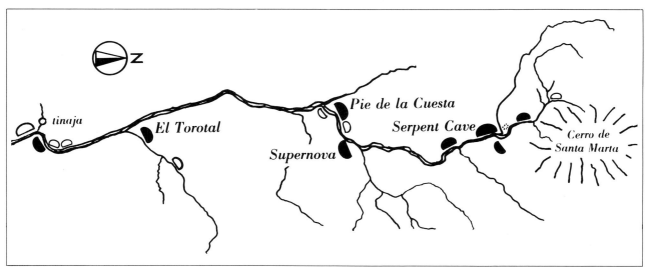

pinoza, could be of more direct help. He had guided a helicopter-borne Erle Stanley Gardner group to an outstanding site called The Serpent Cave. He could take us there and to many of the places his father knew. At San Lino also we picked up Tránsito Quintero an ancient mule skinner who could help Tacho. Thus informed and assisted we set out on the second day of November, 1972.

The trail climbed from the arroyo to the mesa by way of one of those steep zig-zag trails that are called *cuestas*. For a few moments from the rim there was a view back over the tops of thousands of date palms to the pueblo with its stately mission church. Then it was gone and we were alone on the mesa.

To the south the lost view was replaced at a greater distance by a misty profile of the Sierra de Guadalupe dropping down to Laguna San Ignacio and the Pacific. To the east rose the highest mountain in the region, the solitary volcanic form of Cerro de la Vírgen. To the west the phantom-like Picachos of Santa Clara pierced the morning fog that had ventured off the ocean overnight.

Attention, however, was soon riveted on the mountains ahead to the north and the trail which led into them, a scene dominated by two peaks. On the left and the more distant was the abrupt and jagged Cerro El Batequi; nearby on the right was the odd tooth-like picacho of Cerro Santiago. The foreground appeared to be one vast mesa gently sloping upward to blend with the foothills of the sierra.

Stretching ahead was a broad old trail which had the familiar character of a Jesuit road, surveyor-straight and carefully made. The builders must have laid it out about sixteen feet wide with stakes or string and then removed all the rock between the boundaries. The shifted stones were piled in neat rows as markers along either side.

The author of this construction may well have been Padre Fernando Consag who encouraged the chiefs of all his neophyte tribes to build roads which would connect their *rancherías*, or seasonal encampment areas, with Mission San Ignacio. At any rate the road continued into the arroyo, divided, and scaled two mighty passes to arrive at the mission ranches of Santa Marta and San Francisco.

The better stretches of this road imparted a strong presence of history and romance. Here was a great mesa, surprisingly green and blooming from recent rains. In every direction the wild and exotic character of Baja California was evident, and we could have felt like pioneers except that underfoot and as far ahead and behind as the eye could see, ran this incredible road. Despite the toll of time and the elements, it was so mighty a labor that it seemed to have become a permanent feature of the landscape. To test the sense of isolation, I stopped and got out my binoculars. It was true. No other trace of man's world was visible in any direction, not pole or wire, not ranch or town, not mine or mill. We were alone with the lively spirits of the old roadbuilders.

Our experience on the mesa ended as suddenly as it began. The great Arroyo del Parral curved up from the southeast, and at about that point headed due north toward its origin in the sierra. It had been cut perhaps a hundred feet below the mesa and was a broad sandy wash between vertical walls of lava. We came upon it quite abruptly, hidden as it was by the flatness of the mesa, and went down into it immediately by a well-made switchback *cuesta* probably as old as the road itself. What a change! After over two hours of open mesa with panoramic views of fifty miles or more, we were suddenly enclosed by towering red-rock walls. The boxed-in feeling was enhanced by windings of the arroyo; we were seldom able to see far ahead. We rode toward apparent walls which became turns as we drew near.

The contrast between my map and what we were experiencing was marked. The general plan of the sierra as seen from the air is roughly an ellipse with its axis running southeast to northwest. The elevation of the sierra is also a rather simple form; a regular volcanic mound interrupted only by the somewhat eccentric distribution of a few peaks. But on close inspection the apparently simple overall form of the sierra is obscured by a fantastically complex pattern of water erosion. The basic structure of the range is made up of successive flows of hard and soft volcanic rocks. The water courses cut down through these layers to great depths. Since hard basalt tended to remain and cap the softer tuffs, the erosion produced a generally step-like pattern as it plunged to depths as great as 1,200 feet below the high mesas. The walls of these arroyos whether stepped or not are very sheer; if one flew low over the range, it would be difficult to imagine any sort of surface travel at all.

On either side of the arroyo there were petroglyphs pecked into the vertical rock faces and on large fallen boulders. They were not particularly noteworthy for artistic merit, but the numbers and variety augured well for the arroyo's reputed richness in old rock paintings and drawings.

Just three hours out of San Ignacio, Chato reined up and pointed to an unusually steep *cañada* dropping into the arroyo from our left. Up there was a beautiful and seldom visited *tinaja*, a catchment pool worn into the bedrock. Experience had suggested that Indian remains of all sorts were particularly likely to be encountered in such places. We stripped our animals of saddles and burdens and climbed the hillside. The *cañada* had been scoured out of solid rock and was free of any debris, an oddity in itself, as they were usually littered with boulders. The *tinaja* was a classic, beautifully carved, and perfectly round; it measured about twenty feet across and six feet deep.

As I returned to the floor of the arroyo my eye was caught by a small cave on the opposite or east side. Its ceiling was exposed to view and it glowed in its shadow with a rich red hue. I crossed the wash and climbed up for a look. There above was the first cave painting of the trip and it was a curious sight.

The entire roof of the cave, an area of perhaps two or three hundred square feet, was covered with layer upon layer of painted figures, mostly human and as large or larger than life judging from those that could be clearly distinguished. I had seen overpainting before, indeed it was a feature of most sites which displayed Great Mural works, but never had I seen such an incredible display as this. There was no telling how many figures had been depicted nor in how many layers they had been done. The entire ceiling was absolutely covered with paint, some black but largely red. If I half-closed my eyes the cave appeared as a fireplace with tongues of flame darting from its mouth.

Tacho had noted my preoccupation with the little cave and he came over for a look at the flaming ceiling. *"Que tantas manos de monos!"* was his remark. That translated literally as, "What a lot of layers of human caricatures!", and it raises the question of a controversial word. A *mono* can be a monkey or a person who apes or mimics the actions of others. Cartoon figures in comic strips are widely referred to as *monos*, at least in Mexico, probably because they depict humans with the exaggerated antics associated also with mimes and monkeys. The rural folk in many parts of Mexico apply the name *mono* to any pictograph of a human figure. In the sierras of Baja California this is the only specific term in use. Educated Spanish-speaking people are sometimes offended at the use of this word in the rock painting context. No doubt they feel that it is a form of slang beneath the dignity of the subject. I feel otherwise. The word is short and simple and it substitutes neatly for such awkward phrases as "human figures," "man forms," "representations of humans," etc. A final argument is more compelling. The word is in common use among a large number of people including all those who find these works and guide us to them.

Just upstream from our stopping place, we passed through an impressive *angostura*, or narrows, where the walls seemed almost to lean together. Lodged in crevices twenty feet or more above the floor were bits of flotsam from a recent *chubasco*, reminders of the dangers in such a place during the rainy season. After traversing these narrows and a series of bends, we came to the first great fork in the arroyo. To the right was a huge *cañada* called Torotal, which means a stand of *torote* trees. We bore on to the left into deeper and more massive ravines of El Parral. Clearly, the sierra gained altitude at this point more rapidly than the arroyo and the gorges here became really impressive.

We continued to see occasional petroglyphs and small paintings along our way, most of no great interest because of their faded condition. As we rode along and discussed rock art and the terrain, the word *respaldo* cropped up repeatedly. In answer to my query, Tacho explained that a *respaldo* was an overhung rock face. He pointed out a number and they invariably proved to be the broken edge where layers or flows of volcanic agglomerates had been cut by the watercourses. The importance of the term attached to the fact that these surfaces were often slightly recessed, the top overhanging the lower part. The Painters had obviously favored such places and many of our future exertions were to be expended in investigating poorly accessible but promising *respaldos*. A few other terms useful in rock art pursuits in Baja California are *falda*, for the steeply sloped sides of a watercourse, *caja* for its bed or wash, and *ancón*, for any level surface or bank raised above the level of the wash. Most arroyo trails including the one on which we were riding are located on the generally smooth *ancón* rather than in the boulder strewn wash.

By now we rode entirely in the deep shadows cast by our towering surroundings. Occasional vistas to the east showed dazzling afternoon light on layer after layer of rich red volcanic rock. When we came to a second great fork in the arroyo before dusk, it was time to camp. We rode up onto a shelf just above the wash, and broke down our things.

I climbed a little knoll just above our camp and looked around. To the east lay the Cañada del Corralito where we would go to see the painting of the serpent. To the north El Parral wound inexorably on into the sierra. Chato saw me surveying his world, and climbed up to give me a few proprietary pointers. He indicated a cave above us and to the east in the mouth of Corralito. I put the glasses on it. A huge red figure of a man with upraised arms seemed in the act of springing from his lair. Other smaller, but significant figures showed below. I was suitably impressed. Nothing we had seen during the day was nearly so large or well preserved.

The next morning Chato explained his plan. The Serpent Cave and one or two other painted places were up Cañada del Corralito and our visit would be a round trip returning to our camp at the foot of the *cuesta*. We passed the nearby painted caves without a stop because I had been told that the Serpent Cave was best lighted in the morning. For a while we made fairly good time; the trail was open and there were few temptations to pause. An hour or so after leaving camp, Chato pulled up in a clearing at a fork in the *cañada*, and pointed at the sheer wall just above us to the west.

We looked up and saw a small, shallow cave not more than thirty or forty feet above the wash. The entire wall including the cave was made of a sort of rough, broken conglomerate. The colors were speckled; dark stones set in a warm sandy matrix. On this unpromising surface it was possible to make out a rather formless painting. I will have to admit that I was disappointed. I had frankly expected a more impressive cave, a better working surface and a larger painting. With Chato's feelings in mind, I gave no sign of my thoughts. It was just as well.

In a few moments I had untied my camera bags and scrambled up to the cave with them. Closer inspection of the paintings completely reversed my preliminary judgment. I crawled along the ledge below the work with a growing sense of excitement.

The whole painting was in exceptionally fine condition. The uneven rock was apparently hard and very resistant to weathering. As a result, the colors were still vivid and the outlines perfectly sharp. The scale was impressive: the total length of the mural was twenty-six feet. My first estimate of its size was badly in error due to the viewing distance and the fact that there were no real masses of color or form.

The composition of the work, when seen close at hand, was both striking and full of interest. A serpentine figure was the literal spine of an assemblage which was fleshed out with well over fifty doll-like human and animal figures. These lesser bodies were clearly articulated to the sinuous form of the serpent with little or no overpainting. The small figures did not interfere with the movement of the large one; indeed their placement created an odd, rocking effect which rather enhanced the overall waving motion.

All of this was unique. In my eventual travels in Baja California, I have seen over fifty groupings of painted figures that could loosely be called compositions. None of them is nearly as homogeneous, as literally tied together as this one. The feeling of oneness goes far beyond the basic composition. The colors are consistent throughout. The degree of weathering is more or less equal on all parts. Finally there is the more difficult question of style; all of these figures could easily be the work of a single artist.

There are other intriguing features. The wall actually bore two snake forms separated by a gap of about five feet. The right snake was complete with a head sporting ears and antlers and had a bifurcated tail. The left snake-form also had an elaborate set of antlers, but most of its body was completely lost because a section of the rock surface had fallen away. The left serpent also lacked the small figures around it but there was a suggestion that it had been left incomplete in this respect; there were sketched but incomplete figures nearby.

The conception of the serpents was astonishing. In any context those eared, antlered, and fork-tailed monsters would have seemed bizarre and fanciful concoctions. In the land of the Great Murals, where animals always have literal outlines, they were downright iconoclastic.

For half an hour I studied the mural, looking at it from every feasible angle and using the cameras in making tentative compositions, but for a time photographs could not be made. The morning sun burned on the front of the cave so close to the painting that no film could cope with such contrast and it was necessary to wait for shadow.

Chato had mentioned a large stone corral in the vicinity. I suggested that we look at it while waiting on the sun. The structure proved to be about forty feet square and made of really large stones. It is so old that even Chato's grandfather knew it only as an ancient work; he had supposed that it dated from Indian times. No tradition survives to tell us if it once served a ranch, or whether it was a stopping place for animals driven between the high and low country. Unless someone stumbles on records now unknown, hundreds of such puzzling monuments wait in odd places as venerable question marks to confound the rare visitors.

Presently, it was time to make photographs. As I returned the painting once again looked insignificant; it simply did not "carry" over any distance. I climbed up and photographed it as well as possible but it would have gone a whole lot better with a twenty-foot stepladder. Anyone who visits any of these Baja California cave painting sites will understand this perfectly. It is frequently impossible to get far enough back to compose a picture without falling down the mountainside. Between working and musing over the art, nearly an hour passed.

I climbed down from the cave shelf and started to the right along the cliff face; an apparently easier descent than the one used before. Just south of the cave was a prominent rock. The legend "Oregon Archaeological Expedition" was printed large upon it in oil paint. Beneath that line were listed all the members of the group.

I felt ashamed that my countrymen had come in and defaced a place that had been known and visited for so long. Chato's grandfather knew the place of the Serpent and probably knowledge of it has never been lost to the sierra folk from ancient times. The fact that Chato and Tacho had guided those people into the site and were included as members of the offending group does not in any way excuse the act. The Mexicans were provincial folk with little wordly experience. It is simply not a part of their cultural background to interfere in the acts of visitors.

From the wall high above the modern painting an old mural looked down. A faint row of giant men with arms uplifted kept an ancient vigil. It was a touching sight and in my mind I saluted the Painters' grave images and resolved afresh to find them and record them and their cryptic messages. Across the arroyo Chato was motioning toward another find. In a low cave with a partially fallen roof there was a variety of small paintings. The prize was a pair of black deer in full flight across a ceiling so low that it was seen best from a reclining position.

Half the way back to our camp we stopped at a cave left behind in the morning's rush. On the east side of the wash and not far above it was a long overhang with a flat roof like a miniature of El Batequi. On its smooth ceiling were a striking pair of deer in marvelous condition. The smaller on the left was rendered in a rich brick red and painted over that ground color was a grid of black lines dividing the internal space like a checkerboard. In addition, parts of the body and legs were firmly outlined in black and the head was depicted as if pierced or struck by a short, stout stick of wood. The larger deer on the right was even more elaborate. It showed clear signs of having been originally chalked in white and then strongly outlined in red-brown. The interior space was divided lengthwise into three broad bands of color, the outer two black and the central band in the same red-brown. This deer was depicted with a showy set of antlers and an arrow or spear piercing its back and emerging with a well-drawn point or head from the belly.

Elsewhere in the shelter were a group of three fish or dolphins divided half red and half black, a pair of large *monos*, one red, the other divided red and black, and numerous small paintings. Among the latter were some carefully wrought *monos*, some badly eroded fishlike forms and a pair of symbols which immediately struck me with their novelty and possible significance. There on the rear central area of the ceiling was

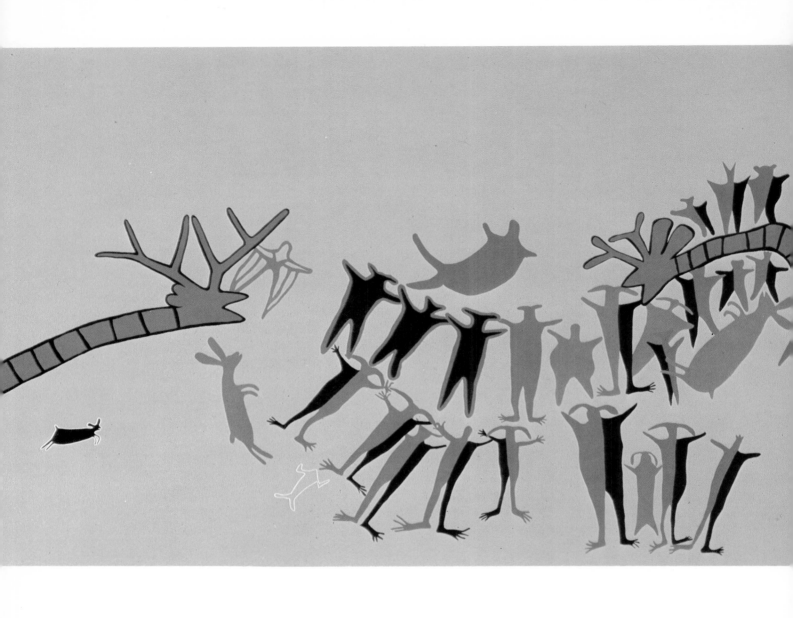

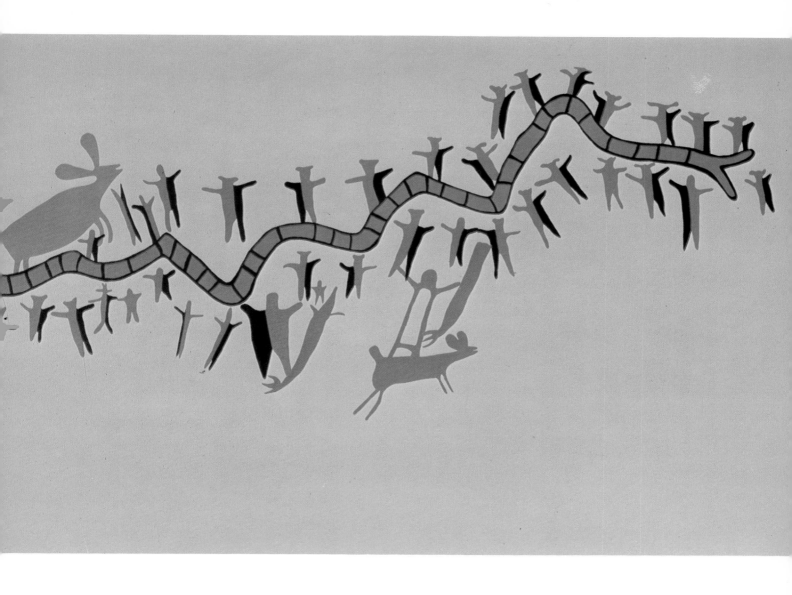

THE SERPENT CAVE

A twenty-six foot long painted panel in a slit cave located in the Arroyo del Parral is the most extraordinary work in the Great Mural area. No other site displays a clearly fanciful creature such as these deer-headed serpents, nor do others show large groups of interrelated figures like those which cluster around the sinuous body of the snake-monster at the right. As if to heighten the enigma of this unique conception, the smaller figures closely resemble the Painters' work at many other places. The photograph at the left is a detail taken from the area between the serpents. It shows the rough surface on which this great work was rendered as well as the fidelity with which the artist has created the facsimile above.

a circle perhaps ten inches in diameter, outlined neatly in red-brown and divided into halves, one unpainted and the other filled in with the same red-brown paint. This unique figure suggested a representation of the half moon, and its associated symbol made the suggestion stronger. Almost tangent to it was a much smaller circle depicted as having rays like a conventional sun symbol. It seemed reasonable to assume that the painting might represent the beginning or ending of an eclipse. Much later this painting was to figure in speculation which may have great significance for students of the Great Murals and the Painters who made them. (See chapter "Who Were the Painters?")

Beneath all the paintings was a thick layer of a soft tuff, actually the material which had weathered away to form the shelter. Its exposed surface was heavily engraved with lines, symbols and patterns of drillings, a phenomenon which I was later to note at nearly every painted cave that offered this invitingly workable rock.

Passing below the cave with the gigantic human figure gesturing from its ceiling, I had a decision to make. We were ready to leave El Parral and there was enough time left in the day to go up the *cuesta* and arrive at a stopping place with food and water for the animals. Visiting this cave would mean another night in the arroyo. I looked up at the red phantom in his den. I thought of all the Indian art we had seen that day, and all that was yet to come, and decided to go on. It was a mistake, and I paid dearly for it. Almost as soon as I left, I could feel a tugging at my mind. Long after, far away in time and distance, I was troubled by recurrent thoughts of the monster and those figures seen only dimly at his feet. If I had just climbed up and had a quick look, I might have exorcised this demon completely or relegated him at least to a sensible niche in my memories.

That experience ended the first exploration of El Parral. The trip continued to Arroyo El Batequi as will be told shortly but there is more to the Parral story. Exactly three years later I returned with Tacho and my friend, Dr. Ray F. Weiss, a geochemist at Scripps Institution of Oceanography. As an assistant we had Tacho's youngest son Ramón, a man who had figured prominently in many of the searches during the intervening years. This second Parral trip followed exactly in the steps of the first as far as the large and hidden *tinaja*. Then began a series of curious and revealing occurrences. I took Ray up to see the water catchment and, while we examined and photographed the place, Ramón made his way to the south along the base of a cliff. When he had gone a hundred yards he returned to tell us that he had found a large painted site. We followed him back and found that an overhung rock face was painted with dozens of *monos* and a number of animal representations. The rock was a very coarse and rough conglomerate and the paintings were in poor condition. Nevertheless, it was an astonishing experience. Three years before I had passed in plain sight of those works at a distance of forty or fifty yards and I had had no inkling of their existence. To make matters even more embarrassing, the paintings proved to be quite noticeable from the bed of the arroyo where we had dismounted on both occasions. A rabbit impaled by an arrow had been skillfully painted on a smooth inclusive rock and it stood out once we knew where to look.

As we rode up the arroyo the comedy played on. In the first quarter of a mile we took turns discovering new paintings in three separate small caves. The climax of this experience was reached at the mouth of Cañada del Torotal. It was late in the day and the low sun was shining on the north side of the *cañada*. The first cursory inspection revealed a large and important painted group high on the wall a quarter of a mile away. It seemed completely impossible that we had missed all these things before. The experience provided a measure of what we had learned in three years.

A nasty climb on a crumbling and steeply inclined approach made possible a close inspection of the painting in El Torotal and the group proved to be attractive and full of interest. It occupied a poorly protected rock face well above the watercourse.

This generally rough *respaldo* had a smooth area in the form of an arch superimposed above the entrance of a small cave. On this flat surface were painted seven or eight stately *monos* with their usual appearance of a solemn ceremonial group. One had a headdress that hung rakishly to one side and resembled an old-fashioned nightcap. The type was familiar from several other sites but this was an outstanding example. For ready reference the title "sackhat man" had been adopted for this configuration and we greeted him here as an old friend. The mural also displayed three large deer and several smaller animal forms but all were so worked into the overpainting that they were difficult to distinguish.

Our next stop was at the foot of the Cuesta de la Higuerita at the cave of the red giant which I had spurned three years before. When we had climbed up and stood at his feet it was obvious that my fears had been justified. The large *mono* which could be seen from afar was less interesting than dozens of vividly colored red and black deer and *monos* painted not only on the wall below but extending into a narrow cave that opened off the larger shelter. The site was felicitous in several ways. From its ample "porch" there was a fine view of the handsome canyon scenery. The visitor could enjoy that balcony panorama and then turn to the choice collection of paintings which more than repaid him for his climb. And all the while the great red figure above stood with sheltering outstretched arms like the messiah or protector of El Parral.

Our plan on quitting the arroyo was to go to Santa Marta by way of the ancient *cuesta* perhaps built by Consag in the 1740's. Because it had been so little used we broke up at its foot. Ramón, Dr. Weiss and I went to see the Serpent Cave and Tacho got out his machete and set out to clear the grade. No sooner had we left him and rounded a turn in the *cañada* than we once again discovered a painted site in full view of the trail. On the west wall about sixty feet above the *caja*, or wash of the watercourse, was a smooth, light-colored *respaldo*. On it, paintings were evident though not well-defined or colorful. The climb to the painted *respaldo* was over a crumbling bedrock incline. Had it been any steeper it could not have been scaled without special equipment.

Despite severe weathering the figures at this site were well worth the effort needed to inspect and record them. There were several deer, two *borregos*, one large *mono* and a pair of smaller figures which appeared to represent coyotes. Many of these were involved in complicated overpainting which reduced their stature as art works by making it difficult to distinguish their separate outlines. Nevertheless, two of the deer and both the *borregos* were beautiful. One of these fine deer was depicted in black except for a pair of large red patches on the body, patches with rounded rectangular forms. One of the *borregos* reversed this pattern, being painted red and having two black patches. It was a shame that the apparent coyote figures were not clearer and more complete. They seemed to have been skillfully depicted and would have been especially welcome since most paintings that are assumed to be of coyotes are rather crude

EL PARRAL XIV

On the following page, the pair of deer provide a clear illustration of a peculiarity in the "realism" of the Painters' school. The outlines of these and almost all other figures were drawn of recognizable animal forms which were then infilled with completely arbitrary and fanciful patterns. The device below may be one of the most important of all the Painters' works despite its modest scale, limited palette and mediocre condition. It could represent the datable astronomical event discussed on page 166.

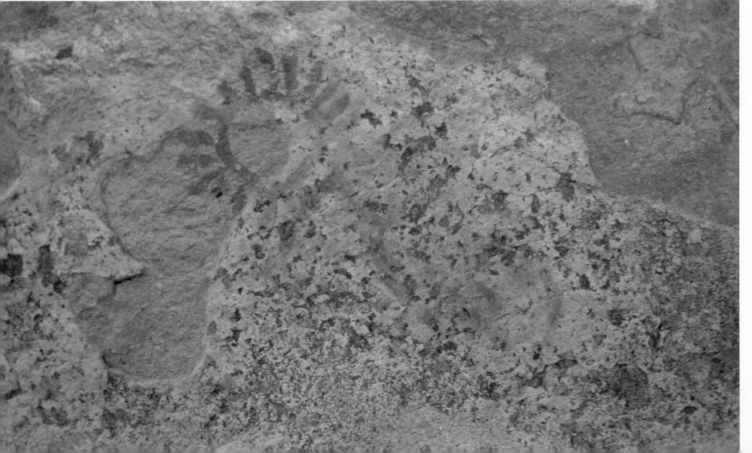

EL PARRAL

The Red Man in the cave at the foot of the Cuesta de la Higuerita is not unusually large but his placement makes him visible from much of the broad arroyo below. Experience shows that this was not a chance occurrence. The Painters habitually placed human figures, especially when in groups, in such a way as to dominate large sweeps of terrain.

and graceless.

We proceeded to the Serpent Cave about four hundred yards to the north and devoted an hour to mapping its large and complicated mural. Our technique involved making nine overlapping photos with the camera exactly six feet from, and perpendicular to, the painted surface. The facsimile in this book was derived from our results.

Meanwhile Ramón was off exploring and when we were nearly finished he returned to tell us

of a discovery. We followed him for a quarter of a mile up the more northerly fork of the *cañada* to reach a large *respaldo* low on the west wall. There in very faded condition were six beautiful deer in a graceful running frieze. Some were black, others red and, even though all were rather faint and incomplete, the group retained its charm. One of the dreams that compelled me to photograph such disappearing art was that of recording enough to create facsimile restoration. It must be said, however, that photography is not the ideal medium. An artist working at the site could detect vestiges which simply do not appear in the best photographs.

The art in El Parral is difficult to put in perspective. The arroyo has obviously been an avenue into the sierra since ancient times. As testimony, a search of the two adjacent arroyos produced little in the way of art remnants, whereas over twenty rock painting sites were identified in El Parral. However, none of these was really large and that is an unusual situation in a major access arroyo. On the other hand the artworks were more diverse and contained more unique forms than any other comparable area of the Sierra de San Francisco.

Perhaps its location at the southern extreme of the sierra helps to explain some of these pe-culiarities. We know from accounts written early in the period of European contact that the oasis of San Ignacio attracted many bands of people on either a revolving or simultaneous basis. Thus El Parral may have served more different groups as a path to mountain foods than did most of the other arroyos. It is possible that during the painting period the sierra and the lowlands to the east had their own population which created the more typical art. Extensively painted centers could have represented their isolation and security. El Parral, however, also serving people of the south and west on occasion, would have come under more influences and been less attractive as a location for large ceremonial centers.

THE ARROYO EL BATEQUI

Cerro Santa Marta, whose southern drainage formed the Arroyo del Parral, gives rise on the west to the very different Arroyo del Batequi. Whereas El Parral is deep and narrow with many convolutions, El Batequi is wide and makes its way into the desert to the west with only a few curves. The heads of the two watercourses are separated by the Mesa de la Higuera's three-thousand-foot elevation and from that vantage point most of El Batequi's extent can be seen. The panorama is Grand Canyonesque in form and color, though on a smaller scale.

Near its origin on the spine of the sierra, El Batequi is divided where two smaller *cañadas* combine to form the single large arroyo which makes its way westward. The more northerly of these tributaries is called La Higuerilla and during the search for the Great Murals it contained a ranch inhabited by two families. The south fork is called La Natividad and its only ranch had been abandoned for two generations. Both *cañadas* have permanent springs which must have attracted Indians.

Tacho brought me to La Natividad in 1972. He had visited the ranch back in the 1930's and one of the sons of Verulo Ojeda, the founder, had taken him a short distance to see the Indian remains. All Tacho could remember was that the place was vast and had paintings.

We approached from the east down a shallow slope. When this suddenly deepened, Tacho indicated that we would proceed on foot. We dropped to the floor of the canyon and started downstream, Tacho striding ahead. In a moment we turned a little corner and he pointed up.

WITHIN THE SIERRA

Crossing the surrounding desert, climbing the rugged slopes and descending steep-walled canyons does not prepare a visitor for the quiet beauty of palms and pools and sculptured rock. At dusk, after the fierce light and heat of the day, a great calm mantles these depths. The visitor has arrived at the hub of the Painters' world.

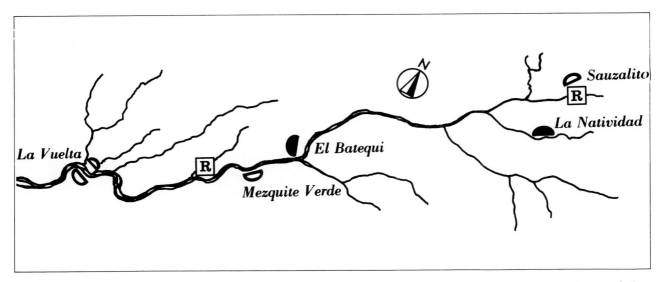

Above was a very steep *falda*, and high above that was an immense overhang, the upper part of the cave we were seeking. It was quite a scramble up the steep bank but in a few minutes my guide and I were standing on the floor of possibly the largest rock shelter in Baja California.

The basic natural formation was an overhung rock face about five hundred feet long and nearly one hundred feet high. The extent of the overhang varied from only a few feet to as much as forty or fifty. The covered area gave the impression of being arched over. People familiar with the great caves of Betatakin, Keet Seal and Inscription House in Navajo National Monument will know the feeling in Natividad Cave. At the west end of the shelter was an enormous pile of fallen rock which choked the floor area and made passage difficult. The rest of the floor was quite clear. Retaining walls had been built from large pieces of the fallen rock and laboriously back-filled with earth to provide a broader and more level floor. Such stone and earth work is very rare in Baja California although it is common in Sonora in such places as Las Trincheras.

Another man-made feature was unusual. There were walls of rock once forming either animal pens or human dwellings. These were laid up using the back of the cave as one wall. The work was sturdy and reasonably neat but not up to the craftsmanship of the cliff-dwellings at the Arizona caves mentioned. My first thought was that the rancher who had lived below must have built these as goat pens but Tacho insisted that no one would have gone to such a monumental amount of work for that purpose.

There was a further oddity involving wall building. For a stretch of many feet the soft floor-level layer of rock was eroded so deeply that a sort of sub-cave existed within the larger volume. Its ceiling height ranged from three or four feet to almost nothing and yet walled-in shelters a few feet wide had been built with head-room down to as little as two feet. These small pens may have been used as sleeping quarters with the entrances closed by piling rocks for protection.

At one time the entire five hundred linear feet of wall had been more or less heavily painted. Along that great length hundreds of figures could be made out, the vast majority being deer. Some had been painted on an enormous scale, larger than any at El Batequi. Sadly, most of them were in bad or very bad condition. It was frustrating to stand below a gigantic mural of a rampant *borrego* and barely be able to make out the outlines and detect the color.

In one small area near the west end at about eye level there was a myriad of tiny figures painted with amazingly fine lines. The usual subjects were represented but they were no more than four to eight inches tall. Later we were to find similar work in the Arroyo de San Pablo and far south in the Arroyo de Guajademí of the Sierra de Guadalupe, but this was our first encounter with a large group of these miniatures.

Providentially, as at El Batequi, there was a

LA NATIVIDAD

At a point apparently late in the Painters' time, the continuing processes of cave formation caused a great section of the backwall to disengage and collapse into giant fragments which still choke the west end of the sheltered area. The large fresh surface above was then decorated with the figures of deer painted in a homogeneous style. Other parts of the cave retain faded or fragmental remains of works far more varied and densely applied.

35

part of the painted display which had survived almost intact. At the west end in the vicinity of the fallen debris the wall was sprinkled with rather sketchy paintings of deer. These were all done using the equivalent of a dry-brush technique which produced less firm outlines than were usual to the Great Murals. They were also filled in with color in a very sparing fashion, each one either black or maroon. A similarity in all these well-preserved figures suggested that they might have come from one hand, certainly from a single period. The art was competent and attractive but it did not impart the excitement sensed at El Batequi. However, close inspection of the older, more deteriorated work at the east end of La Natividad did indeed suggest a relationship to the great black deer of the Batequi mural. Objective comparisons will be difficult because the comparable figures at La Natividad are so heavily overpainted and in such bad condition.

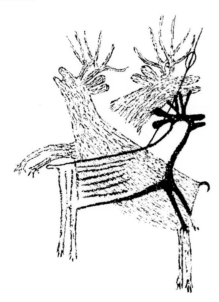

Art is not the only attraction at the grand old site of La Natividad. From the "front porch" created by the retaining wall there was a fine view down the arroyo system to the west and, in the other direction, of the more open space by which we had entered. The bank opposite the cave was composed of an abrupt series of grand rock faces tiered up like the layers of a wedding cake. I measured the elevation of the place at 2,600 feet, stood a little longer scanning that panorama, and then turned and had a last look

at the cave. Its sheer size was awesome, turning away for a moment had brought it back into perspective. My eyes scaled its hundred-foot height and then returned to features like the retaining walls, pens and low shelters. I can say now what I could only guess then: the amount of human labor expended is unique in the painted caves of Baja California. Probably no other site so strongly suggests human habitation. I wondered then, as I do now, if that was all aboriginal work or whether some had been done in historic times. As if to underscore the latter possibility a small inclusive rock protruding from the wall of the cave over ten feet from the floor displayed a pair of unmistakable Christian crosses painted in bright yellow, the only glint of that color in the cave.

Rancho Sauzalito is situated less than a mile north of the Cañada de la Natividad in the Cañada de la Higuerilla which is virtually its twin. Jorge Arce responded to questions about ancient paintings at Sauzalito by pointing up the north wall of the *cañada* which was less than two hundred yards from his home. There, he informed us, were many paintings, but *muy boradas*. This description, meaning very worn or erased, was unwelcome but it was destined to become very familiar in all the Great Mural area.

Looking up at the steep canyon wall, it was easy to believe that there were many examples of cave art. Tier after tier of *respaldos* were piled up and each seemed to overhang a slit cave several hundred feet long. Jorge Arce volunteered to show us how to get around on the precarious cliff.

On the first level the long shelter was weathered from a very soft powdery rock and most of it was smoke-blackened in addition. Only a few fragments of paintings indicated what once must have been many works. The second level was similar, but the third and fourth were considerably more rewarding. Despite deterioration, their long galleries still displayed unmistakable evidence of dozens of very large paintings, mostly groupings of red-and-black *monos*. We ranged along these open passages both fascinated and frustrated by the painted remains. In spite of very large numbers of figures not one was clear enough to promise a decent photographic image.

Finally Jorge Arce conducted us to the last and most distant bastion, a large open cave at the east end of the top level. There a few paintings, notably of deer and birds, had survived quite well. A single hard rock about six feet long was imbedded as part of the cave wall in the painted area. It had held the paint extremely well and those figures on it, or the parts of figures that extended onto it, were unusually clear and brightly colored.

The elevation of this cave was very close to 3,000 feet.

Below Sauzalito a few hundred yards the *cañada* makes a sudden drop of nearly a hundred feet creating what, during a summer storm, must be a spectacular falls. For an hour's ride the canyon remains narrow and deep and the trail, while very beautiful, is slow as it winds through a rocky defile picturesquely planted with fruit trees by the ranchers above. Then La Higuerilla joins La Natividad to form the broad Arroyo del Batequi. It is another two-hour ride to its foremost painted place, the cave of El Batequi.

My second visit came only a few months after the first. We arrived late and passed the night at the great bend of the arroyo just below the cave. At dawn I rolled out and started the climb to the murals. All sorts of thoughts raced through my head as I labored up the hill and not the least of them was fear, fear that El Batequi could not possibly measure up to my idealized memories.

The sun rose for all the higher parts of the sierra. Cerro Batequi, just to the south, was rimmed with gold on its east face, but the depths of the arroyo were still wrapped in the blue-gray light of dawn. When I arrived at the great painted rock shelter it's mural ceiling was shadowed and dim. I felt as if I had been admitted to the Louvre before the lights had been turned on.

While awaiting the sun I read my altimeter and recorded an elevation of 1,800 feet; then I fell to examining the lower parts of the shelter. I remembered that the soft tuff of the back wall had engravings on it but it was astonishing, during a real inventory, to see their number and complexity. The first form that identified itself was that characteristic figure of so much of the world's rock art, the vulva symbol. The universality of this symbol is a bit of a puzzle. It had been engraved and painted by hunting and gathering people who lived on different continents and as much as 25,000 years apart. Did it evolve with each culture as a separate if obvious inspiration, or was it used to represent procreation so early in man's history that he was able to take it with him on all his roamings of the earth?

On the back wall of the shelter dozens of such symbols were worked deeply into the soft rock. Above, on the ceiling, a number of vulva symbols had been painted in white, an occurrence which has proved far rarer than engravings of the same theme. There were innumerable drilled holes perhaps a half inch in diameter. At first it seemed that the latter were a natural occurrence but I soon found that they formed lines and patterns too perfect for chance. There were also numerous sets of slightly divergent lines. Some of these hundreds of figures were sharp and clear, most were weathered to the point of having their engraved lines distinctly softened and rounded. A few were so eroded that they could only be detected later when the surface had strong side lighting.

The sun rose and struck the shelter. The light now reflected strongly from the floor and back wall and the mural on the ceiling had its greatest illumination of the day. My earlier anxiety was forever ended. For me, that is a supreme example of primitive art. I went over it again and again. I suffered once more with its lost and damaged parts. I rejoiced again at its essential survival, its power and its unity.

The overpainting, especially at the right end, attracted attention. In that strong light shadowy figures could be seen that underlaid what I had perceived before. At least five different layers of paintings could be counted and the thought crossed my mind that they must represent a rather large span of time. The freshest, the uppermost layer must be several hundred years old and yet its total weathering appeared far less than

EL BATEQUI

This detail from the right end of the cavalcade illustrates several of the Painters' conventions and practices. Four or five different layers of overpainting can be distinguished. White outlining is conspicuous, as are two examples of twisted perspective. The breasts of the woman at upper left appear to emanate from her armpits due to their depiction in double profile. The same perspective distortion causes the dewlap claws of the deer to appear unnaturally splayed, producing the curious handlike hooves.

the difference between it and the oldest.

The works of that right end invite wonder and comment. They are quite unique in their style which seems the most formal and sophisticated of all the Great Murals. The great deer and the arresting *monos* alike have a refinement and a classic simplicity which may be the highest expression of this culture.

The other parts of the grand cavalcade are curiously different. The central section includes two *monos* and a large deer which are positively crude and the left end seems to have been decorated by artists of widely varied talents. At first it seemed very odd that these differences should be so marked in different parts of the mural rather than in different layers. However, a more thorough examination suggested a partial answer. The quality of the rock changes gradually across the mural. The smoothest and hardest is at the right and it looks progressively softer to the left. The condition of five nearly identical tall brown-and-pale-red *monos* tends to bear this out. Two at the right are in a good state of preservation and the others are successively poorer as they are found farther to the left. It is possible that the entire ceiling was decorated during early periods of the painting epoch and that what we see at the right dates from those times. Corresponding works on the left must have been lost to erosion and replaced by successions of later paintings. In any event it is that beautiful right end which will probably command the greatest attention and stir the strongest emotions.

At last it was time to go, I gathered up my things and, with many a backward glance, left my proudest discovery. I am amused now at my parting thoughts. What I confidently took for final farewells were only the preliminaries to four more pilgrimages.

As we rode down the arroyo no more than a quarter of a mile west of the great painted site, Tacho remembered another. Thirty years before he had had to chase a wounded deer and, while returning, had noticed some paintings. He pointed at some poorly sheltered *respaldos* on the south side and perhaps eighty feet above the *caja*. The place was called Mezquite Verde. I got out my binoculars and scanned its hundred yard length. The wall was in deep shade and at first I could make out nothing but the speckling of numerous rocks cemented into the general matrix. Then I saw the head of a deer painted on one of those inclusive rocks. With that I dismounted and climbed up a steep rock face to reach the level of the paintings.

The place once was a large center of primitive art. The entire length of the *respaldo* had intermittent showings of painted groups, some on as grand a scale as those at El Batequi or La Natividad. All were in the last stages of deterioration. There was not really a single profitable subject for a photograph, but finally I forced myself to select three or four representative groups to record the site.

One unique feature remained quite visible. At the western extremity, the rock face was eroded into a fantastic tracery of pockets and baseball-sized lumps. The smooth, rounded ends of the protuberances had been painted in different colors which had faded but still gave the place the air of a bizarre parody of the pointalist school of French painters. It was the only example of such painting that I have yet encountered. Caves at Cuesta San Pablo about fifteen miles north have similar knobs, but no paint.

The poor condition of the art at Mezquite Verde precluded any simple estimate of its worth, but it did offer some more evidence as to the causes of destruction. After analyzing El Batequi, La Natividad, and Mezquite Verde in the same arroyo, I can report an opinion on the deterioration of their art. Essentially it applies to most other sites as well.

The principal culprit was the rock itself. At some sites, the rock was hard and strongly resisted all the weathering agencies exerted on it. At others, it seemed to disintegrate at a fairly uniform rate due merely to exposure to air with its attendant changes of temperature and humidity. The site at Mezquite Verde offered dramatic proof of the differences due to the character of the rock. The painted walls were a conglomerate of volcanic debris: ash, pebbles, and some fairly large inclusive rocks, occasionally softer but usually harder than the matrix. In some places a figure could be made out dimly on the wall as a whole, but was clearer and showed strong colors where the design carried over the harder inclusive material.

Exposure to sunlight alone seemed to have been a negligible factor in most cases; parts of paintings exposed to direct sun were little different than those in year-round full shade, other factors being about equal. Direct exposure to rain or run-off from rain was disastrous and most paintings so exposed were virtually erased.

Paintings on western sierra slopes were, on the whole, in poorer shape than those on Gulf slopes. That could have been due to rock differences but humidity may have played a part also since the Pacific slopes are generally quite a bit more moist.

A few minutes' further ride brought us to Rancho El Batequi which stood *solo*, or unoccupied just then despite its water, corrals, and sound buildings. Our animals needed water so our objective was the *batequi* which gave the place its name.

A *batequi* is a shallow pit dug in search of water in the bottom of a watercourse. It seems likely that the Spaniards learned the technique from the Mexican natives, at least the word *batequi* appears to have had an Indian origin. Many Baja California arroyos have hard rock bottoms over which water flows underneath a bed of sand. The Indians, and later the *gente de razón*, found many of these sites and used them as water sources. A few served full-time as watering places for ranch stock, as at El Batequi. The construction here was classic. Three sides of the hole were fenced to prevent animals from breaking down the edges. The fourth side was dug back to form a long shallow ramp by which the stock could approach the water.

About two miles below Rancho El Batequi the arroyo takes the form of a very large dogleg by turning north and then abruptly back to the west. For the purposes of mapping and record keeping we call this place La Vuelta del Batequi, The Turn of El Batequi. On the west wall just before the second of these turns is a series of small caves. In them we found a number of paintings in poor condition. The principal subject was deer and one figure was noteworthy. The usual distribution of red and black in a bi-color deer was reversed; this one was principally black with red on the belly and the inner legs.

Across the arroyo to the northeast is another shelter with unusual form and content. A low bluff protrudes into the sweep of the arroyo. At its extremity a cave has formed which passes through like a tunnel. The chamber is not large and the two entrances are no more than fifty feet apart, but that small volume has seen an amazing amount of ancient activity.

The inner space is divided into a broad passageway at ground level and a shelf two to three feet above that floor. This raised portion, which is on the north or uphill side, has had its entire surface engraved in a lavish and complex design of pits and grooves. Such work is not unknown in other places within the Great Mural region, but nowhere, to date at least, has such an elaborate and extensive example been found. The carvings are also unusual in their depth; most are chipped or scratched at least two inches into the rock surface.

All this work creates a puzzling spectacle for today's visitor. Such engravings may appear decorative to our receptive and tolerant minds, but that could be a purely incidental by-product of their creation for specific ceremonial purposes. Similar works in other regions of the world have been associated ethnographically with tribal rites of several quite different kinds. Here we can only look and wonder at what is clearly a meaningful artifact.

The rich array of rock carving distracted us from other modest remains. On the walls above were vestiges of paintings and on the floor were several extremely worn *metates*. Present also were the rarer *manos*, or handstones used in grinding on the *metate* surfaces. Probably *manos* are less common because they are smaller and hence more easily scattered, buried, or taken away for use at today's ranches.

The art of El Batequi stands in the most marked contrast to that of El Parral. The number of sites is small; no more than five or six really separate locations can be counted, but four of these are major painting centers, each with over a hundred figures.

The site which I have chosen to call simply El Batequi is distinguished by many masterfully executed figures. More importantly it shows an unprecedented degree of cooperation between its major artists. Men painting unknown numbers of years or generations apart not only respected but added to what they found; the product is a powerful composition. This attribute is absolutely spotlighted amongst the Painters' work because the norm is diametrically opposite. In a land where overpainting was the rule, successive artists simply obliterated the works of their predecessors. El Batequi shines down from its ceiling as the glorious exception.

Immediately to the north of the Arroyo del Batequi is a small arroyo called San Esteban

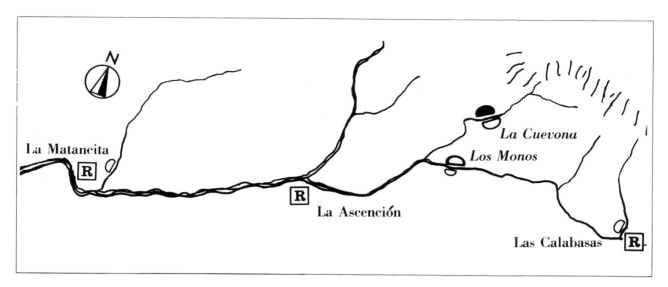

which does not penetrate to the heart of the sierra. North of that, however, and generally parallel to both the others, is a major arroyo born (as they say in the sierra) on the south flanks of Cerro de La Laguna. That mountain has an elevation near 6,000 feet and is the highest and most central expression of the sierra. The arroyo which drains the southern slope of the peak is called La Ascención after an old ranch located at its deepest point. A curiosity, at least for people alien to local usage, is the fact that below the ranch the same arroyo is called La Matancita after another ranch. This practice is common; the name of an arroyo in a given locale typically reflects no more than that of the ranch that it contains. At the turn of the century, what we now know as the Arroyo del Batequi was called La Natividad, as was the mountain now known as Cerro Batequi. But Rancho La Natividad fell and Rancho Batequi flourished.

THE ARROYO DE LA ASCENCIÓN

Juan Leree at Rancho La Ascención was surprised at our interest in rock art, surprised that anyone would ride for weeks in the sierra seeking all the paintings strewn about by antiquity. But he did not laugh at us. He knew three painted places and, on reflection, he decided that we would never find two of them without help. He offered to devote a day to our cause.

The arroyo divides at the ranch. The north fork is called the Cañada de la Tinaja and the main trunk continues east to divide again. Our instructions were to pass that second north fork, the Cañada del Cerro, and follow the trail until we found a cave with some paintings. That place was called Los Monos; we could see it for ourselves and pass the night nearby. In the morning Juan would join us.

Los Monos must once have been an attractive place with a small but choice collection of art. A modest cave-shelter on the north side of the arroyo had been painted with figures of deer, rabbits, birds and men. Now, however, the works were severely damaged by rock deterioration and further obscured by heavy deposits of soot from fires built within the shelter. Only a single attractive red and black bird had survived both scourges.

The whole subject of fires and smoke in the caves of Baja California badly needs study by appropriate scientists. Places like Los Monos de la Ascención lead us to suspect that ranchers of the historic period were responsible. After all, this cave lies only a few feet from a trail connecting Rancho La Ascención with Rancho Las Calabasas and then continuing to Santa Marta, long a portal to the sierra. But such smoked caves form only a small fraction of the total. Most caves are far from any modern trails and some are in places where modern man would have no conceivable activity. In addition, while many painted caves are smoked, the majority are not. And smoke-blackened caves without signs of painting are frequently found near unsmoked caves that are heavily painted. It seems certain that both the soot on the walls and the charcoal

LA VUELTA DEL BATEQUI

The palaeolithic cultures of every continent have produced pit-and-groove rock engravings, but even very similar works seem to have been done for different reasons. A creative act, which in one group was a mandatory part of a puberty rite, in another may be a shaman's means of divination. So perhaps with rock art. No matter how similar, works of different times and places may have had entirely different inspirations. The media for expression are far more limited than the particulars of human motivations.

LA CUEVONA

A huge windswept void in a steep wall of the Cañada del Cerro has the distinction of being the largest and handsomest cave in which Great Murals have yet been found. It is also one of the least accessible. If a few giant men and deer painted on its walls are not outstanding mementos of the Painters' work, La Cuevona, and the experience of reaching it, create beautiful memories of their land.

mixed with the earth, as eminently datable materials, have a story to tell. It is to be hoped that it will be deciphered soon and that it can be directly related to the Painters.

Directly across from Los Monos a soft rock stratum had eroded so as to produce a long low recess about fifteen feet above the wash of the arroyo. At one point in this shelter a group of small paintings were visible on a large inclusive rock which was weathering from the greater mass. These depictions were of deer and perhaps rabbits and they were a graceful and attractive lot. The intention of the painter seemed obvious as most of the plump little figures were depicted as spitted by arrows.

Juan Leree came at an early hour and we were climbing a bedrock shute on the northern side of the arroyo before the sun got down to those depths. The ascent was slow and precarious with much loose material to avoid and many level changes involving dubious hand- and foot-holds. When we arrived at an impassable palisade we turned west and rounded a point. For an hour and a half the climb continued until we reached the spine of the hill separating the arroyo from the Cañada del Cerro. The whole hike was impeded by not only the exceedingly steep and rough terrain but also by an unusually heavy growth of *garabatillo*, a long-limbed shrub with wicked hook-like thorns.

Finally Señor Leree brought us to the edge of a precipice that dropped more than three hundred feet to the floor of the *cañada*. We had arrived, he said, at a painted cave, it was directly beneath us. There followed a quarter of an hour of confusion. Leree had discovered the cave while seeking strayed goats. He had come to it while working his way along what even he described as a difficult ledge. He had left the place by climbing up a flue-like crack to a point near where we stood. For some time he could not find the hidden stair and we all looked along the perilous edge at what appeared to be an impossible descent.

At last the missing access was found and we let ourselves down in a very cautious fashion and, by that means, came into La Cuevona, the largest true cave in the Painters' realm.

For once the setting stole the show from art or even the possibility of ancient treasures. The place was vast and it was beautiful. Under the brow of that cliff the elements had eroded an ovoid volume about two hundred feet long, sixty feet high and eighty feet deep. The floor was windswept and clean of all traces of recent activity, no footprints and no animal droppings. The initial impression was that we were the first humans ever to disturb the place's isolated serenity. A brief tour dispelled all that. Set about here and there were several *metates* and, from the walls, paintings of three giant *monos* and five deer stared down.

A thorough examination of the entire cave surface produced no further evidence from the Painters' hands. We were scarcely surprised; the wonder was that man had labored up to such a place to paint at all, not that he had failed to return in repeated cycles. Those figures which had been rendered were unfortunately in a very diminished state, the erosive forces which had created so great a cave had not spared the art. It too was loosening bit by bit and falling to be scoured away by the winds which whipped those heights. One of the *monos* was only a shadow, two others still asserted a degree of their half-red and half-black presence in the center of the cave's back wall. Well off to the right, the deer, in a procession, were gradually fading.

We left, profoundly moved by the grandeur of the cave, by its enigmatic past association with man and by the effort expended to reach it. The elevation at its floor was 3,500 feet; we left it and followed Juan Leree by a devious path to the *caja* of the *cañada* below.

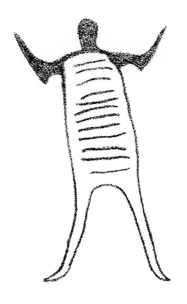

Directly across from La Cuevona but only fifty feet or so above the floor of the waterway was an open rock shelter, an unimpressive geologic event but a far livelier place from the standpoint of rock art. On a wall a little less than a hundred feet long were painted several dozen figures large and small dominated by two fine large deer and three *monos*, two large and one smaller, which gave the impression of being a man, a woman and a child. The large male *mono* was unique in being drawn only in a heavy red outline filled in by horizontal bars that led us to dub him "ladder-man." The deers' distinction came not in any unusual character but in the sure and simple way in which their grace was depicted.

Another painted site in this arroyo was visited on a different occasion. Farther east than Los Monos the Arroyo de la Ascensión narrows to become a spectacularly deep and twisting gorge. Beyond that it emerges in the uplands as an open valley created by a pair of minor seasonal streams. Exactly at the place where the narrows end is Rancho Las Calabasas, inhabited at the time of my visit by Tacho's brothers Ignacio and Loreto and their families. High on the north side of the arroyo and looking directly down on the ranch is a small, undistinguished cave hollowed from the usual cemented volcanic materials. Loreto Arce pointed it out and then showed us the trail.

The granular walls of this shelter displayed several *monos*, deer and a rabbit. Three of the *monos* had an unusual distinction. Though divided vertically in the common San Francisco fashion, they were painted in brown-and-black rather than the usual red-and-black. Elsewhere the Indian remains were scarce. We found a number of horseshoe-shaped engravings on a rock outcropping along the bed of the arroyo a mile below Rancho La Ascensión. At La Matancita there was a *respaldo*-backed site of at least seasonal occupation replete with *metates* and much charcoal. Though La Ascensión is a major arroyo and penetrates to the heart of the sierra, the surface evidence suggests that it was not a major access route nor a place where the aboriginal people spent a lot of time. Over the mountains to the north another waterway provides a striking contrast.

From the drainage of the north slopes of Cerro de la Laguna arises a watercourse which cuts down to depths of over a thousand feet and traverses two thirds of the length of the sierra. Its extent is suggested also in the number of names by which it is known beginning at its source before it passes out into the Vizcaino Desert: Agua Verde, El Cartucho, Santa Teresa, San Nicolás, San Pablo, and, according to some old-timers, El Salón. Along the way there are numerous tributary *cañadas*, El Dátil, La Banderita, San Jorge, El Bajío, La Soledad, El Cacariso, San Julio, Los Vainoros, and San Nicolás, which make it not only the longest but by all odds the most complex drainage system in the Sierra de San Francisco.

THE ARROYO DE SAN PABLO

At the head of the Arroyo de San Pablo is the ranch village of San Francisco seasonally occupied by as many as sixteen families. There is a school and, in recent years, an airstrip. Here in the early 1960's Erle Stanley Gardner landed on his way to visit a group of caves which were all in the San Pablo drainage. Leon Diguet also came here in the 1890's. One of the sites he visited and specifically identified is only a twenty-minute walk from the village. It is called Cueva del Ratón.

The cave lies southwest and above the little collection of ranch houses. It is on the eastern edge of a ridge dropping down from the high ground of Cerro de la Laguna and it is more of an overhang or rock shelter than a true cave. The painted area is about thirty or forty feet long and it displayed a small but choice collection of the Painters' art. There were representations of deer, *borrego*, rabbit, and man. The rock seems to be above average in its resistance to weathering and the paintings were more complete than at most sites we had seen. In spite of this advantage, the works were dulled and their contrast reduced by an unusually heavy smoking of the cave's walls. A few little walls of piled rocks were evidence that the place had been used to shelter humans or domestic animals. That, and the proximity of San Francisco, once a ranch and visiting station of the San Ignacio mission, suggested that the unwitting vandalism might have come in historic times.

One large *mono* represented a rare type. The figure was divided into red and black areas along the vertical axis in the usual fashion, but a black oval had been heavily painted over the

CUEVA DEL RATÓN

Some of San Francisco's great painted centers seem linked by the work of specific artists. The mountain lion shown here is virtually duplicated at Cuesta Palmarito and the rare black-faced human is repeated at La Candelaria. Cuesta Palmarito also shows strong ties with La Palma. The art in some other caves seems exclusive; no counterparts are known for the great works of El Batequi or the Serpent Cave.

SANTA TERESA I

A few of the Painters' works seem designed to flaunt the difficulties faced in their creation. Some can be found at amazingly inaccessible sites and others, as here, seem unnecessarily high on a wall otherwise unpainted. This group also raises broad questions about the reasons for overpainting. These figures were intentionally arranged in what, to a viewer, is a confused grouping in spite of the vast available area.

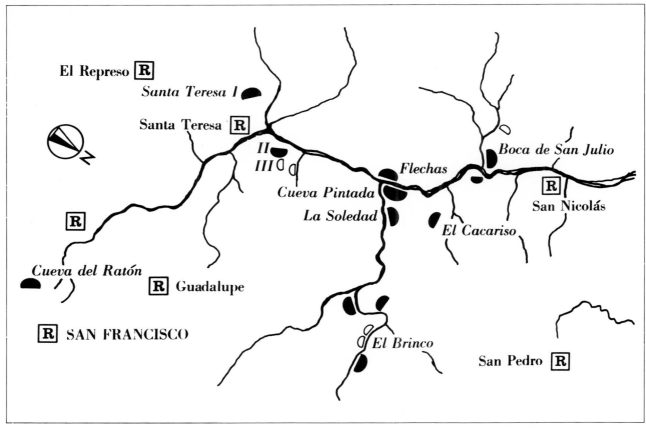

area where we would imagine a face. In addition both the red and black portions of the body had been colored in fine vertical stripes rather than solid paint. This curious face patch has turned up at only three other sites: Cuesta Palmarito, which is about four miles to the southeast, La Candelaria about the same distance north, and Los Monos de San Juan, which is fifty miles south in a different sierra, that of Guadalupe. As a further curiosity, the coloring in vertical lines is much commoner in the Guadalupe region than it is in the Sierra de San Francisco.

A black mountain lion also commanded attention. The painted representations of these animals occupy a special niche in the Painters' repertory. For some reason which I cannot possibly surmise, león figures vary less than any other, animal or mono. They all have the same long, stiff, extended tail, the short legs cocked at a similar angle. There is virtually no neck and the round, short-muzzled head is set with small round ears. Most leones are black but several red examples have turned up; the oddity is that

these animals are never bicolored. They are unique in this respect.

Below Cueva del Ratón, the great arroyo drops to the northwest. At San Francisco it is no more than a bunch of deep scratches on the backbone of the sierra, but within a mile these have consolidated into a sizeable canyon called Agua Verde, a name taken from a large tinaja in its floor. Within two miles the arroyo has cut a thousand feet below the mesa to form a spectacular winding corridor with nearly vertical sides. That

48

extends for two more miles in a run called El Cartucho. With its vistas of towering red-rock walls, its course choked with boulders twenty, thirty, even fifty feet in size, and its groves of lofty palms, El Cartucho should eventually become a national park. As a better solution, the entire Sierra de San Francisco should achieve that status and El Cartucho would be one of its jewels.

Below, the arroyo opens up suddenly into an amphitheatrical space called Santa Teresa. This twelve hundred-foot-deep dish is the result of the confluence of four *cañadas* with the main arroyo. From the east descend El Dátil and El Bajío and, from the west, larger La Banderita and San Jorge. In this space Fernando Arce Sandoval founded a ranch around 1940. At the time of our visits it was one of the two or three most beautiful ranches in all the Baja California sierras. Don Fernando and his sons had built four substantial buildings of mortared masonry, plastered, painted and beautifully thatched with fronds of the abundant native palms. They had also created two *huertas*, or garden-orchards, and built over a mile of flume to carry water to them from a spring.

These men, upon being queried about rock art, deferred to the grandsons. They had been busy building and farming, they said. The boys herded goats all over the arroyo, up into the *cañadas*, up the *faldas*, and onto the mesas far above. Thus it was that one or the other of two teenage brothers, Santo and Bernardino Arce, took us to see the nearby sites, including those visited by Erle Stanley Gardner and Dr. Clement Meighan.

Directly above Rancho Santa Teresa and to the southwest there is a typically steep and precarious trail which leads to Rancho El Represo on the mesa above. Halfway up that *cuesta* in a ravine to the right there is a very high *respaldo* with some minor caves at its foot. A curiosity of this place was the presence of a fan palm, grotesquely bent and distorted, which grew from the rock at the base of the *respaldo*. Since palms are usually restricted to watercourses we sought its source of water and found that a tiny spring wept from the rock at the level of the caves.

This place was also known to the Painters. On the smooth surface above the caves were three major groups of paintings. At the left was a large ceremonial assemblage of *monos*. In the middle was a group of two deer and a *borrego* in an attractive design created by the partial superimposition of all three figures.

Such "compositions" will always remain an enigma; we will never know if they were the product of chance or whether some artists in re-using a surface consciously or unconsciously took advantage of the existing art. At El Batequi simple statistics told us that the result was by design. The odds would be astronomical on aligning twenty or so figures in the same direction by pure chance. But with small groups, like that at Santa Teresa I, direction is not involved and evaluations are entirely subjective. Certainly it can be said that most of the hundreds of groups created by overpainting are not successful as compositions and that the total effect is to diminish the individual figures without creating artistic composites.

The third or right-hand group seemed to illustrate the latter conclusion; it consisted of a formless melange including *monos*, deer and *borrego*.

Entirely across the arroyo, on the east side just south of the opening of the Cañada del Bajío, there is another site also located halfway to the mesa and at the foot of a high vertical rock face. This place, which we called Santa Teresa II, was a mixed bag in every sense.

The basic shelter is unusual and, because of its exposure, very conspicuous. For hundreds of yards along the top of the *falda*, there runs a very high smooth layer of rock with a vertical face. At one point an arch-shaped piece of this face has dropped away leaving an alcove sixty feet high, sixty feet wide and twenty feet deep. This regular depression can be seen readily from any part of the valley.

Within this shelter, both on its back wall and the two wing walls there were a score or more of *monos* and deer, all very faded. Some of the *monos* were quite large; one female figure was around ten feet tall. Nearby there was the depiction of a doughnut-shaped figure about a foot in diameter, oddly abstract in a land where realistic art was the rule.

To the left of the great arched alcove a low overhang contained some additional small works including more non-representational figures. Most conspicuous was a set of parallel and partially broken waving lines, a most unusual apparition among the Painters' display. Just beneath, a delightful, long-legged figure, probably

FLECHAS CAVE

The central figure is impaled and overlaid with arrows, one of the many enigmas in the Painters' art-symbolic vocabulary. Animal figures transfixed by arrows are common in the Sierra de San Francisco, but humans are very rare. In the sierras of Guadalupe and San Borja both are common. Some sites in all regions fairly bristle with figures wounded by spears and arrows, yet El Batequi does not show a single one. The figures at Flechas Cave act out an elaborate charade of which we have not yet guessed the first word.

representing a fawn, was very much in the expected realistic style. Elsewhere a rabbit in red was ringed by the black forms of several bat rays.

Our young guide then took us another level up the mountain to a cave just below the trail to Rancho Guadalupe. There we saw three medium-sized red-and-black deer crudely painted. This site also displayed a most curious cave, wide and deep with a low ceiling of such a rough rock-hung conglomerate that not even the most ambitious Painter could have rendered a figure on it.

The Cañada del Bajío is short and steep. According to the brother guides it had little to offer, perhaps a handful of faded figures. I was too curious to pass without a glance so I had Bernardino take me up for a look. About two or three hundred yards from the mouth of the *cañada* on the south side we came to a long low overhung wall. A few painted figures were as reported, small, faded and uninteresting. Later, I was to hear that farther up was a cave with a handsomely worked group of fish.

Bernardino led us a mile and a half down the arroyo from Santa Teresa. After a half-mile the trail quitted the *caja* level and worked its way along an irregular shelf on the canyon's west wall. As we made our way along the very bumpy and occasionally perilous path, it was easy to believe that the level *caja* a hundred feet below would have been a better choice. This form of self-deception is common among the uninitiated in country as rough as that. Any other route tends to appear better than the one with which

you are afflicted. Experience has shown conclusively that the local people know what they are about. On one occasion I tried to return by that same *caja* and found out how tiring it is to walk on sand and over and around large boulders.

Our guide led us off the trail, down a bedrock chute, and across a small broken *falda* to a cave and painted *respaldo*. The first glance showed the very fine groupings of figures which Dr. Meighan used as a frontispiece in his book, *Indian Art and History*. We were standing on the floor of the site which he called Flechas Cave.

Visitors to this place will always find themselves distracted. Most of the art is above average in conception and execution; it is well displayed and in generally superb condition. The view from the cave is a work of art in its own right. From its shelf one looks readily down a great canyon cut deeply through colorful layers of rock. Below are the heads of tall fan palms which form a line which serpentines out of sight with the curves of the arroyo. And, as another distraction, in the midst of the principal view is the overhung form of Gardner Cave with some of its copious art in plain view.

Flechas cave itself is an interesting study. The massive layer of volcanic agglomerate from which its main walls are derived overlies a softer layer which is only three or four feet thick. The latter has been eroded selectively and to rather great depths. At the south end of the Flechas site this layer is hollowed back into the mountain for over thirty feet forming a most curious cavern fifty feet wide, thirty feet deep and only three to four feet high. When this cavity grows large enough, the whole structure will not support the harder layer above and it will drop great scallop-shaped blocks of its substance onto the apron of the cave or into the chasm below. The scars where such events have taken place in the past are the typical *respaldos* that we see on all sides. It is a characteristic of this material, when unsupported, to fracture from its own weight and release a fragment much thicker at the base than at the apex. That is why most *respaldos* are overhung or sheltered.

Once the visitor turns his attention to rock art he finds himself in a fine gallery, not large but very choice. The principal group mentioned before includes three of the most elegant *monos* to be found anywhere. Beside their noble proportions and great stature they exhibit some unusual distinctions. The two at the left have tiny figures inverted over their shoulders like elaborate epaulets. These appear to be a *mono* and a deer in the case of the central giant and a *mono* and an indeterminate animal in the case of the even larger red-and-black figure on the left. The two right *monos* in this trio are shown as impaled or overlaid by half a dozen black arrows each. A pair of the arrows overlying the central *mono* have carefully painted points representing arrowheads similar to the obsidian projectile points found quite commonly in the greater area. These primitive Saint Sebastian figures suggested the name Flechas, or Arrow Cave to Dr. Meighan because they were the only human figures so mutilated in the four caves that he visited. In his choice of names he was blessed with singular fortune. In the sierras of San Borja to the north and Guadalupe to the south such arrow-impaled representations are quite common and make up a high percentage of the known human figures. But in the Sierra de San Francisco these *monos flechados* are, to my knowledge, found at only three sites.

Far away to the south in the Sierra de Guadalupe there is a site called El Carrizo where I noticed a combination of features which may indicate that it was a counterpart to this group at Flechas Cave. At El Carrizo there is a pair of big *monos*. The larger and higher has no arrows, is red and black, and has a headdress similar to that on the red-and-black upper figure at Flechas. The other Carrizo *mono* is in red only and has black arrows with carefully drawn points painted over it. This red figure also has one of those tiny "epaulet" animal figures inverted over one shoulder; the only instance of this peculiarity that I have noted other than on the two figures at Flechas Cave.

A further peculiarity in the Flechas group is the black cap on the otherwise-red central figure. And it is worth noting that all have particularly fine, if not rare, types of headdresses. The central *mono* was painted over an interesting animal figure in such a way that its head was completely defaced. This is more than usually unfortunate because the animal's body is highly stylized and probably represented the relatively rarely painted *gato montes*, or bobcat.

Elsewhere the site is distinguished by a fine red-and-black *borrego* with two relatively rare peculiarities. One horn is red and the other

black. The vast majority of such bicolored *borrego* paintings have both horns the same color. It is interesting that just across the arroyo at Gardner Cave there is another of these rare exceptions. The forelegs of the Flechas *borrego* are also unusual. They appear to have been painted twice, once straight down and the other time extended forward. This is not the result of over-painting another figure, it may have been an attempt to simulate action. As we will see, several devices of the Painters suggest that they sought after animation in their drawings.

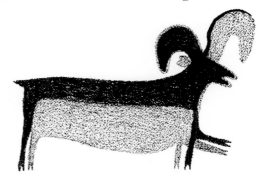

A second possible method of implying movement is common at Flechas Cave and throughout the Great Mural area. Two, or more figures were painted in succession. These are usually nearly identical deer or rabbits and they were often cocked in slightly different positions which produced the sense of an animated progression.

At this site there are at least four such pairs and one is especially interesting. Two rabbits were drawn in sure, fine lines of red paint which included an arrow in each. But this outline was

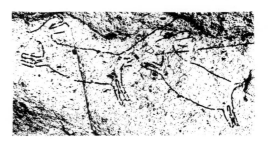

never filled in with paint. Such incomplete figures are found here and there throughout the Great Murals and they suggest that all paintings began with outlines. These few must have been interrupted by exigencies of the moment, pauses that became eternal.

The remaining figures and groups at Flechas Cave include a large black deer, a red deer painted over a large black bird, and numerous small figures representative of all the usual subjects. These miniatures, ranging in size from about eight inches to a foot and a half, are very common at most sites and should not be confused with the truly tiny figures, drawn in outline only, which were noted at La Natividad. Dr. Meighan drew attention to the fact that a number of the small *monos* at Flechas Cave had only one side painted in red. The presumably intended black half was missing in each case and he assumed that it had never been painted. After inspecting hundreds of figures and sites, I would submit an alternate opinion. Black paint apparently weathered more quickly than red; this was particularly true where charcoal was used as the black pigment. As a result, it is very common to find figures with strong red parts and weak black parts. Sometimes the black is barely detectable. In instances like that at Flechas Cave, I think it likely that the figures were completed and that the black side has entirely weathered away.

Across the arroyo and down a scant quarter of a mile is Gardner Cave. Stating the distance, however, gives little conception of the experience of traversing that stretch. First, there is a descent of about a hundred and fifty feet to the *caja* over a crumbling, slippery bedrock inclined at a phenomenally steep angle. The *caja* then has the small obstacles of water, boulders, and thickets of a woody plant called *guatamote*. Then, the climb to Gardner Cave is nearly as steep, if not as high as the descent from Flechas. However, all is forgiven and forgotten in the contemplation of the new surroundings.

This grand cave may be considered the focus of the Great Murals. It is the most painted place in the most painted part of the entire range in which these giant realistic artworks are found. The larger physical setting, as with nearby Flechas Cave, is very beautiful as well. This slightly lower cave has an even more intimate view of the deep canyon, palms, and pools of water. The cave itself, while nearly five hundred

feet in length, is not as impressive as that figure implies. At no point is it very deep, perhaps forty feet at most, and for half its length it is very low-ceilinged and shallow as well. Both La Cuevona de la Ascención and La Natividad are caves of much greater volume. But no other cave has so much appreciable art.

The quantity of art is a function of two factors that extend beyond the will of the Painters; the size of the cave and the durability of its rock surfaces. In the latter respect it has proved especially outstanding. Many other sites were as heavily painted per square foot of wall space but in very few has the ratio of survival been so high. This is due in part to a rather recent event in the history of the cave's formation.

At the south end of the shelter there is a section of the back wall some one hundred feet long which is covered with very fresh paintings of large *monos*, deer and *borrego*. Though there is a considerable amount of overpainting to a depth of at least three layers, the group is in the best condition of any considerable number of figures to be found in the entire range of Great Murals. Just below most of this stretch of back wall there is a line of huge fallen rock fragments. Inspection shows that they have released relatively recently from the wall above, leaving it as a very clean, little-eroded surface. It appears that the excellent condition of these paintings is due in large measure to the fresh character of the rock on which they were painted. Most of the other *respaldos* apparently were quite weathered when painted on. This meant that they were already in a partial state of disintegration and, as it proceeded, the paintings suffered. All the rock at this great cave is relatively durable but that south end is in phenomenally good condition.

The rock in part of this special area appears especially fresh and it is interesting that the style of painting on what seems to be the very freshest rock surface is very homogeneous and the range of color is amazingly limited. Only black and a single red are evident. The situation invites the thought that this particular section collapsed during the painting epoch and that the Painters decorated the new surface in a fairly short period of time. Someday this hypothesis could be tested by tunneling under one of the huge fallen fragments to see if its lower side is painted. Should this prove to be the case, the problem of dating might be simplified. Any or-

CUEVA PINTADA

First brought to public attention by Erle Stanley Gardner in 1962, this most painted of all Great Mural sites is also known as Gardner Cave. Here an extent of five hundred feet of wall and ceilings is almost continuously painted with a variety of figures and styles. The great south panel pictured above is remarkable for the fine condition and the homogeneity of its painted figures. Despite the fact that three separate layers can be distinguished, all the works seem similar in style and pigments.

CUEVA PINTADA

Overpainting was as much a part of the Painters' way as the heroic size and representational character of their figures. While a number of grouped paintings and an occasional entire site, like El Batequi, seem to show the intent to create a composition, most overpainting was destructive. It is puzzling to consider that the Painters at times showed little concern for the visibility of either the existing works or those being added and yet, at other times, created elaborate constructions to reach the unused parts of cave walls.

ganic materials lying on the floor covered by the fall would almost certainly be from the Painters' time.

Elsewhere the art of the cave contrasts strongly with that just described. The subject matter is much more varied; more styles are observable and more colors were used. Just to the left of the abnormally fresh appearing works there is a gigantic figure rendered in a light sketchy red, a chalk-like technique similar to that used to produce the well-preserved group of deer at La Natividad. This monster, the largest figure in the cave, appears to represent a whale. The forepart, head and fins, are admirable but the tail region is drawn more like a pair of elephantine legs than the fluke of a whale. Farther to the left, after a rather large area with little or no painting, is a group of additional *monos* and deer in the pale, chalked style. Prominent among them are several examples of "sackhat man," a *mono* type widespread among the Great Murals and usually worked in this sketchy fashion.

The entire northern half of the cave has an unusually low ceiling which is, for the greater part, very heavily painted. The colors are exceptionally rich, the figures range from large to small but the latter predominate. Overpainting is the rule and in places it is as heavily applied and wildly confused as any to be encountered among the Great Murals.

The smaller figures include an unusual variety of subjects and styles, forming a sub-gallery of special interest. Birds are represented more frequently than usual; over a dozen can be discerned. Fish figures on the other hand, are few; the three or four examples are undistinguished in concept or execution. Five times the number of fish can be seen on the walls of a single small cave at the Cuesta de San Pablo, a few miles down the arroyo. Rabbits are really common at Gardner Cave. From fifteen to twenty depictions can be counted, the disparity allowing for differences of opinion about representations of rabbits and fawns. I suspect that the Indians preyed heavily on the baby deer which could have been run down readily as compared to the older animals. It seems to me also that a rather large percentage of the paintings which outsiders instantly assume to represent rabbits or hares actually are of fawns. Most of us are not familiar with the mule deer which figures as the only species available to the Painters. Their ears are

very large, and, in the young, the proportion to the head size is at least as great as the comparable proportion in a rabbit.

Gardner Cave by no means contains all the different sorts of figures known in this sierra. It does not necessarily display the best or most artistic examples of those that are represented on its walls. In spite of that it remains the greatest single example of a Painter site. It is the place that a visitor would choose to know the phenomenon best with a single visit. It probably contains three times as many clear, well-preserved figures as any other site. Even the indifferent people of the sierra, or the few who knew it, were moved to call it La Cueva Pintada; to them it was The Painted Cave, despite the many other shelters which were known to contain Indian art.

Although it is obvious that this large, long slit cave on the wall of a remote arroyo was an important center in prehistoric times, it has a very short history in either written or oral tradition. The missionaries missed it because their roads ran either east of the sierra or over its mesas far above the *caja* of the arroyo. It would seem probable that some of the Cochimí neophytes at either the mission *rancho* of San Francisco at the head of this arroyo, or that of San Pablo nearer its mouth, would have known of the paintings. But apparently they either ignored them or their reports failed to interest the missionaries who already knew the phenomenon from places closer to their beaten tracks.

When Buenaventura Arce acquired legal title to Rancho Santa Marta around 1840, its vaguely stated extent included the old mission station of San Francisco. No one today knows whether the great painted caves of the arroyo were known to Arce, his family, or his tenants. Everyone assumes that Cueva del Ratón was known all along because of its proximity to the ranch, but the deep parts of the arroyo had no inhabitants and few visitors in those days.

In pursuing this history I have queried all the sierra's old-timers and got a fairly consistent report. By about 1890 at least two men knew of a large cave with many paintings in the Arroyo de Salsipuedes, and it was already known as Cueva Pintada. Tacho's father, Severiano Arce, at age ninety, recalled that when he was a child his father Cesario discovered such a cave and it was talked about for a while as other sierra men occasionally visited it. Cesario was a grandson of Buenaventura Arce, and during the old man's life moved up to the mountain ranch as the first family member in full-time residence. He was an *andariego*, a restless travelling type, according to family legend, and knew every trail between San Borja and La Purísima.

Pedro Altamirano, living at San Pablo, was sure that his father Francisco, who was apparently the first post-mission rancher in the lower arroyo, also knew of Cueva Pintada. Pedro was born in 1890 and believes that his father knew the cave and had traversed the entire arroyo well before his son's birth.

Subsequent neglect is not difficult to understand. The Arroyo de Salsipuedes was passable only on foot and then with great difficulty. No one had any real reason to abandon the far faster mesa routes which connected all the sierra ranches. When Diguet visited San Francisco in 1893-94 he missed Cueva Pintada. This does not tell us that no one knew it at the time. We do not know his guide for this trip as a whole, nor whom he saw in San Francisco. Only two or three families lived at the ranch in those days and then, as now, they had to move seasonally to pasture their animals. It is also true that Diguet's list of painted places included few, if any, which were not on or near main trails. A study of Sierra de San Francisco place-names derived from the various Diguet publications reveals his probable route. He entered the north end of the sierra at Cuesta Blanca and came up the Arroyo de San Pablo as far as Rancho San Pablo. Then he ascended the cuesta to the south which put him on the mesa of San Julio. He took and published a photograph of Rancho San Jorge on that mesa which shows that he passed to the west and a thousand feet above Cueva Pintada. From there he stayed on mesas all the way to San Francisco, passing through Rancho Santa Ana on the way. This route incidentally was a main road from Calmallí to the San Ignacio area and many people could have guided Diguet competently over that trail who had little knowledge of the country on either side.

When Fernando Arce Sandoval founded Rancho Santa Teresa in the heart of the Arroyo de Salsipuedes around 1940, he changed the travel patterns significantly in the area. His wife was an Altamirano from San Nicolás only four or five miles down the arroyo. A regular trail was established between the two ranches and every

passerby could literally have seen into the great cave from the trail. Thus, by 1962, when Erle Stanley Gardner got wind of the place a lot of people were aware of La Cueva Pintada.

Sam Hicks, of Temecula, California, was a member of the Gardner party which first flew into the sierra and was told about cave paintings. He, the helicopter pilot, Bob Boughton, and J. W. Black, and John Straubel went to San Francisco the day after Gardner and were taken to Cueva del Ratón as Gardner had been. But then they were told about giant Cueva Pintada far down the Arroyo de San Pablo. As they flew back to tell the others in their party of this revelation they took the route described to them by the people of San Francisco. By good fortune Hicks spotted the cave; they landed and took a few pictures.

That incident opened the door. The photos convinced Gardner that he was on to something big and he organized the return expedition with Dr. Meighan. Nat Farbman from Life Magazine was along and national coverage resulted. For a brief time the affair commanded international interest. I and millions of others read about this discovery on our neighbor's land and settled back assuming that studies were undertaken.

My historical inquiries raised a thorny subject. Dr. Meighan had named three caves, Flechas, as we have seen, Gardner Cave, and another nearby which he called Pájaro Negro. The question reaches far beyond the mere problem of these three caves. It is a very general question of how places in remote regions are going to be known, mapped and reported. When three caves are concerned it seems simple, when hundreds are involved the situation cries out for a philosophy, a system which will bring order and be acceptable to everyone involved.

It seems to me that the first criterion in naming a place is local usage. If a name is employed regularly by local people, even if they are few in number, that is its legitimate name.

A second criterion is a general place name. Few caves, for instance, were named directly like Cueva Pintada. But many are known by their locality: "The Cave in the Cañada de la Natividad" communicates perfectly to a man who knows the sierra well. Since that *cañada* has only one cave of any consequence, the Cueva de la Natividad makes an ideal name. This can be legitimately shortened to La Natividad in any context where it is clear that caves are the subject.

When a named geographic area like an arroyo embraces several caves the problem becomes complex and some more arbitrary decisions have to be made. Additional designations are called for and numbers or Roman numerals seem to be indicated. I prefer the latter, hence such designations in my notes as Santa Teresa I, Santa Teresa II, etc. However, I recognize that Roman numerals become cumbersome if large numbers are involved. The simplest way to apply any sort of numerals is the order in which discoveries are made. That also leaves the door open to the indefinite extension of the system.

This nomenclatural digression properly ends as a review of Dr. Meighan's names for three caves.

Gardner Cave already had a recognized legitimate name, Cueva Pintada. The translation, Painted Cave, is certainly not a marvel of originality or distinctiveness but that is not the question.

Flechas Cave apparently had no name of its own even among the people who lived a few miles above or below it. It was known as "the-cave-across-from-Cueva Pintada," which is scarcely a satisfactory designation for such an important place. Since Dr. Meighan's name is descriptive and distinguishes the place from others, it seems perfectly appropriate to vote for its continued use.

Pájaro Negro is the only painted cave in the main trunk of the Cañada de la Soledad. The local people call it the Cueva de la Soledad, or simply La Soledad, if caves are being listed or discussed. Even if this name were not in use,

Pájaro Negro would be debatably appropriate. There are several other caves in the same sierra which display prominent black birds. Furthermore, the cave in the Cañada de la Soledad has a red bird of similar proportions and prominence only a few feet from the black one.

The Cañada de la Soledad enters the Arroyo de San Pablo at a right angle from the northeast where it has made an abrupt drop between very steep walls. The intersection takes place only a few dozen yards upstream from Flechas cave. A quarter of a mile up this *cañada* and on its north side, a large rock shelter can be seen at the top of a *falda* so steep that it would almost classify as a cliff. This shelter is the Cueva de la Soledad, otherwise known as Pájaro Negro.

The basic volume is very simple. An agglomerate layer, comprising some thirty feet of the height of the rock sectioned by the *cañada*, has also been cross-cut by a smaller watercourse at right angles to the main drainage. This second cut has produced a free-standing corner of rock out of which large pieces have fallen away to create an alcove about thirty feet high by eighty feet wide. The backwall is in two quite different sections; the southerly end consists of a simple curved surface which goes to the full height of the shelter. This wall displays most of the art which includes about a dozen clear *monos*, half as many deer, and a striking pair of nearly identical large birds, one red and one black. The latter figure was responsible for Dr. Meighan's choice of names.

The northern end of the backwall is much rougher and has a complex form. Its lower half is undercut and eroded to form a tiny cave-within-the-shelter. On the roof of this recess is

CUEVA DE LA SOLEDAD and FLECHAS CAVE

The typical painted shelter in the Great Mural region is formed by the collapse of volcanic rock layers undercut by erosion. These photographs show the steep-walled arroyos, the layered character of the rock, the process of cave formation and examples of painted sites. Flechas Cave is the left of the three shelters in the lower picture. Note the proximity of the native palms which could have been used in the making of ladders for painting high parts of cave walls.

an extremely rare sort of painting, a checkerboard made up of ochre-yellow lines with the boxes filled in neatly in red and black. The whole is about four feet long and a foot-and-a-half wide. One row of squares has been partially drawn in yellow but never completed or colored in.

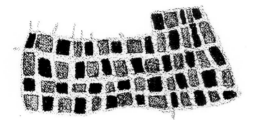

On the same surface as the checkerboard are a pair of ornate red and black birds, a red rabbit, and a rich confusion of overpainted works which cannot be identified. In a higher alcove almost outside the north side of the shelter are three figures: a red-and-black *mono*, a black *borrego* and a black deer. The latter two are notable for the vigor of their representations.

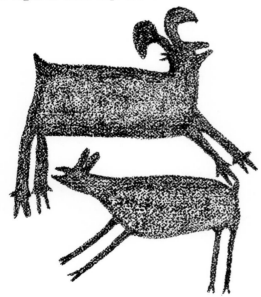

On the principal wall the greatest artistic interest centers on the birds and three black deer apparently from the same hand. Spaced well across the forty-foot space and moving from left to right are a buck, a young animal and a mature doe. The representations are executed in a simple, secure style which suggests a thoroughly practiced artist. Particularly noteworthy are his careful depictions of details such as antlers and dewlap claws.

Above the Cueva de la Soledad the *cañada* has formed a region of twisting, steep-sided gorges. About a mile from the cave the watercourse divides into two and before long the northern branch divides again. All of this branching and twisting and cutting deeply into the many-layered rock produces the most labyrinthine passages in the entire sierra and, on the peninsula, rivalled only in the Sierra de la Giganta far to the south. For large parts of the length of the Cañada de la Soledad a man literally cannot climb out of the *caja* and, where he can, the exits are precipitous. In precisely those places where no exit is possible some excellent paintings are found in galleries high above the restricted waterways.

The middle branch of the *cañada* is called El Brinco because, at its head, there is a trail which used to scale a very precarious palisade layer of rock. A short steep ascent was the *brinco*, or jump. Recent trail work with large iron bars had made this into a respectable stair which no longer challenged a sierra mule, but the name persisted.

The mountain people have little reason to enter the Cañada de la Soledad, much less El Brinco. They apparently never enter from below. The Arces of Santa Teresa knew nothing about it and I might have missed it altogether but for Leandro Arce Sandoval at San Pedro, a *rancho* high on the mesa and north of this whole drainage complex. The subject came up on my second visit to San Pedro when, for a second time, I was attempting to penetrate Don Leandro's vague references to paintings in the region. We had disposed of the mesa as totally barren and he professed to know no Indian remains whatever in the Arroyo de San Pedro, a *tinaja* of which provided water for his ranch. My host truthfully was not interested in paintings and only politeness and my persistence kept him on the subject. Finally there was a flicker, a recollection. Years before, many years before, he had lost a number of goats, a dozen or so. He had searched for days and finally ventured down from the top to look into the abysmally deep Cañada del Brinco. After a long scramble he found them on an "island" created by the deep-cutting vagaries of the *cañada*. During the chase he had noticed a large cave with some paintings; he could remember nothing about them. I immediately wanted to go, but Leandro, at sixty-and-some years, obviously did not relish acting as a guide. Tacho knew the trail over the *brinco* but nothing of the *cañada*. It finally developed that a grandson of Leandro knew the terrain but he was far away. I would have to wait.

The wait lasted two years and through two more visits. Finally the young man was available and the trip began. The trail used was that which connects Rancho San Pedro with the village of San Francisco; it follows the absolute spine of the sierra and permits wonderful views of the gulf coast and the sierras of San Juan and San Borja.

Shortly before coming to the actual *brinco*, our guide led us west on foot down a slope which became steeper and steeper, finally having to be descended with the utmost care, one halting step at a time. After twisting downward for forty minutes and nearing the notchlike bottom of the gulley, we suddenly found that our trail had brought us to the floor of a large cave shelter.

The place had an unusually regular form; a high *respaldo* arched over a wide, level floor area. On the tall curved plane of the wall were a large number of figures. Most were in very poor condition and required some effort to interpret. There were a number of red-and-black *monos* and several deer. Higher than most of the other figures a fairly clear "sackhat man" stood out in the uniform almost exclusive to his kind. His red upper body changed exactly at the waist to black as if he were wearing trousers. Elsewhere a red *león* was fairly clear and, to-

ward the extreme east end of the shelter, was a large manta ray, a rare form indeed. The initial drawing of this great fish was in a rich orange-pink, then the diamond-shaped form had been bisected vertically by a straight line from the center of the head through the center of the tail. One half was then painted red and the other black. The figure could be made out readily and it was clear that it had been elegantly painted, but all parts were badly faded and the tail was missing. The rareness of such representations made the loss especially galling.

After much study of the poorly preserved works, I realized why a few of the deer looked so familiar. Their style was very reminiscent of La Natividad and I had not made the connection because of their radically different condition. At the other site they looked like yesterday's work and here more like ancient artifacts.

A hundred yards down the *caja* we were shown second and third El Brinco painted places; small, worn paintings were all that remained. We climbed out of the wash and worked our way along a shelf on the north side. The *cañada* turned south and we followed around the turn. Our guide stopped and pointed up to a steep cliff. Under its brow was a small shelter, his own discovery. Like his grandfather, he had come down to look for lost goats. A group was trapped on that ridge and he had gone up to investigate, noticing the paintings as he passed.

After the sad losses at El Brinco I and the poverty of II and III, this place was an absolute joy. The small shallow cave fairly glowed with color and, for a blessed change, most of the figures were quite clear. On a single panel six feet high, which represented the weathered edge of one rock layer, was a continuous frieze of figures some thirty feet in extent. The subject matter offered few surprises; *monos*, deer and perhaps rabbits made it up. What was a surprise was the curious palette. There was very little black. The contrasting colors were rich browns, a deep umber and a burnt sienna.

The parade of forms was easily dominated by the largest and darkest, a strikingly composed deer in dark umber. The only real curiosity at the site was associated with this painting. A square, whose sides were made up of two or three parallel black lines, was painted to exactly fit within the body of the deer. This is the only occurrence of this, or any similar device, of

which I know.

While we photographed El Brinco IV, Ramón Arce was out scouting further along the ledge. He returned having found nothing on our side of the *cañada* but reported a huge cave on the other side about four or five hundred yards downstream. Our next exertions help to give a fair picture of the terrain. There was no question of a direct descent, a sheer drop of eighty feet intervened. We returned as we had come, a quarter of a mile upstream to reach the bed of the *cañada*. Then we had to ascend that wash another two hundred yards before it was possible to climb the opposite bank. The walk to the new cave was a fairly easy half-mile march over a sloping shelf high above the *caja*.

The cave was the most impressive of its kind that I have ever seen. Two successive layers of fairly soft rock underlay a very thick layer of harder material. The former had eroded until the hard layer above overhung them by twenty feet or more. Since the two layers thus removed had a thickness, in sum, of twenty feet and since the whole outcropping was about four hundred feet long, the void was huge. The whole was formed of a very pale gray-beige agglomerate, almost a white. The floor was level and smooth and, as we walked along it was like traversing some great open gallery. A marvelous view was to be had on one hand and an art collection on the other.

Actually the painted works were concentrated in a run of only fifty feet or so, the rest of the gallery was spotless. But what paintings they were and in what condition! The inventory was short: six *monos*, four deer, three rabbits and one fish. Beside these, a *mono* and two additional rabbits had been neatly painted in white outline only and abandoned in that incomplete condition. These "ghost" rabbits, as at the Flechas site, included arrows as an integral part of their initial drawing.

The joy of this place is created by the quality and condition of its few works as well as by their beautiful surroundings. As a group they are better preserved than those of any other site. They are almost as colorful and complete as those of the great southern wall panel at Cueva Pintada. Overpainting is limited to a slight confusion of the feet of two *monos* with the figures of the two large deer, no problem for anyone who has puzzled over some of the Painters' really complex overlaid mazes.

Three *monos* show the conventional vertically divided red-and-black pattern and one of these has a truly droll little headdress that looks like a miniature palm.

The other three *monos* all represent women and are painted in a red ground color overlaid by vertical black stripes. One of these also has an unusual black line emerging from the top of the head. It could represent an arrow or a very simple headdress.

LA CANDELARIA I and EL BRINCO IV

Representations of berrendo, *the pronghorn antelope, are rare; the author has found three which he can confidently identify. This example from La Candelaria I, at top, shows the long neck and short body common to all three works. Visible also are two of the rare ochre "checkerboards" whose abstract style may post-date the Painters. Below, Ramón Arce inspects and Enrique Hambleton photographs the painted wall at El Brinco IV, where the style, pigments, and overpainting suggest that it was the product of just three easily distinguished artists or groups of artists.*

A pair of deer or fawns are beautifully realized. The use of black accents around ears and tail is especially noteworthy.

The fish is bicolored but the division of red and black is highly individual.

A rabbit carefully painted on an inclusive rock has both an unusual drawing and color combination. The dark upper part is painted in a rich red-brown and the pale belly in a soft beige.

Our guide from San Pedro had never heard of this cave although he had a name, Banco del Carrizo, for the slope and hill on which it was found. We learned later that the people of Rancho Guadalupe on the mesa to the south did know of this place and had taken visitors to it a year or two before. They, in turn, knew nothing of our El Brinco IV site, all of which illustrates the rugged and isolated state of the upper reaches of the Cañada de la Soledad.

Back in the principal flow of the Arroyo de San Pablo and about a mile below the mouth of the Cañada de la Soledad, a trail climbs out of the depths of the arroyo and commences the long and notably indirect ascent to the north which eventually leads to the Mesa de los Gajos. The greater part of this *cuesta* lies in a short, steep *cañada* called El Cacariso, the pock-marked, after an oddly eroded bluff at its mouth. The trail ascends the north wall of the *cañada* and, as it does so, it affords a good view of some *respaldos* on its south side and perhaps a third of the way up. On the basis of a tip from young Bernardino Arce at Santa Teresa we went over and checked these potential sites.

We worked our way along the lower of two *respaldo* levels without success and climbed with difficulty to the second. There, in a large overhung shelter, were *metates* and numerous rock chips but no paintings. However, perhaps a hundred yards farther to the east, we found what we sought, a small but heavily painted *respaldo*.

On the principal face were fifteen deer and five *monos* including a clear red representation of the ubiquitous "sackhat man" in his usual position high amongst the other works.

The rock was soft and the paintings were badly eroded, particularly a lower row. The general level of artistry appeared to have been rather low and the figures entirely routine except for one oddity in red and black which was about four

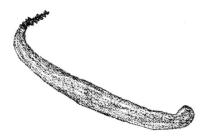

feet long. The most logical assumption is that we found at El Cacariso another of the very rare rattlesnake paintings. This would scarcely compete as art with the superb rattler from the Sierra de Guadalupe which is illustrated elsewhere.

The same trail which goes up the Cuesta del Cacariso divides near the bottom of the *cuesta* and the left branch, as one rides north, proceeds along a shelf some hundred feet or more above the *caja*. A half mile below the opening of El Cacariso, another *cañada* enters from the southwest through a narrow channel. This is the Cañada de San Julio, taking its name from that of a prominent volcanic cone on the mesa to the west.

As we rode along on my first visit to the area I was inspecting every suspicious rock surface with care, inspired by viewing the great sites around Cueva Pintada during the previous days. Looking up San Julio, I thought that I saw several possible shelters, one high and distant and others near the *caja* and closer. I wanted to investigate but was frustrated by the terrain; there was no descent at that point. Finally, after riding another quarter of a mile north, I was able to climb down to the *caja* and hike back to the opening of the *cañada*.

This part of the Arroyo de San Pablo is impressive for its depth and for its wild character. There are pools of water hundreds of feet long and up to twenty feet deep; there are huge boulders scattered about, numerous stands of palms and thickets of dense undergrowth. Working my way back was neither quick nor easy. Finally, however, I was able to start up the actual *cañada* and soon found that, on its floor, was a stand of *palo blanco*, a beautiful white-barked tree. After scrambling up the *cañada* about a hundred and fifty yards I looked to my right up the steep wall and saw a beautiful cave shelter carved from a soft cream-colored rock. With difficulty I climbed the bank and entered a place which I call La Boca de San Julio, the Mouth of San Julio.

There is no more beautiful painted place in all the mountains. The cave is about seventy feet long and eight to twelve feet high. The floor is a level, spotless expanse of pale sandy stone raised above the shelf outside. The whole is so inaccessible that neither cattle nor goats have used it for shelter. The ceiling curves gently downward, its slope accelerating as it approaches the floor. The little cave faces south and its interior is brilliantly lighted all day by sun reflected from the floor.

This cheerful place was once liberally painted and a considerable showing survives. Unfortunately the stone of Boca de San Julio is not of the best. It is quite soft and sheds its substance in a constant sloughing of grains. All its paintings have been damaged in the process.

At the west end is the greatest concentration of works, a multitude of large and small deer much overpainted. Two stand out for their fine condition, a heavy-bodied doe in red that could well be drawn as pregnant, and a red-and-black buck arched as in flight. Around and under them are a large number of small figures which include rabbits, *monos* (actually half-*monos* as at Flechas Cave), birds and an odd figure whose damaged state prevents it from being identified as a grotesquely fat *mono* or perhaps a turtle.

At the right end is an exceptional show. On one small rock panel there are four birds rendered in dark red, pink, and white. All are badly damaged but the two larger ones mercifully are in good enough condition that facsimiles can be made. These depictions, with about thirty-inch wing spreads, appear to represent some sort of shore or water fowl; perhaps one is a cormorant and the other a duck or goose. In each case the painting is very beautiful; the basic drawing being in dark red and the whole being outlined in pink and white. The technique makes the display of flight feathers appear to be alternately red and pink.

A long climb to the farther, higher cave showed that it was empty but, on the way up, a very exposed shelter facing the trail produced striking sentinels, a large red-and-black *mono*, his black half nearly eroded away, and a larger female *mono*. With their upraised arms this weather-beaten pair seemed to be blocking the passage to some secret place beyond.

Later, a real curiosity turned up just a few yards above the trail which faces the opening of the Cañada de San Julio.

There on the ceiling of a small cave clogged with a huge fallen block of rock, there is an absolutely unique group of tiny red-and-black *monos* scattered in a tight but apparently random pattern. Drawn across them in dazzling white are two groups of lines resembling musical staffs. The effect is peculiar in the extreme. The *monos* look like dancing notes on two bars of music.

A mile below the mouth of San Julio is Rancho San Nicolás, and four miles below that is Rancho San Pablo, the home of Pedro Altamirano. This man, who was past eighty years of age when I first met him, was a living legend in the entire region. He associated himself with the revolutionaries of 1910 as a young man and served them

with distinction. In two well-remembered incidents he risked his life to save men of the region from government reprisals. When a degree of normalcy returned, Pedro was decorated and received in his old age a pension from his grateful nation.

We found the old man sitting in the sun on a chill morning wearing a much-favored knitted cap. He was hard of hearing but soon understood who we were and made us welcome. After a stiff-gaited excursion into the house for his glasses he commenced a lively account of rock art in the area and his family's experiences with Indian remains in general. First he remembered a string of caves in a *respaldo* just off a *cuesta* that ascended the south wall of the arroyo, "the old Cuesta de San Pablo," he called it. Then he and his first cousin, Tránsito Quintero, who was Tacho's assistant on the trip, fell to discussing a site in a place called El Salón. They had not seen it for sixty years and the recollection proved vague. Finally he gave us some pointers on finding numerous small painted sites farther down the arroyo off of the Cuesta Blanca. It was obvious that the old man had never really paid any great attention to paintings, but he was intelligent and kind enough to rack his memories for clues. I am very grateful. Cuesta San Pablo alone proved to be a tremendous gift.

A mile and a half below Rancho San Pablo there is an inconspicuous part of the arroyo which has seen an unusual amount of historical activity. Riding down the trail, the sign which best identifies this place is a high sheer outcropping of very red volcanic rock, a material so colorful that it may have been ground to produce some of the Indian paint. This solitary geologic feature is on the east side of the wash; on the opposite *ancón* and downstream a couple of hundred yards are the remains of a large adobe chapel. This is the site usually indicated by those who interpret history to include a mission called Los Dolores del Norte. Actually the name, as well as that of Mission San Juan Bautista located in the Picachos of Santa Clara, seems to have arisen from a chance series of events in the eighteenth century.

Padre Fernando Consag was the most zealous of missionaries and he took his responsibilities to explore for converts very seriously. And, while very humble personally, he was an enthusiastic promoter of plans to enlarge the Jesuit mis-

EL BRINCO V

A vast cave-overhang high above a minor watercourse in one of the least accessible parts of the Sierra de San Francisco contains a striking display of Great Mural art. A durable rock surface and good protection explain the fine condition of paintings that show men, women, deer, rabbits, and fish in the Painters' highest tradition. The remoteness of such places from scenes of hunting or food gathering and the relative absence of artifacts suggest that they were visited only to produce and possibly commune with the huge paintings.

sionary horizon. During the 1740's, as a result of thorough explorations, he apparently recommended the establishment of at least three missions north and west of San Ignacio. Somehow, during deliberations and actions on Consag's proposals, a garbled report must have leaked out of Jesuit circles. A 1757 map, now widely reproduced, shows the three missions as *empezadas*, or begun. The mapmaker was clearly misinformed on all counts. Consag's most northerly proposal had, by 1757, been established as Mission Santa Gertrudis and run for five years. The map calls it Santa María Magdalena. The other two Consag proposals were never acted on. Both were close to existing missions and the supposed site of San Juan Bautista in the desert peaks of Santa Clara had no adequate source of water.

These ruins in the Arroyo de San Pablo were almost certainly what Gerhard and Gulick call them in their *Lower California Guidebook*, "a visiting station of Santa Gertrudis mission." As evidence a large, beautifully made road constructed in typical Jesuit fashion connects chapel and mission.

The chapel structure is about one hundred and thirty feet long by twenty-one feet wide and consists of three rooms of approximately equal size. The adobe walls were erected on stone foundations and still stand to three or four feet along the sides and to nearly full height at the four gable walls. Just south of this church is a massive stone corral and on the *ancón* of the opposite, or east side, there are the remains of a *huerta* buttressed by rock against the ravages of flood and also of an irrigation system, much damaged but quite visible.

Another great artifact scars the hillside to the west. A conspicuous trail diverges at the chapel and leads up the slope. After an extremely steep series of switchbacks, steep even for the Sierra de San Francisco, the trail heads up onto a mesa and then south by way of San Jorge. This was once the main road in use between San Ignacio and such northern places as Calmallí, El Arco, Rosarito and Punta Prieta. During small mining booms it was heavily travelled and continued in use until the need for an auto road caused a new construction entirely west of the sierra.

The part of this road which led up the *falda* to the southwest was the Cuesta de San Pablo. About two thirds of the way up the *cuesta* the trail is forced to make a radical turn to the north in order to get over a vertical impasse breached only at one point. Following Altamirano's instructions, Tacho, who had never seen the caves but knew the trail, led us to the right along the base of the cliff which so blocked the access to the summit. In less than a hundred yards we arrived at a small cave with its floor raised above the head of the *falda*.

The walls of this cave were eroded from a grey conglomerate of fine particles. The form of the eroded surface was unusual in that it mimicked the character of draped material. This curtained pattern parted to leave two fairly smooth clear areas about twelve feet high. The left was decorated with a rather stylish if unintentional grouping of three distinguishable figures, a deer, a *gato montes*, or wild cat, and a *mono*. The bobcat much resembled the Painters' depiction of a mountain lion except that it had a well defined, stub-like tail. The right grouping was larger and more confused. It appeared to consist of at least three deer and a *mono* with smaller figures frolicking at their feet. Despite the confusion of overpainting, both groups were attractive; their color making an effective contrast with the warm gray of the walls.

Another fifty yards of scrambling took us past a huge fallen rock mass and into a second cave. This one too had curiously formed walls, this time the entire surface was textured by a pattern of protruding knobs four or five inches in diameter. The paintings, however, were so striking that they put the subject of the textured wall quite out of mind. Although there was a large black deer and several attractive smaller bicolored deer and rabbits, all attention was first focussed on four similar and extremely rare depictions. There, grouped together in the central part of the cave were four superb paintings of *mobula* or manta rays done in elegantly simple detail. Precisely indicated were the cephalic fins on either side of the mouth cavity and the extended whip-like tail. One clearly showed the trailing claspers of the male fish. All were outlined in white with a single sure line; two had been painted in red and the others had had only one half colored with the same hue. Below were perhaps two dozen smaller fish of more conventional types as well as a few nicely drawn birds and small *monos*. The great rays, however, absolutely dominated the small cave.

By pushing farther along the top of the *falda*

we came first to a cave so smoked that its interior was still a solid black. Through that heavy patina a few vestiges of painting were visible and, as an oddity, a number of engravings had been added by cutting through the smoked surface to the pale rock. These as a result stood out boldly. After a hiatus of a hundred yards in which no remains appeared, we found a final cave, the largest and most deteriorated. Its back wall had a long group made up apparently of deer only, mostly bicolored and heavily overpainted. The impact of this last cave shelter was distinctly dispiriting. The figures had been elegantly conceived and executed by artists with a real sense of style. But that finesse was nearly obscured by the confusion of superimposed lines and colors and by the heavy losses to erosion.

From the chapel, the afore-mentioned Jesuit road made a five-mile run down the broad *ancón* on the east side of the arroyo. Then it headed obliquely up the *falda* over a striking white way that gave the ascent its name, Cuesta Blanca. Near the pass on the north side was a long line of small caves in a soft light-colored rock layer. Most of them had been painted but the attrition in the art was nearly complete. Scattered in various shelters were deer and *monos*; one black figure was probably either a *borrego* or a rare depiction of *berrendo*, the pronghorn antelope.

One group of these deteriorated paintings may be of special interest to archaeologists. In a small, open shelter were a couple of *monos*; one was red and black, the other black. The soft, fine, sand-textured surface on which they were painted had almost entirely weathered away to a depth of at least a few millimeters. Almost all the paint was lost with it but a strange "ghost"

of the black image has penetrated deeper and remained as a perceptible stain. This stain could provide a clue as to the binder used by the Painters.

No summary is needed of the art in Arroyo San Pablo. It is the epicenter of the Great Mural phenomenon and the works it contains are so numerous that their characteristics create the norm against which others are compared.

THE ARROYO DE LA CUESTA BLANCA

The north end of the main mass of the Sierra de San Francisco takes the form of a grand flow toward the northwest. In its original state it must have been a rather featureless fan of volcanic rock gradually descending to the level of the surrounding plains. Today that early simplicity is scarred by a series of nearly parallel water-eroded arroyos which cut deeply through the successive layers which make up its thickness. San Pablo is the largest. Just to the east and over Cuesta Blanca the next arroyo, with a certain paucity of imagination, is called the Arroyo de la Cuesta Blanca. At just about the point where the old Jesuit road descends from that *cuesta*, the arroyo is joined from the east by the next major water-course, the Arroyo de San Pedro. The latter runs far into the sierra remaining roughly parallel to the Arroyo de San Pablo. The Arroyo de la Cuesta Blanca, sandwiched between these larger neighbors, extends only about five miles to the southeast where it originates as a group of rivulets collecting off the surface of the great flow.

The eastern slope of Cuesta Blanca also contains a series of cliffs which run southeast and proceed almost unbroken up the west wall of the

ROSARITO and CUESTA DE SAN PABLO II

Though the Painters' selection of animals is usually limited to a few kinds often repeated, there are rare and welcome exceptions. The fine rattlesnake described on page 113, shares a wall with common deer. Some, however, are rendered in a rare yellow pigment. Seldom encountered paintings of manta or mobula rays make up the principal show at Cuesta de San Pablo II. These works detail the fishes' anatomy with great accuracy despite being more than twenty-five miles from the nearest arm of the sea. See following page.

CUESTA DE SAN PABLO I

Tightly composed groupings of apparently unrelated figures is a recurrent theme among the Great Murals. That they are not simply accidental overpaintings seems certain since many are thus compactly rendered on large walls where much clean space was available. Furthermore many seem to be composed of figures of similar age, style, and paint. What was the relationship which the artist or artists saw between this man with his unusual basket-like headdress, the handsome bicolored wildcat and the strange red creature which seems to have both cloven hooves and a long tail?

71

arroyo. That part of the cliff nearest the *cuesta* has various caves and the larger ones show abundant traces of past human activity. *Metates* and *manos* are commoner than at most other cave sites which is to say that they are plentiful indeed.

About a half mile from the prominent white scar of the *cuesta*, this line of cliffs lies close to the bed of the arroyo and it turns a rather sharp corner to head more south than east. Exactly at that point the rocks of the cliff begin to show a multitude of petroglyphs, perhaps the largest and most interesting collection within the boundaries of the sierra proper.

We poked along the base of the cliff for an hour or more inspecting and photographing these engravings which were nearly all on the *in situ* rock of the bluff rather than on the numerous large fragments scattered about. This alone was atypical. At most petroglyph sites the larger free boulders were usually chosen with at least as great frequency as the living rock. But a greater distinction lay in the subjects of the glyphs themselves. Though there were many conventionally representational figures such as deer and grotesque human dolls, and many abstract lines, grids, circles, and so forth, there were an unusual number of semi-realistic symbols which strongly suggested such things as the sun, flowers, and plants. One grouping would surely be taken as a vernal celebration in any part of the world.

A hundred yards south of the greatest concentration of these engravings the cliff became honeycombed with caves. A search revealed the surprising fact that only one was painted. It con-

tained a superb red-and-black deer fully eight feet long and in excellent condition. Several *monos* in a more exposed location were terribly damaged as was an interesting red deer. Its body had survived well and displayed a pattern of red and black that ran down its side like a racing stripe, but the head and forelegs were entirely missing.

Another cave in the complex yielded additional realistic petroglyphs showing a procession of tiny deer, and two caves had networks of pits-and-grooves dug into their rock floors. Neither of these, however, was ten percent of the display which we found at La Vuelta del Batequi.

About a quarter of a mile farther there was a large *respaldo* covered with a veritable tapestry of painting in terrible condition. Soft rock and exposure had ruined any chance for a good survival. We stood in frustration looking at what once had been an amazing display. Photographs disclose its extent but not too much else. Our on-the-spot analysis linked its artists to those of Cuesta San Pablo I and IV and, interestingly enough, to Santa Gertrudis Norte, a site twenty miles to the north. The similarities extended to pigment colors, groupings and individual stylistic features in the drawings.

Two miles to the south the arroyo divided and a short but steep grade, the Cuesta de Marcial, zig-zagged up to the mesa. That trail took us on to Rancho San Pedro, the goat ranch midway between the arroyos of San Pablo and San Gregorio. Just before starting up the *cuesta* we found a final *respaldo* site in the same rock formation on the west wall which had contained all the others. This one was extremely similar to the previous site and possibly in poorer condition. Its place in my notes only serves to emphasize the amazing degree to which the Painters decorated this sierra in the practice of their obscure beliefs.

The painting of the Arroyo de la Cuesta Blanca is generally in very poor condition. Its chief contribution may be to assist in showing a very close linkage between the painters of this region and those of Santa Gertrudis. The petroglyphs are unusual and will have to be carefully considered when a major study is made of this other field of aboriginal art.

I have not had the opportunity to explore the northeast corner of the sierra. Beyond Cuesta Blanca, the arroyos of San Pedro, Buenos Aires and two others whose names I do not know, flow into the general Pacific drainage. Over the peninsular divide there is an arroyo with the totally provocative name of Los Monos, which flows into the Llano de San Gregorio. None of these to my knowledge has been surveyed for paintings, but the probability is high that some exist. As evidence we have seen that each of the arroyos to the west had several painted sites and the next arroyo which will be considered, San Gregorio, is adjacent to Los Monos and is extremely heavily endowed with painted art. In addition, the Sierra de San Juan, which will be covered later, lies just to the north and has numerous painted sites some of which are no more than four to eight miles from the various parts of the unexplored area. To temper the enthusiasm that these suggestions might engender, there is a sobering reality. The region involved has what even the natives of this arid land consider a dangerous lack of water.

THE ARROYO DE SAN GREGORIO

The eastern slope of the sierra has almost the character of a wall. Its arroyos start just as high as those of the west but they drop to an elevation of one thousand feet in an average of about one third the run. These then are places where occasional storms produce thunderous floods and where the terrain is so broken that all travel is difficult and the choice of routes is severely restricted.

The Arroyo de San Gregorio results from a confluence of four relatively short cañadas. One of these, the most southerly, is considered as a separate arroyo, San Gregorito, and follows under its own heading.

The array of painted art in this drainage basin is absolutely bewildering. Although it is only a fraction of the size of Arroyo San Pablo, the Arroyo de San Gregorio has as many sites. Along some stretches of its watercourses, caves and shelters run with chain-like continuity and most of them have at least a few paintings still in evidence.

Rancho San Gregorio, which was prominent in the introductory chapter of this work, lies at about the geographic center of the areas' rock art locations. Less than a quarter of a mile up the arroyo to the south is the great site which so amazed me when I first visited it. This place, designated as San Gregorio I, consists of a low

cave about a hundred feet long located at the base of a formidable respaldo. The ceiling of the shallow cave is heavily painted with large and small figures of nearly every sort found in the Great Mural area. Most of these are in reasonably good condition and this assemblage alone would constitute a major example of the Painters' range and skills. However, on the respaldo outside and above this ceiling exhibit there is a cavalcade of men and beasts which perhaps equals the composition at El Batequi in its power and thrust. Like El Batequi, the effect was aided by a sort of tacit cooperation between the artists who painted different areas or repainted those already used. It is noteworthy that the flow of running, pressing animals here is from right to left, or the reverse of El Batequi.

In further comparison, San Gregorio has a harder but rougher rock and its colors are the more vivid as a result. The drawings at El Batequi seem finer and surer. In balance both these grand canvases are profoundly impressive; San Gregorio may be the more immediate and striking but Batequi seems the more sophisticated expression. Unfortunately a large area to the right of the existing mural at San Gregorio has fallen away and lies in huge fragments on the apron of the cave. Several painted figures are broken at the line of this fallen area showing that the work proceeded to the right; it is possible that it was once nearly double the size that we see today.

The ceiling menagerie within the cave proper is difficult to appreciate and requires careful study. The problem, as with a few of the figures at Flechas Cave, is that the ceiling is so low that a good view is difficult to obtain. This becomes a critical problem for photography. Several really beautiful figures are painted so far back that the camera must be less than two feet from them. Even with wide angle lenses it is impossible to photograph some groupings.

A thorough inventory of all the overlapping figures has not yet been made but a couple of curiosities can be confidently reported. There are an unusually large number of birds represented. At least a half dozen are prominently displayed and others are at least partially visible. There are also at least five or six unique animals. All are carefully delineated but several fall into no obvious category. One, which can be classified, still has no known precedent in this sierra.

SAN GREGORIO I

The rock face which overhangs the cave proper retains much of the form and color of a huge melange of aboriginal art. This sixty-foot wide group of interlaced, tangled forms, on analysis, proves to contain dozens upon dozens of independent figures painted one over another during long periods of time. However, the aggregate of all this artistic effort becomes a powerful mural to modern viewers conditioned to synthesize separate images into meaningful wholes.

SAN GREGORIO II

It is not surprising that the monsters of the deep impressed the Painters. A whale or one of the great rays stranded would have supplied a whole band with unprecedented quantities of protein. This painting seems to show a whale broaching, an event which the artist could have seen at Scammon's Lagoon. But, since fish are always shown thus, head up and tail down, the leaping illusion is probably accidental.

It is a white serpent, very sinuous and neatly and heavily outlined in red. Unfortunately, while some parts are very clear, others are heavily overpainted including head and tail. In spite of this a bulge is noticeable which may be designed to indicate that the snake had fed. Two other beasts rendered in black remain in excellent condition but still defy identification.

It seems clear that the painters of San Gregorio I were not as bound by convention as most of their fellow artists. Or, of course, it is possible that something about the magical or ritual character of this cave permitted or encouraged depictions of unusual creatures.

About a hundred yards north is another long, overhung shelter which we call San Gregorio II. This contains at least thirty distinguishable figures but all are dominated by one great group, a giant fish or dolphin, a large red *borrego* and a huge whale, perhaps the biggest single figure among all the Great Murals. As in the whale-like painting at Cueva Pintada, this one has strange rear appendages which scarcely recall the fluke of a whale.

A little over a mile below Rancho San Gregorio is an inconspicuous *cañada* called La Palma which enters the arroyo from a southerly direction. Two hundred yards up that unprepossess-

ing watercourse is one of the richest galleries left by the Painters. The site consists basically of a two-hundred-foot *respaldo* located fifty or sixty feet above the *caja* and on the east side. Near the north end of this wall the lower part is undercut to form a deeper shelter and at the north end itself a small cave has formed which penetrates the base of the *respaldo* to a depth of twenty feet. Each of these areas is painted in its own important and distinctive fashion.

The large outer face of the *respaldo* has an array of *monos* at its right end which display a degree of order unmatched at any other site. Two rows of greater-than-life-sized figures are ranged one above the other. These *monos* are spaced at about arm's length. The style, paint, and proportions of all these figures are similar. The rows are the result of plan, not accident. The only break in this regular scheme is the figure of a large *borrego*, over which the human grid was apparently superimposed. These *monos* are typical of what was apparently a late phase of the painting phenomenon. All are lightly colored, the paint applied sparingly and in streaks which suggest the character of chalk strokes. Several figures have headdresses of the "sackhat" variety. One has the lower half of the body and legs painted black, a decorative scheme that gives the figure the appearance of wearing trousers. In a very rare combination, the only female figure in this group, clearly identified by breasts, also is wearing a headdress, three small feather-like projections. This is one of very few instances so far observed of a female *mono* with any sort of headgear.

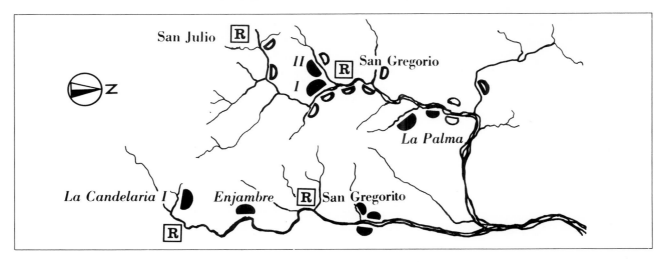

This group displays at least one other peculiarity. Two of its figures are clearly represented as impaled by, or overlaid with, arrows. As was discussed in connection with Flechas Cave, this was extremely uncommon in the works of the Sierra de San Francisco.

Farther to the left, the outer wall is profusely decorated with other less regularly placed *monos* and several large *borrego*. These representations of big-horn sheep are as fine as those at any other place and they occur here in impressive combinations. One pair overlaps to appear like a brace of animals moving in tandem. Both seem launched on a simultaneous leap as if startled by the same stimulus. Nearby is another group of three *borrego* barely overlapping and all raised so as to best display noble representations of their distinctive horns. Another noteworthy feature of the middle wall area is the presence of four rather crudely drawn fish. One of these almost certainly represents a shark and is rendered as a profile, a very rare occurrence.

The lower, better sheltered part of the *respaldo* is principally decorated with a remarkably integrated group of *monos*. Unlike the rows of their regularly spaced fellows described above, this group of eight is arranged shoulder to shoulder in a partially superimposed fashion which strongly suggests an actual event. The appearance of real people is enhanced by other factors. The group is painted very near the level of the shelter's floor so that one confronts them more on an eye-level than is customary. The figures are unusually naturalistic; their heads are rounded and set on perceptible necks. Also, the decorative pattern of two of the figures strongly suggest clothing, and finally, a small black *mono* is placed in such a way that it creates the illusion of being a child. The total effect of this assemblage is very compelling; it is perhaps the most human of all the Painters' efforts. My companions and I have come to call it The Family of Man.

Just above and to the left of this most appealing work is one of the very rare representations of a pronghorn antelope, the *berrendo*, now nearly extinct on the peninsula. Fortunately this skillful and lively representation is in excellent condition.

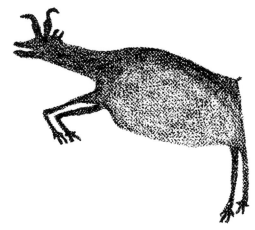

The small cave at the north end of the La Palma site has a ceiling formed into a low vault perhaps twenty-by-fifteen feet in extent. This surface has one of those incredibly painted and overpainted histories which result in a flame of color but little distinguishable art. Even if this were the whole story, the rich interplay of velvety black, orange-red and white-outlined fragments would create a beautiful artifact. But there is more and the place is transformed by it. Late in the painting cycle two very large and beautiful black *borregos* were added. Nothing covers or obscures them and they stand out like two black appliques on a background of rich brocade. This juxtaposition creates one of the most opulent effects in all the surviving Great Murals. La Palma, already abounding in fine paintings of the mountain sheep, with these becomes the Painters' apotheosis of all that is *borrego*.

The remainder of San Gregorio's thirty sites are minor by contrast, but many contain works of considerable interest. One of the highest of these painted places, a shelter located in the Cañada de San Julio, has an elegantly crafted checkerboard design with alternate red and black squares. The basic grid is painted in ochre yellow, a little-used pigment in Painter land. It is noteworthy that most of the half dozen of these abstract works in the Sierra de San Francisco utilize this rare color. The combination of aberrant subject matter and paint might indicate an invasion or visit by an alien group.

A small cave near Rancho San Gregorio has been heavily smoked and only a single figure, quite near its less blackened mouth, survives.

LA PALMA

A cave-within-a-shelter has blazoned on its domed ceiling a rich mural which, even in its present damaged state, glows with color and the genius of primitive design. Three huge black forms crowd the vault; these finest of the Painters' evocations of bighorn sheep are magnified by their surroundings. The art bursts the bounds of the space.

"THE FAMILY OF MAN"

An artist with an individual and compelling style created this oddly affecting scene at La Palma. His secure, bold representations have an unusually human air about them, while their arrangement and the presence of the child-like figure suggests a family group. The practiced technique of the painter indicates much experience yet only a single other figure located at Cuesta Palmarito can be laid to his hand. Perhaps others will be found in the poorly explored canyons on the gulf slope of the sierra.

That one painting could brighten a far greater place. With its triumph over the forces of time and fire it could serve as the phoenix of the Painters' spirit.

When we look at the map of the sierra and its painted sites, an additional significance is suggested for the Arroyo de San Gregorio. No other avenue into the sierra is so art-lined, not even the Arroyo del Parral which led to the major oasis of San Ignacio. Further map study shows that the most direct route to the coast from all this region would have run down this arroyo and across the Llano de San Gregorio to the gulf shore near Punta de la Trinidad. Shell mounds in that region have not yet been associated with the Painters, but they in no way dispute the proposition that the arroyo's art suggests. Certainly the entire sierra is littered with evidence of ancient interest in marine harvests. Shells are found scattered along every trail even to the ultimate heights. They are found here and there on *ancones*, *faldas*, and mesas in a surprisingly random fashion. They are not found in midden accumulations; the distribution is so widespread and uniform that it fits the proposition that these were a people constantly on the move.

THE ARROYO DE SAN GREGORITO

This watercourse is actually a large southern tributary to the Arroyo de San Gregorio entering the latter's flow at a point about four miles downstream from Rancho San Gregorito. It originates, like the Arroyo de San Gregorio, in a series of extremely steep runoff gullies at the very crest of the sierra.

During all my early explorations of the sierra I picked up no real information about paintings in San Gregorito. But in the fall of 1973, during the survey of another area, Tacho and I encountered Angel Ojeda, a resident of the village of

San Francisco, and fell to discussing cave painting. Angel surprised us with the statement that he had seen a painted cave near his seasonal ranch at La Candelaria in the headwaters of the Arroyo de San Gregorito. We got directions and in the spring of 1974 arranged to come up the arroyo to investigate. My wife, Joanne, and daughter, Ristin Crosby Decker, were on that trip preparing to do illustrations for this work and, as artists, enjoying a grand tour of this most painted sierra. We had high hopes for Angel Ojeda's cave in any case but were particularly anxious for my wife and daughter to share the excitement of a new discovery.

Near the mouth of San Gregorito a trail drops into the arroyo from the southeast. This is the direct linkage to El Camino Real.

Three miles upstream Rancho San Gregorito is located on a shelf above the north side of the *caja*. This prosperous goat ranch was founded around the turn of the century by Patricio Arce, the father of Loreto.

At the ranch we made the acquaintance of Jesús Arce, a nephew of both Loreto Arce and Pedro Altamirano, and his cousin Salvador Arce. Both, of course, were kin to Tacho and eager to help as soon as they understood the nature of our mission. We sat around and discussed what we had seen elsewhere and they were put on their mettle to produce results in their area. Despite early protestations that the place had little more than *pinturitas*, small works of no great interest, it soon developed that they knew several sites.

First we were directed to a point only a quarter of a mile below the ranch. There the arroyo branches and a minor *cañada* runs to the west. In the immediate environs of this fork we saw six small shelters, each with a handfull of paintings. Since none was difficult to reach a very

80

pleasant couple of hours were spent finding and enjoying an outstanding group of smaller works. Many were in unusually good condition. The prize of the collection was a very precisely drawn group of black figures including a four-foot deer, and a *borrego* and a stylized *mono* each about one foot in extent.

The following morning we saddled up for a ride to La Candelaria and some other places up the arroyo that the cousins knew. An hour's ride brought us to a spot called the Enjambre de Hipólito, meaning the place where Hipólito collects wild honey. Jesús Arce pointed high on the north wall of the arroyo and said that there were paintings above a ledge and out of sight. He proposed that we see it on our return. Shortly we passed through a wildly beautiful *angostura*, a place where the high rock walls virtually lean together. In that shady canyon great *zalate*, or wild fig trees, grow to fifty-foot spreads with their white-barked roots running madly over and through broken rock to the sources of water below.

Beyond the *angostura* the arroyo broadened and we soon came to La Candelaria, the ranch of Angel Ojeda, then standing empty. A few hundred yards beyond it we arrived at a stand of fan palms and a spring of clear water. The cousins had us dismount and tie our animals.

For a quarter of a mile we labored up a rocky *falda* climbing abruptly to the northwest. My wife and daughter had worked hard to condition themselves for this trip and here for the first of many times they were rewarded as they managed a stiff climb in the hot sun without delays or undue exhaustion.

When we arrived at the head of the *falda* we were up against a wall and our guides led us to the west along its base. Turning a corner we found ourselves in a small cave with a few paintings in mediocre condition. At first we imagined that we were seeing Angel Ojeda's painted cave and we were thoroughly disappointed, but before that idea took root, Jesús and Salvador took us a few yards around a corner into the actual and marvelous cave of La Candelaria.

At its mouth the cave is about a hundred feet wide and forty feet high and the interior is very complex in form. The opening faces west and the northern part of the cave is quite shallow with a nearly vertical back wall. The southern portion is much deeper, running back fifty feet or so from

the entry. Between these dissimilar areas is a structure unique to La Candelaria among all the painted caves which I have seen. A sort of natural staircase leads from the central part of the cave up to a point quite close to the ceiling and near the center of the back wall. This ready-made scaffolding was not wasted on the Painters. Exactly at its top we found the supremely beautiful deer of La Candelaria, a figure which, in spite of its damaged condition, will assert itself in any company as an expressive work of art.

Elsewhere the cave proved to be a treasure house. Much, much art was, as usual, irrevocably lost to erosion, but the surviving works include a high percentage that are beautiful and represent rare types.

The last major figure at the north end depicts a *berrendo*, or pronghorn antelope, in the Painters' best bicolored tradition. This and the all-red *berrendo* at La Palma are among the few representations of this animal that I have found in peninsular art. On the south side of the "staircase" is a very curious group of figures. Two are checkerboards, quite unusual as has been suggested, but a *mono* on this small wall is absolutely unique in the Painters' world, looking like nothing so much as a piece of mesoamerican pottery. Such breaks with convention are inexplicable but they do add a great deal of spice to the quest.

Directly behind the beautiful deer is a neatly executed red fish about five feet tall, and directly in front of the deer, superimposed on its front legs, is a bicolored fish or dolphin about half as large. The former is a rare type but the latter

LA CANDELARIA I

Whatever their motives for painting caves, in the process the Painters developed an artistic affinity for the creatures that they represented. Deer are shown as impaled by arrows or spears, or with legs broken as by throwing sticks, or gasping with mouths open, perhaps run down in a chase. Nevertheless, the grace and symmetry of the animals shine through in much of the art. These are not pieces of meat on the hoof. The deer were given spirits; there was a bond between artist and animal.

closely resembles fish figures in El Parral, San Julio, El Infierno, and San Pablo. In fact, these widespread fish and the many "sackhat man" representations argue more than any other works for the idea that some of the Great Mural figures were products of itinerant painters. It is obvious that the tradition with all its conventions influenced many people over a rather large area. These figures suggest that, in addition, some individual painters may have actually practiced their art over much of that area.

The south wall, the closed end of the deep half of the cave, is the sad chapter in the Candelaria story. The fragments or faded remains of two to three dozen large figures can be made out and the indications are that they were a fine lot. But, as was so often the case, the rock proved false and a painted wall with excellent protection from the elements was nevertheless reduced to a hint of its original state. One figure which, while faded, remains clear is the red *mono* with a black face referred to earlier in connection with its rare counterpart at Cueva del Ratón.

On our return trip we spotted some paintings on an exposed wall just upstream from the beautiful *angostura*. Close inspection showed that there once had been a group of fifteen or twenty large red-and-black *monos* ranged in a tight group. Now there were only faded remnants.

By the time we returned to the Enjambre de Hipólito it was late and the sun was nearly down. We attacked a steep treacherous slope and arrived at the upper level exhausted and breathless with just enough light to literally snap a few pictures.

The site consisted of a *respaldo* painted for about sixty feet of its length. At the right end of the painted area was a deeper alcove about ten feet tall and twenty feet broad. This recess was

very heavily painted with large handsome figures primarily in red and outlined strikingly in white. The massing of the figures and the form of the shelter suggested a primitive shrine and a close inspection showed that, within this niche, a high percentage of the figures were notable for artistic merit and good preservation. Though there were fine deer, *borregos, monos,* and striking depictions of birds, this site was dominated by the unusual prominence of large heavy-bodied fish. It was a rare experience to see fish depicted almost as large as human figures and given equal footing in the presentation.

Before the light failed entirely our inspection produced a final observation. At least two of the smaller fish had been damaged by deep transverse scratches which broke through the paint and the rock surface. This apparent vandalism was impressively old. The rock had eroded perceptibly in the scratched area.

In review, the art of San Gregorito would seem to relate to that of San Gregorio. Both display several examples of subject matter unknown or rare elsewhere in the sierra. One explanation for this is not only the adjacency of the two waterways but also the fact that the one literally opens off the other. People coming off the Llano de San Gregorio could have used either as a staircase into the sierra, the choice depending on the desire to reach a more northerly or a more southerly destination. To reinforce this supposition the next arroyo to the south, El Balcón, is difficult to approach from the gulf and requires a very hazardous climb to make an exit at its top. We were able to find no sites in the entire arroyo with more than one or two negligible paintings.

THE ARROYO DE LOS CERRITOS

Three or four miles south of the Arroyo de San Gregorito and over a low pass from the intermediate Arroyo del Balcón is another short steep watercourse called the Arroyo de los Cerritos. Its name is taken from a row of low bare hills of a distinctive light color which partially block its passage to the east. The description given above of El Balcón applies almost as well to Los Cerritos. It too is an arroyo which offers poor access to any lowland places which would seem to have promised a livelihood to aboriginal people. And, at its head, the pass into the sierra is almost as bad as that of El Balcón. However, Los Cerritos does have a better water supply and it offered the Painters a true cave to decorate.

The main trail from San Gregorio to Santa Marta and on to San Ignacio cuts across the mouth of Los Cerritos at a point only a mile and a half below a seasonally occupied ranch which lies at the foot of the great wall of the sierra. This ranch, *solo* at the time of our visit, is only about a quarter of a mile from a cave which is located up a slope to the south.

The cave of Los Cerritos is exceptional in that its form is actually that of a conventional cave rather than an open overhung shelter like most of what are called *cuevas* by the natives. This cave furthermore has two entrances on quite different levels. The lower is a low arch about twenty feet wide which leads to a stair-like chute from the cave space twenty feet above. The upper entrance is a thoroughly odd natural formation consisting of a large arched entrance divided in the middle by a pillar to produce two small arched doorways that lead directly into a domed inner room some thirty by forty feet in extent. The Painters, however, did not really take advantage of the protected inner space. They painted a few small rabbits inside and concentrated their major efforts on the partially sheltered walls just outside.

A further curiosity at an already curious site is the fact that the character of the paintings is quite different at the upper entrance. The figures around the lower portal and on the adjacent *respaldo* are very conventional; red-and-black *monos* predominate but there are deer and large birds. At the upper location only one red *mono*, out of nearly two dozen figures, is close to life-sized. The rest, almost exclusively in red, are about two feet in height or length. The predominant subject, as within, is the rabbit, though there are also a few small deer and *monos*.

In sum, the paintings of Los Cerritos seem less exciting than the singular site at which they are located. This is due not only to the generally poor condition of the painted works but also to a rather monotonous range of subjects. Other major sites on the gulf drainage display such variety and even instances of originality that, subjectively at least, the art of Los Cerritos seems routine. At least one exception is well displayed high on the wall above the lower entrance. A fine large bird reminiscent of the phoenix of San Gregorio overlies the dashing figure of a *borrego* or possibly the rarer *berrendo*.

THE ARROYO DEL PALMARITO

Less than two miles below the painted cave, Los Cerritos merges with an arroyo called El Palmarito which flows from the south. The trail ascends this arroyo for nearly two miles and then climbs out of its depths by way of a high *cuesta* to the southeast. Near the base of the *cuesta* the Arroyo del Palmarito divides into two deep canyons which die against the eastern wall of the sierra. The northern branch is called the Cañada de San Antonio while the southern simply retains the name El Palmarito. Neither of those very beautiful, palm-filled canyons has been explored for paintings.

The *cuesta* which leaves El Palmarito to the southeast has a long and poorly reported history. Actually this entire trail along the lower east slope of the sierra is an historic alternate route of El Camino Real, as a Jesuit road dating from about 1750, and probably far earlier as an Indian trail. The massive character of the existing construction clearly betrays its mission origin. Though the basic route of The King's Highway lay a few miles to the east, this rougher, less direct alternate was essential from the beginning. The key to its existence and use was water.

From the time El Camino Real left Santa Marta until it arrived at either San Juan de las Parras or San Juan de las Palmas twenty-five miles to the north, the only reliable spring was encountered at El Rosarito, ten miles from Santa Marta. This was adequate in cool weather or after rains when the *tinajas* were full. But in the summer heat or during years without rainfall the high road was a godsend. It offered water in the Arroyo del Palmarito, literally at the trail crossing and, with short detours, other springs in Los Cerritos, San Gregorio and San Gregorito. During the nineteenth century various strangers lost

84

their lives in this region and others had harrowing experiences trying to get from San Ignacio to Santa Gertrudis. Unguided, they followed the larger, better marked version of El Camino Real instead of taking the trail which jumped from Santa Marta over the Cuesta del Palmarito.

The Painters, of course, knew all about water sources and we find their characteristic work near every one of these springs. The watering place of El Palmarito alone offered no inviting caves or *respaldos* but the Indians spotted an eminently suitable substitute at the top of the *cuesta*. There a mammoth *respaldo* ran south in an unbroken arc about a half-mile long. In this prominent rock layer were numerous small caves and one that was very large, the Cueva de la Cuesta del Palmarito. This great shelter was about one hundred and fifty feet long, forty feet high and perhaps fifty feet deep at the extreme of its inward curve. Furthermore its opening and prominent overhead *respaldo* were very visible from the trail.

No important painted place was so exposed to the missionaries' view. It is quite probable that the Jesuit Fernando Consag knew this place or at least noticed it. It is almost certain that his successor at San Ignacio, Joseph Mariano Rothea knew it well. His description of Great Murals quoted earlier fits this site better than any other despite the fact that his measurements are all at about half scale. Allowing for error created by the passage of ten years and the occurrence of events which shattered the man's career and moved him and other Jesuits eight thousand miles away, the description is admirable.

During his 1893-4 trip of exploration Leon Diguet visited the Cueva de la Cuesta del Palmarito. From his published work it is clear that he understood the relationship between the cave and the *cuesta*. He wrote, "But on the eastern slope of this sierra one can discover, from a steep hillside known under the name of cuesta del Palmarito, a number of pictographic representations forming the ornamentation of a rock shelter located on the upper part of the cliff." What he apparently did not know was that the place itself was not Palmarito but only a point on the *cuesta* leading in and out of the Arroyo del Palmarito. As a result he referred elsewhere to the site simply as Palmarito and others have followed suit. None of the sierra people practice this usage and it should be discouraged. At present it is simply inaccurate; if any painted places are found in the Arroyo del Palmarito it will become actively confusing. A short and completely satisfactory anglicized title for this historic site is Cuesta Palmarito.

Erle Stanley Gardner and those who flew with him somehow confused Cuesta Palmarito with Cueva del Ratón. Since both were visited by Diguet and correctly identified, this is difficult to understand. A possible explanation lies in the fact that both these otherwise dissimilar sites are in the general vicinity of the village of San Francisco and have conspicuous black mountain lion figures. In an illustration Diguet showed the *león* of Cuesta Palmarito and Gardner's group may have seen the one at Cueva del Ratón and jumped to a conclusion. It has already been noted that the *león* figure varies less from place to place than any other.

There are two paths of access to this important cave. One system is to approach as close as possible by trail and then climb directly up the *falda*. The other is to start at the pass and skirt along the base of the *respaldo* until the cave is reached. I have tried both and the latter is preferable by far.

While following the latter path a small painted cave is passed at about the half way point. It contains several sizeable paintings including crudely delineated *monos*, some small deer and a large fish. None is in any way artistically important or memorable, but at the feet of all the large fig-

CUESTA PALMARITO

Major trails during both prehistoric and Mission Period passed within easy view of this cave's great arched entrance probably making it the most visited of all Great Mural locations. Highest of a legion of paintings is a collection of human figures unusually varied in headdresses and decoration. Some appear clothed, a possibility so welcome to the decorous Jesuits that it contributed to their belief that the region had once been populated by a higher culture.

ures runs a chain of tiny deer exquisitely conceived and executed. Ten of them in black outlined in white follow each other in a thoroughly intentional procession. No two are exactly alike and they are cocked up and down successively so as to impart motion to the whole line. The painter of the tiny deer almost certainly understood what he was doing and he was an independent inventor of animation.

The principal cave was once as great a showplace of painted art as any in the Great Mural region. The entire concavity was heavily painted to a height of twenty feet and a large number of later works go from there to a height of thirty-five feet. The lower paintings are so mutilated by rock erosion that few can be appreciated but most of those above are still quite clear and many are in exceptional condition. The age and style of the upper figures appear to be similar to that of the carefully spaced *monos* at La Palma. These are not arranged in rows but they too avoid overpainting to a marked degree.

There are a few animals among the high figures. A pair of large red deer which stand face to face as if contesting are handsome examples of the Painters' skill and inspiration. There are other deer and the black lion mentioned before but they are pedestrian entries in the catalog. The real show at Cuesta Palmarito is the collection of *monos*. Although only about fifteen stand out clearly they are as diverse a group as can be found at any site. Headdresses abound; there are half a dozen "sackhat men" and, uniquely, a "sackhat woman." There are several examples of *monos* with the horizontal division of painted areas which results in the illusion of a man wearing a red shirt and black pants. Others are painted in vertical stripes which some viewers imagine as representations of capes or robes. These, almost certainly, are the paintings described by the missionaries as depicting a decently clad folk who walked the land before their naked and shameless neophytes. Any contention that these are truly the representations of clothing has two difficult questions to answer. Why are the outlines of such elaborately painted *monos* identical to those colored a simple red or black? Why are animals frequently decorated with all the same devices which are interpreted as clothing on man?

Four of these upper *monos* at Cuesta Palmarito exhibit a fascinating ornament or accessory.

Over the bicep of the up-raised arm on the viewer's right there is suspended a black sphere about the size of the *mono's* head.

Of all the Painters' sites none compels more awe than this for the solution of the extremely difficult problem of gaining access to a sloping surface higher than a three-story building. As a further complication, the floor of the Cueva de la Cuesta del Palmarito is composed of slippery crumbling material, irregular and sharply slanting. The feat that overcame such obstacles was no simple thing but we must not make it sound superhuman. Obviously a solution was invented; it is worth noting that El Palmarito in those days was full of fifty-foot palms and then, as now, the forty-foot wands could be extracted from the skeletons of the ubiquitous *cardón*.

THE ARROYO DE SANTA MARTA

The balcony view afforded by the Cueva de la Cuesta del Palmarito looks out over the lower part of the mountain-ringed amphitheater of Santa Marta. Cerro de las Cabras, a dark bulky mountain, rises in the midst of the scene. Beyond, the Arroyo de Santa Marta flows east and then swings south on its way to join the Arroyo de San Ignacio, twenty-five miles away.

As far as paintings are concerned, the Arroyo de Santa Marta is a large puzzle. It drains an area which contains numerous signs of an extensive human past. Its walls are liberally sprinkled with caves and shelters and many of these, especially a few miles east of Santa Marta proper, are rife with *metates*, charcoal and other evidence of past human occupancy. But, thus far at least, very few paintings have been found. The only sites worth mentioning are a painted wall on the Cuesta de Sán Antonio and a small painted cave near the mouth of the Cañada de los Platos, six or seven miles downstream from Santa Marta. The former site is in a very faded state though *monos*, a deer, a *borrego*, and perhaps a sea turtle can be made out. The Los Platos site is in plain view of the trail. It is situated about a hundred yards to the west as a depression in a *respaldo* a hundred feet higher than the bed of the arroyo. The principal chamber has been heavily painted and over-painted and much of its color survives. Even from the trail the interior has a fiery look, but on close inspection the figures are badly melted together. Just to the north a more exposed shelter shows the much eroded remains of several smaller paintings.

For the present that is the Santa Marta story, a major access arroyo almost without aboriginal art. The possibility remains, however, that people who explore its many tributary *cañadas* will discover more. There are rumors of other paintings; logic and probability are in their favor.

THE ARROYO DEL INFIERNO

After El Camino Real, headed south, crosses Santa Marta it climbs a short *cuesta* and enters the headwaters of an arroyo called El Infierno. The old road, and almost certainly an Indian trail before it, follows the arroyo out of the sierra, then turns south and proceeds over fairly level ground to San Ignacio. That part of the road which traverses the uppermost part of El Infierno is a troublesome stretch, steep, tortuous, and rocky. The name Infierno probably was bestowed by the Jesuits more for trials imposed by these hazards than for the heat of the place which is no worse than that of any boxed-in canyon on the gulf slope of the sierra.

With El Infierno, this work has made a clockwise circuit of the Sierra de San Francisco's arroyos. Our entrance was by El Parral which was the southern drainage of Cerro Santa Marta. Now we arrived at El Infierno which drains part of the east slope of the same eminence. The Jesuits tried both of these arroyos as routes for roads to the north. Their constructions are still in evidence leaving San Ignacio and bearing for the respective mouths of these natural avenues into the sierra. After building the El Parral road, the Infierno route apparently was chosen as better; it is the El Camino Real of history. The Indians, or at least the Painters, appear to have made the reverse decision. El Parral, as we have seen, was heavily painted; El Infierno has only a few modest sites.

In innocence, I rode through the arroyo three times before I ever looked for a painting. Tacho and I had asked about such things both at Santa Marta and at Rancho Carrizito in the mouth of El Infierno. No one had any suggestions and we accepted the judgment which that implied. Subsequent experiences in other places made us suspicious of such local advice. None of our informants ran livestock in the arroyo, and their only real business in the place, like our own, had been to use it as a road.

In the spring of 1974, we made an all-day project of the short stretch from Carrizito to the head of the arroyo. We examined every suspicious rock formation with ten-power field glasses and climbed to investigate those that showed any evidence of paint. The result was the discovery of three sites, two of which had been in plain view to us and every other daytime traveller since the paint was fresh.

In the upper three miles of the arroyo the trail, which is to say El Camino Real, stays on the south *falda*. At one point a considerable stretch was built up, or reinforced, by a retaining wall made of carefully laid large fragments of basalt. This sort of construction is called an *ademado* and it has given that place a name in local usage. On the opposite bank across from El Ademado is an unimpressive cave and to its left a *respaldo* which angles back toward the hillside. A magnified view of the cave showed little, but an obvious red painting appeared on the *respaldo* and an investigation was made.

The paint proved to be part of a very good red-and-black *borrego*, not a memorable figure but a nice trophy from previously barren El Infierno. But the cave yielded one of those unexpected treasures, a unique and beautifully crafted figure. On the west wall of the cave was an ochre *león* about five feet from tip to tip. The pose was conventional but the drawing was as unusual as the color. This cat was not the heavy, club-footed creature we were accustomed to see; it was lean, almost gaunt, and all its parts were drawn with unusual attention to detail. A careful examination showed that the feet were armed with claws.

A few hundred yards to the west Ramón Arce spotted a small steep cleft in the arroyo wall and went up to investigate. Around a corner and after a steep climb he found a large cave with a few paintings including some rather original but crudely made *monos*.

Near the head of the arroyo there is a sharp turn from west to north. The obstacle around which this turn is made is a very high steepsided bluff. As we rode up the arroyo we could see a cave near its top and when we were as close as possible on the trail we inspected it with our glasses. Paintings fairly leaped out. We parked our animals at the turn and made a laborious climb.

The contents of the cave, or cave complex as it turned out, were enough to remind us once again that we have no simple explanation for the Painters' choice of places to paint. This one was high and poorly accessible. In the course of our study we had investigated dozens of others which seemed to offer better facilities in a location easier to reach. We had, of course, also found dozens which were easier to reach and heavily painted. It is baffling; perhaps ours is the wrong logic altogether. Perhaps such choices were controlled in part by magic or divine guidance. We will probably never know.

The paintings in this high and out-of-the-way place were, with a single exception, routine. There were several large red-and-black *monos*, deer and the stereotyped red-and-black fish noted at La Candelaria. Definitely not routine was a huge red form outlined in white which lay, as it were, along one wall of the cave. Several figures had been painted over it and the apparent rear portion was badly eroded but it appeared to represent a whale. Whales at other sites had been in a vertical posture, like fish, with head up and tail down. But here at El Infierno III the size of the wall would permit no such orientation. If the figure is that of a whole it would be a rare case of the Painters' conventions being modified to conform to a practical necessity.

There is another small entry in El Infierno's history. In the fall of 1974 we finally followed Consag's road up El Parral and made its great jump over the mountains to Santa Marta. Prior to this, Ramón was told of a painted cave by Roberto Ojeda from Santa Marta who herds goats on the mesa over which the old road passes. During our crossing Ramón hunted it out high on the cliff which overlooks El Infierno from the west. There, in a modest cave-shelter, were figures of a pair of large and very faded deer and four coyotes, two in the rare ochre yellow paint.

The principal value of our visit to this minor site was the reminder that the Great Murals probably cannot be explained simply or in purely practical terms. This place, like La Cuevona, certainly never had numbers of casual passers-by. Anyone who came here did so in order to express the impulse that lay behind the paintings or he came to commune with the works themselves or the spirits they mediated. So many of the painted places display their works to trails or natural avenues that we might regard that exposure as fundamental if it were not for a handful of these immensely secluded places revealing another practice.

This account of art discoveries has been structured by the separate drainage systems in the Sierra de San Francisco. That plan fits the terrain and the distribution of paintings very well, up to a point. The arroyos certainly are as logical geographic subdivisions as can be devised and

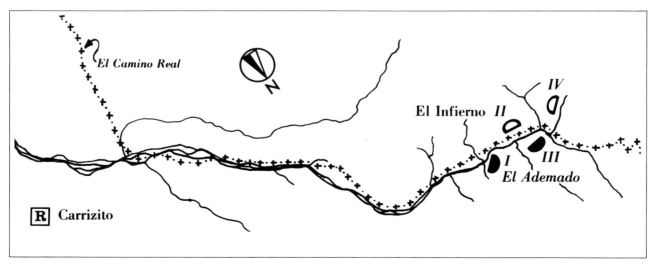

several of them clearly served as avenues for prehistoric man. However, this clockwise circuit of the sierra's arroyos has not revealed the whole story or even all that is observable at the present. At least four arroyos on the west side of the sierra have not been entered in the course of my study and the same neglect applies to the large piece of ground on the northeast corner of the sierra, a region whose potential was discussed earlier.

Apart from areas not investigated, the pattern of this presentation also neglects several inter-arroyo relationships which may someday help us to understand the Painters' activities in the sierra and their relationship to the occupation of nearby lower ground and the coasts.

On the basis of their heavily painted state, it was surmised earlier that El Parral and San Gregorio were major routes in and out of the San Francisco highlands. El Batequí and Cuesta Blanca seem to have been lesser arteries. All of this could be deduced to some degree from evidence found within the individual arroyos. But a great deal of art and hence human activity is found along the Cañada de la Soledad and in the Arroyo de San Pablo within a mile of the *cañada's* mouth. The region thus defined is in the heart of the sierra and, to this point, has appeared very isolated. This, in fact, may not have been the case at all. A look at the map of the whole sierra shows that the Arroyo de San Gregorio, heavily painted, drains the northeast portion of the high ground. Its upper reaches, the arms called San Gregorito and San Julio, both touch the very divide of the mountains and they do so within a hundred yards of the corresponding fingers of La Soledad which drain the western side. Thus the most heavily painted avenue on the east communicated directly with the drainage in which are found the great complex of painted places that included El Brinco I, La Soledad, Flechas Cave and Cueva Pintada. This connection seems to be more than a coincidence. Even without the painted record the route could be calculated as the most direct trail with permanent water to cross the central high ground. Further exploration west of the Arroyo de San Pablo may indicate an equivalent route or routes in the direction of the Pacific.

But no matter what is learned about the paintings, and from them, it is clear that they are only a single piece of the archaeological record, the whole of which is virtually unstudied. At present such a role is merely a prospect for the paintings and their future students. The Great Murals, unlike many humbler artifacts, express a timeless genius which speaks to us even out of context. These works will find an independent audience as art for art's sake.

90

The Sierra de Guadalupe

Stretching southeast from San Ignacio to a point beyond the Bahía de la Concepción is a jumbled mass of mountains with peaks rising four and five thousand feet all along the way. It is the most complex terrain in all the Great Mural area. The missionaries found many people here as well as the resources to feed them. A mission and its satellite ranches prospered materially but the human flock did not. The religious establishment closed and its secular people took over the lonely sierra where their descendants still live, tucked into its isolated pockets of watered land. No one knows the whole of this intricate maze but its people know it bit by bit. Under patient questioning they produce the lines that add up to the sierra's tale; the Painters were here and, range by arroyo, they left their tell-tale art. Now the images flicker and fade, well made by man's measure but not equal to a brush with eternity.

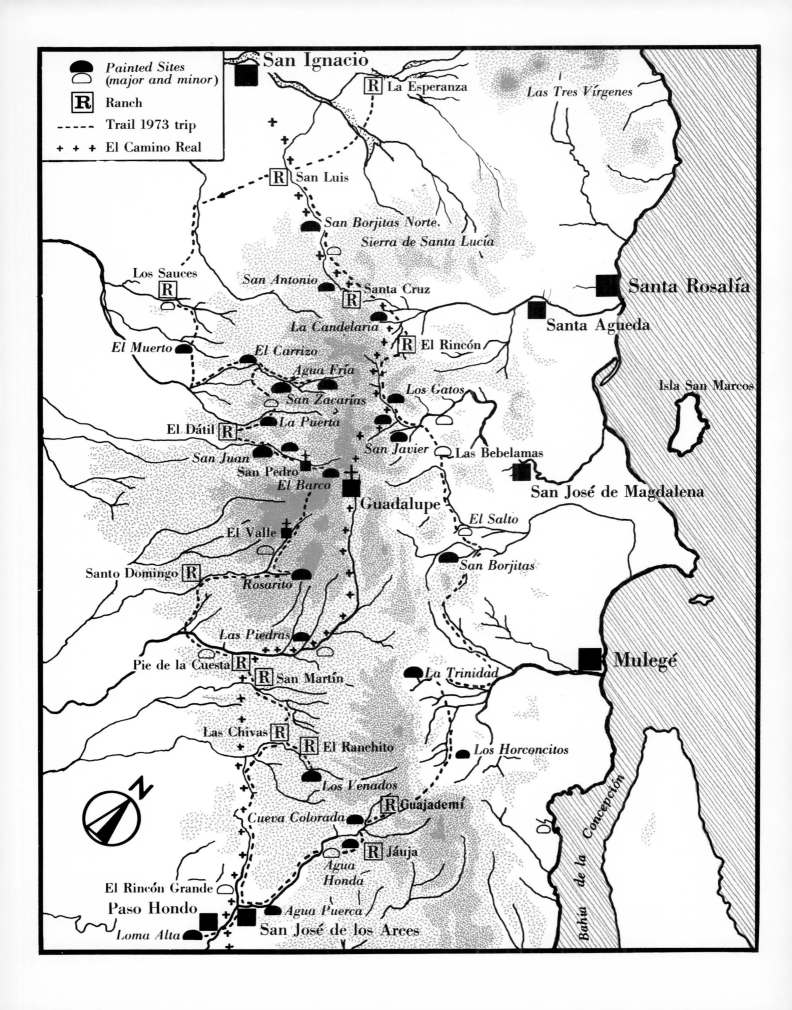

Legend:
- Painted Sites (major and minor)
- **R** Ranch
- - - - Trail 1973 trip
- + + + El Camino Real

San Ignacio

R La Esperanza

Las Tres Vírgenes

R San Luis

San Borjitas Norte.

Sierra de Santa Lucía

Los Sauces **R**

San Antonio

Santa Cruz

Santa Rosalía

R Santa Cruz

La Candelaria

El Muerto

El Carrizo

Agua Fría

R El Rincón

Santa Agueda

Isla San Marcos

San Zacarías

Los Gatos

El Dátil **R**

La Puerta

San Juan

San Javier

Las Bebelamas

San Pedro

El Barco

Guadalupe

San José de Magdalena

El Valle

El Salto

Santo Domingo **R**

Rosarito

San Borjitas

Las Piedras

Pie de la Cuesta **R**

La Trinidad

Mulegé

R San Martín

Las Chivas **R**

R El Ranchito

Los Horconcitos

Los Venados

R Guajademí

Cueva Colorada

R Jáuja

Agua Honda

El Rincón Grande

Paso Hondo

Agua Puerca

San José de los Arces

Loma Alta

Bahía de la Concepción

N

Before the many striking discoveries of the mid-twentieth century, the best known rock art of Baja California was located in a cave at a place called San Borjitas near Mulegé. Leon Diguet visited the site in the 1890's, photographed it, and wrote about its works as among the most impressive he saw on the peninsula. In 1951 it was the subject of a study by Dahlgren and Romero for the Instituto Nacional de Antropologia y Historia. Erle Stanley Gardner visited and described it as a wondrous sight. Even the cave description which Padre Escalante gave Miguel del Barco around 1772 fits San Borjitas closely except for some perhaps minimized dimensions.

A single factor probably underlies all of these somewhat separate occurrences. San Borjitas was close to a population center which retained its importance continuously from early mission times to the present. The cave and its contents were known early to people in Mulegé and the knowledge was never lost. Furthermore, the trip between the two places was not difficult, no high mountains needed to be crossed, and there had always been an important ranch in the vicinity.

San Borjitas today is an abandoned ranch in a greater cattle-raising area known as San Baltazar. Since the late nineteenth century the whole spread has been the property of the Gorosave family of Mulegé, the purchase of Vicente Gorosave, an immigrant born in 1844 in the Basque provinces of Spain. Since Vicente was educated and, according to family tradition, well acquainted with the French colony at Santa Rosalía, it was probably he who informed Diguet of the cave and its art.

After my early experiences with the aboriginal paintings of the Sierra de San Francisco I became curious about this famous place. Especially, I wanted to compare its art to what I had been discovering to the north. During many visits to Mulegé I had had the privilege of meeting and knowing Doña Refugio Gorosave, a granddaughter of Vicente Gorosave. By December 1971 I was ready to visit San Borjitas and a communication with Doña Cuca, as she was familiarly called, soon put me in touch with a man who had worked at the ranch and could act as a guide. We were able to drive fourteen miles north on the main road toward Santa Rosalía and then nineteen additional miles west into the sierra to a ranch called Las Tinajas. From there an hour-and-a-half mule ride to the south brought us to the site of the abandoned ranch, and a twenty-minute walk up a brush-filled *cañada* put us at the base of a slope which led up to the cave.

As usual, the site was unimpressive when viewed from below. As we made our way up, it looked like no more than a *respaldo* at the foot of a high bluff. But from its own level, the form and scale of the place underwent a dramatic change. A broad opening appeared at the base of the *respaldo*, and, as we approached, it could be seen as an overhung cave of impressive depth. Furthermore, the paintings, or part of them at least, were immediately apparent. That part of the ceiling visible from without was already heavily decorated with a maze of large *monos* in random orientation.

Because of the great mass of rock above and

SAN BORJITAS

This best known site of the Sierra de Guadalupe probably shares with Cuesta Palmarito of the Sierra de San Francisco the unusual distinction of having been a major center of aboriginal art and also a well known place in mission times and subsequent ranching periods. Its written history appears to date from the 1770's since it is the site which best fits Padre Escalante's description of a painted cave quoted on page 14.

SAN BORJITAS

More than fifty stiff, slightly bulbous human figures, many with outthrust arms and vertical stripes, define a parochial Sierra de Guadalupe style. A number (including one above) mimic Sierra de San Francisco conventions such as characteristic headdresses and bodies divided vertically into red and black sides. But spread legs and heads divided between the two colors suggest that they are the work of Guadalupe artists only partially familiar with the style. Perhaps San Borjitas shows painted representations of conflicts between the folk of the two sierras.

95

the low ceiling the cave seemed small. The measurements were a real surprise. At one hundred feet wide by about eighty feet deep and an average of twelve feet high it was no match for La Cuevona or even Cuesta Palmarito in the Sierra de San Francisco, but it was an impressive expanse nonetheless. And its broad, unusually smooth and accessible ceiling had made an extremely satisfactory canvas to which a large amount of art had been entrusted. The majority of over eighty identifiable figures were *monos* larger than life sife. There was also a scattering of deer and fish.

The *monos* of San Borjitas are both varied and strikingly related. They are painted in red, black, ochre, gray, white and combinations of these colors. They are filled in with solid areas of one paint, divided vertically into areas of two colors, or made up of stripes, checkerboards or more complex geometric lattices. Despite all this variety there is a characteristic form recognizable in most of these human figures. Their bodies are long and tend to bulge as if they were inflated. The arms are thrust more out than up, and the heads are short, often rectangular in outline, and rest directly on the shoulders without the suggestion of a neck. In all, as compared to the *monos* of the Sierra de San Francisco, these figures are stiff and ill-proportioned. An additional contrast is the emphasis on arrows embedded in the bodies of the *monos*. This theme is certainly widespread in the Sierras of San Francisco and San Borja but not with the emphasis seen at San Borjitas. More than a dozen figures are thus transfixed, some with as many as six arrows.

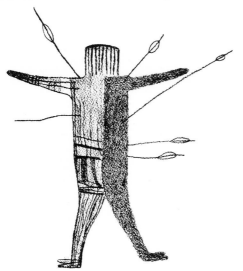

The *monos* of San Borjitas *en masse* present another unique aspect. Their bodies are oriented rather randomly toward three points of the compass. The heads point predominantly west but also south and north. This is probably due to the relatively horizontal plane of the ceiling which allowed each artist to choose his own version of "up." East was avoided by all because a figure whose head pointed in that direction would clearly be upside down. At any rate, the spectacle of adjacent and overlapping figures at right angles to each other is most unusual among the Great Murals and can be considered characteristic only of San Borjitas.

The side and back walls of the cave consist of a soft tuff. Originally the entire void was filled with this material and the ceiling was the contact face of a harder agglomerate layer above. The tuff layer bears water, a spring drips from it year round, and this has contributed to the erosion which has eaten out the cave. The soft side walls, particularly on the north, have attracted the makers of engravings and literally dozens of symbols, predominantly vulvas, can be seen. On the back wall, a fire blackened area has been scratched through to produce handsome figures of a deer and fish.

The visit to San Borjitas produced much food for thought. The paintings were not those of San Francisco. Certainly the great majority of the figures would have looked quite out of place at any of the sites with which I had become familiar. Nevertheless they were simply different, not alien. The impulse and the subject matter were quite compatible, only fine points of style distinguished the works in these areas some seventy miles apart. It seemed virtually certain that other works lay between.

Leon Diguet had reported only five sites in the greater San Francisco area; he listed ten from Guadalupe. This suggested forcibly that the number there might be high indeed, and, beyond that, its area was several times greater in size than that in which I had been working. Suddenly it seemed more important to link San Borjitas to San Francisco than it did to accumulate more and more material from the latter area. The thought created a vision of finding a dozen splendidly painted caves marching in sequence from the northern foothills of Guadalupe all the way to San Borjitas and linking the artistic styles of the two sierras into a continuous chain.

The plan that leaped into being so simply took a long time to put into practice. I had to work on other things to support these adventures and I was not able to return to the Sierra de Guadalupe until the latter part of 1973. During the intervening time I had met Enrique Hambleton, a young, educated Mexican living in La Paz and trying to develop a career in photography. He saw my pictures of rock art and was immediately interested. I liked the idea of having an active, intelligent companion to share in the search and I had no trouble enlisting Enrique for the Guadalupe adventure. Tacho and Ramón were alerted so as to retain their services and get them to rent animals. We also asked them to obtain the guide or guides we would need, since we were leaving their region. When the time came, Tacho was unable to go but fortunately he had been able to arrange for a guide, his distant cousin Arnulfo Villavicencio. This man, nicknamed Coco, was a wiry, forty-year-old cowboy who had grown up near Guadalupe and seemed well acquainted with the northern part of the mountains.

The plan was to start an exploration on the northwest corner of the sierra and to proceed down its Pacific slopes to the region of La Purísima. Then we would turn north and follow an ancient Indian and mission route toward Mulegé. Once on the Mulegé plain we would return to the north by way of the Gulf slopes and finish where we had begun at La Esperanza. The exact itinerary, of course, would be determined by any clues we might get as to painting sites. For a beginning I had Diguet's list, but it did not really help too much in laying out a route because we would not be able to identify most of his named places until we reached their immediate vicinities.

The sierra to be surveyed loomed on the horizon to the south, a line of jagged peaks at the east end giving way to a long slope down toward the Pacific. Maps showed that the mountain mass extended ninety miles to the southeast and that its width varied from twenty to thirty miles. Thus the area involved was greater than two thousand square miles and I was acutely aware that I would be more dependent than ever on local information. If that broken pile of mountains and mesas were deserted, a man could spend years finding all the nooks and crannies. Fortunately it was sprinkled with ranches, many of which dated back to mission times. In addition the

north end of the Sierra de Guadalupe, the part to be visited first, had been the scene of much activity during the heyday of El Boleo, the French copper-mining concern at Santa Rosalía. During the years between 1900 and 1925, the company bought, confiscated, or founded a total of more than fifty ranches in the hinterland around Santa Rosalía. These were used primarily to raise beef but goats and goat cheese were also important and several ranches had enough water to serve as truck gardens. The company lavished a great deal of money on this ranch system. They hired a large percentage of the local people and put them to work building huge corrals of stone and digging wells by hand at each ranch. The company also constructed an elaborate road system for driving stock, part of which still served to connect ranches and was conspicuous in aerial photographs of this arid, rocky region.

For two days we rode south over these Boleo roads and visited onetime ranches of the company. There was no information about rock art but that was neither surprising nor disappointing. The terrain promised little, consisting as it did of large mesas and broad arroyos with few rock formations that would appear to invite painting.

A small change of fortune occurred at Los Sauces, the first ranch that could be said to occupy a corner of the sierra proper. After days of riding over very open, very dry country it was a surprise to come to the edge of a deep *cañada* carved from colorful rock. The trail wound down an incredibly steep road built by the rancher and led to the ranch house and the welcome shade of its *corredor*. The *dueño*, Venancio Zuñiga, heard our questions and in answer led us below his orchard and across the *cañada*. There, on a low basalt *cantil*, were paintings, but scarcely Great Murals. Painted in rose-red on a smoothly fractured surface of columnar basalt were five fish and an unidentifiable zoomorphic form suggestive of a pelican. The figures ranged from a few inches to a couple of feet in height. Vertical stains on the painted panels indicated that they washed by running water during and after rains; as a result there was a deposit of insoluble salts which streaked the paintings. Small wonder; the marvel was that the primitive paint-makers' product had persisted so well despite centuries of annual washings. Four of the painted fish had only a generalized fish-form to identify them;

they could be called fish symbols, but the fifth was a skillfully executed bat ray. Unfortunately all the works had suffered the fate of antiquities near ranches. Someone had scratched fresh outlines around the paintings and there were numerous initials worked lightly into the hard basalt.

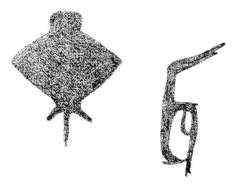

The trail left Los Sauces by going up its *cañada* and heading east. We were now coming into the real foothills of the sierra and each successive arroyo was wider and deeper. Coco was in his element now and for the next two weeks our routes and objectives would be in his hands or subject to the suggestions of residents in the region.

Two hours' ride brought us to a place called Las Tinajitas, a succession of water catchments in a basalt flow. Scattered all around were countless blocks of basalt and, on those close to the pools, a profusion of petroglyphs. Most of the themes were natural if not actually realistic. Many of the human figures were rather grotesque but the animals, deer, and rabbits for the most part, were depicted much as they were in the Great Mural assemblages. It was surprising to

see a pelican-like figure very similar to the puzzling painting at Los Sauces. Such a correspondence in so complicated a figure invited the thought that they came from the same hand.

Another hour took us to the south edge of a mesa and down into an arroyo by way of a steep trail which worked around and through a tremendous slide of detached and tumbled blocks of basalt.

For many yards on either side of the trail as it descended, and on the undisturbed bluffs of basalt above were thousands of engraved artworks. There was Leon Diguet's eighth site, "Cañada del Muerto, about 27°, petroglyphs and cliff with paintings."

From the crest of the mesa to a point over half way down the *cuesta* nearly every boulder of that great slide was covered with pictures pecked into its patinated surface. Human, deer, bird, fish, and perhaps insect forms abounded. There were dozens of depictions of spears and arrows as well as many symbolic devices or perhaps zoomorphic forms too stylized to recognize. Photography was discouraging; a proper recording of the Cañada del Muerto's petroglyphs would have used up my entire stock of film.

We hiked back and forth across the slope looking for prime examples. There were many arrangements or groups of figures but one of the most striking compositions was also the simplest. A pair of nicely drawn deer were superimposed. I was struck by the degree to which they resembled the deer in many Great Murals.

The most unique and fascinating find was also the least conspicuous. Spread over two or three square feet of a flat surface was a delicate tracery representing a spiderweb. Working such fine lines into the hard basalt must have required the utmost in patience and skill.

We moved down to the *caja* of the Arroyo del Muerto. Diguet had promised "A cliff with paintings;" I was too impatient to wait for morning so despite approaching sunset I climbed the *cuesta* exiting to the south and found the paintings where Coco indicated. Near the top of the *cuesta* was an open, poorly protected *respaldo* facing east. On it were painted a singularly appropriate group. From left to right were a red-and-black *mono* with vertical stripes; a figure in all ways reminiscent of San Borjitas (which now lay thirty-five miles to the southeast). Next was an even larger solid black woman, then a red deer and, superimposed on that, a perfect "black warrior" of the type found at El Batequi in the Sierra de San Francisco. The whole thing seemed a perfect introduction to the Great Murals in the Sierra de Guadalupe, a sort of interface between the art of the two sierras. Any joy was moderated, however, by the terribly weathered condition of these exposed works. At best, they were clear but faint.

In the morning Enrique and I found more painted places, all in very bad condition. On the north side of the arroyo directly opposite the *tinaja* was a small cave weathered out of a grey-brown puddingstone agglomerate. The lower and deeper parts were heavily smoke-blackened but the ceiling showed the remains of extensive paintings. At the left, a group of three life-sized *monos* survived well enough to discern if not to enjoy as art. Each was divided vertically into red and black areas, the head on the red side, as usual. Noteworthy were the apparent head-dresses on two of the figures, one with a single tall feather-like plume, the other possibly with a pair. Some smaller human figures were distinguishable at the right end of the opening and all

the *monos* were unusually heavily outlined in white paint of the plaster type. A large *metate* lay broken on the floor, apparently the victim of heat during its use as a fire stone.

About five hundred yards up the arroyo to the east was a slit cave on the south wall. Here was a small painting of a bird in the skillful fashion of Boca de San Julio, although in much poorer condition than its San Francisco counterparts. The basic drawing was in a brownish-red, outlined with a rich pink. Below, a dozen or more vulva symbols were carved into a soft tuff layer of the cave formation.

We left the Tinaja del Muerto by way of the *cañada* to the south, passed the painted *respaldo*, and were shortly on the Mesa del Muerto at an elevation of 2,100 feet. To the east, a mountain panorama was dominated by the pointed Pilón de San Matías and the great flat-topped block of Cerro de la Victoria. Due north, the sentinel tip of La Vírgen was still visible over the top of the intervening range.

We arrived at the south edge of the Mesa del Muerto to find a geography lesson that would cover our travels for several days. Below was a vast and complicated system of waterways carved by the chubascos of countless summers. An arroyo ran east into the sierra; Coco called it the arroyo del Dátil. Branching from it just below us and running north was the Arroyo de Santa Isabel. Other smaller fingers and arms broke from both of these to cut the country below us into a crazy-quilt pattern.

El Dátil contained paintings, said Coco, and it led on to more. But first we must go up Santa Isabel and see its offerings. We descended a long carefully made *cuesta* and turned north at the bottom.

Near sunset, after a break for lunch and resting our animals, and after over two hours of riding up the boulder-strewn arroyo, we arrived at a place called El Carrizo. There was the water we needed to camp and there also were real caves on both sides of the watercourse. The first, only a few feet above the bed of the arroyo and on its north side, yielded prompt but frustrating rewards. It had been painted heavily at one time but its rough and crumbling surface retained only a few patches of paint with here and there a decipherable figure. In the gloom of the cave interior, dimly lighted by the sky at dusk, shone the only real survivor, the white outline of a deer done in the tenacious plaster-like paint. It was at once promising and disappointing. We had been encountering paintings during each of the past three days but not one had been in good enough condition to really enjoy or photograph as art. Coco said that other paintings in his sierra were *mas o menos*, meaning, colloquially, "about the same."

At dawn we were up and searching. The other caves were also painted but in equally poor condition. As I came out of one up on the south side of the arroyo something caught my eye. On the *respaldo* opposite was a suspicious looking patch of red. Binoculars confirmed the suspicion. In that ten-power magnification was a pair of large *monos* with their arms raised in the familiar salute. I scrambled down one bank, crossed the arroyo and worked my way up the loose, sliding rock of the other. Only a few moments after the discovery I stood puffing in front of my prize. And a prize it was. The right hand *mono* was about seven feet tall, bicolored red-and-black, divided vertically, and outlined in pink. It displayed a familiar three-lobed headdress, the center protuberance being short and one on either side longer and curving downward toward the shoulders. The other *mono* was a woman painted in a plain red, also with the pink outline and pierced by at least three black arrows whose heads were carefully delineated over the body paint. Over one shoulder was a tiny inverted figure similar to those over the shoulders of two *monos* at Flechas Cave in the Sierra de San Francisco. Above this pair flew three black *auras*, or vultures, wing to wing. Their heads were painted red, making this one of the rare instances where more than the outline was realistic.

Walking around the site revealed more paintings. Very high and to the left of the *mono-aura* group was a huge black deer with handsome antlers; the legs, however, were gone, the victims of having been entrusted to a softer layer of rock.

Several tiny *monos* were scattered on inclusive rocks and other larger paintings near the bottom of the *respaldo* were now in the last stages of deterioration. On returning to the main group I noticed a fourth *aura* in good condition partially overpainting the calf area of the bicolored *mono*. On the ground were numerous artifacts, choppers, scrapers, *manos*, and, best of all, a *metate* and other stones unmistakably stained with red and black paints.

El Carrizo left a warm sense of having arrived once again among the Painters and a half hour's ride brought a further reminder. At a narrow corner of the arroyo a faded but visible *mono* looked down from a position on the sheer rock wall.

Two hours later we came to the place where the Arroyo de San Zacarías flows down from the north and joins that of Santa Isabel. As we rode past the mouth of San Zacarías, Coco pointed up the high bank opposite. There in plain sight was a mammoth *respaldo* covered with *monos* so large and numerous that they made an impressive showing even from far below.

Thus we came to our first major Great Mural site in the Sierra de Guadalupe. The *respaldo* was long, at least two hundred feet, and it was high. Some of the paintings were twenty-five feet off the floor and they were dwarfed by the height of the wall above them. Rows of giant red and black *monos* stood staunchly abreast braving erosion but theirs was a losing battle. The fine outlines were gone, the colors were washing away and here and there flakes of rock had fallen and taken pieces of painted figures as they went. It was a profoundly moving experience. With its huge dimensions, its sweeping view over two arroyos, and the remains of so much human endeavor, Boca de San Zacarías had the aura of a great ceremonial center.

Despite the destruction there were a few items of artistic interest. The most important was embodied in a different style of *mono*. Near the center of the entire painted assemblage was a pair of human figures; only their heads, shoulders and arms survived. One was solid maroon outlined heavily in white and the other was maroon and black with a lighter white boundary. Their characteristic and different appearance was created by a very short head so deeply sunk into the shoulders that it gave no sense of a neck at all, and also by a strange, floppy "dog ears" sort of headdress on each figure. Below these and the

rows of tall *monos* were animal figures but they were terribly eroded.

Time did not allow an inventory of the Arroyo de San Zacarías itself but, a few steps into it, in a tiny cave on the west wall were a well-preserved pair of small black deer.

Two hours' ride brought us to Rancho Santa Isabel. The *dueño*, Tomás Murillo, gave us instructions for reaching the best known paintings in his region. About a mile and a half away, precisely at sunset, we came to a place that is called Agua Fria. Even before we arrived, Ramón had spotted the paintings. Across the arroyo to the east, and up the usual steep, rocky *falda*, was a conspicuous cave. On its ceiling, well exposed to view, were huge paintings of a deer and a mountain lion. They were brilliantly lighted by the last rays of the sun and binoculars showed that they were in superb condition. I jumped down, grabbed our motion picture camera, and charged the slope. Minutes later and utterly winded, I arrived before the cave just in time to see the light die on the paintings. No matter. Being there was reward enough and I poked around in the pink light of the afterglow. The two huge black figures had survived marvelously and even in the rapidly graying dusk I could make out the forms of several older figures which the lion and the deer partially covered.

Far above the painted cave, perhaps a thousand feet higher, we had noticed a gigantic cave illuminated in the setting sun. Coco called it Cueva Blanca and told a strange story about it. According to local lore the cave had been struck by an *aerolito*, a meteorite, some seventy or eighty years before. The people at Santa Isabel heard a great roar and felt a smashing impact. When they examined the place they found a huge slide of broken rock down the mountain side and individual fragments as much as a mile to the west. Coco himself had never been up to the site and had no notion if the remains of the

cave were painted or not.

In the morning the climb proved to be slow, difficult and tiring. The entire slope was covered with fragments of freshly broken rock set at about the steepest angle that they could occupy and not slide. There were many places where large chunks were precariously balanced and we had to move with caution.

The cave turned out to be an exciting place but entirely barren of art. It was huge, some three hundred feet long and overhung by a *respaldo* more than a hundred feet high. Of the original deepest part of the cave only a pocket remained but that was eighty feet wide, more than sixty feet deep and thirty feet high. A tiny spring dripped from the roof and formed a pool of delicious water which was surrounded by a wreath made up of tiny plants with golden flowers.

The entire area, except the inner cave, was buried in freshly broken rock. The source of the tremendous cubage of fallen stone appeared to have been an overhang which had once formed a gigantic cave. No test that we could apply told us whether the meteorite tale should be believed or not. All the stone that we actually saw could have simply fallen and rolled or slid down the steep slope. But whatever the cause, the event left an impressive scar.

We were thoroughly tired by the time we got down again, but we launched right into the job of recording Agua Fria. The two large black figures offered a surprise. They had been painted with a unique substance. It had the look of some sort of bituminous material, perhaps natural tar or asphalt. Many of the painted caves including Agua Fria contained blotch-like exudations of a similar appearing material. However, when we have examined these stains they have invariably proven to be hard and dry.

Lower than the two figures which so dominated the cave, were a nicely painted small rabbit and the eroded remains of a deer with elegant antlers, both in the same curious paint. The older works, which I had seen the night before, turned out to be two deer, one a little larger than life and the other huge, even bigger than the black giant. Both these were well preserved but painted in a soft pink which did not give a lot of contrast with the warm beige patina on the cave wall.

Early in the morning before the climb, I had had my binoculars out looking at Cueva Blanca

AGUA FRIA I

The massive black forms of a mountain lion and a deer, each ten feet long, exemplify the diversity found among Great Mural expressions. Although many conventions were observed by nearly all the artists, their works are surprisingly individual. No other site known at this time displays figures which seem akin to these or that are colored with the strange burnt umber, pitch-like paint used in their depiction.

AGUA FRIA II

Rock paintings like these in the northern region of the Sierra de Guadalupe show stylistic similarities to those of the Sierra de San Francisco just to the north across the San Ignacio plain. But subtle differences are already apparent and, as an observer moves south, each additional site has more new elements. The human figures in this group illustrate a commonly observed fact in the survival of paints. The larger were originally bicolored in red and black, but the black sides have virtually disappeared.

and the hillsides in general. Just a couple of hundred yards south of the Agua Fria Cave I spotted a *respaldo* at the same level with a suspicious stain on it. When we finished our photography at the first site, we scrambled along the rough *falda* and through the thorny plants until we reached the other.

It did indeed prove to be painted and it also contained a mild surprise. Here were conventional red and black *monos*, divided vertically, displaying more than usually elaborate headdresses. Here also were deer painted in the usual Great Mural fashion. It seemed odd to us that all of the figures at Agua Fria I were so unusual and those at Agua Fria II should be so familiar. Only a small pink deer seemed to form any sort of a bond between the two sites.

Agua Fria II, like I, was an excellent survival; the colors were strong and the outlines distinct. we tore ourselves away reluctantly; nothing we had seen thus far had proved nearly so fine.

Now we had to backtrack to a spot beyond the Boca de San Zacarías before we could continue south. We mounted and started back to Santa Isabel. In not more than a half mile Ramón pointed across the arroyo to a *respaldo* behind some trees. Just over a canopy of leaves he had seen a telltale *mancha*, as he called them, a spot or stain. Binoculars proved him right. Enrique and I dismounted and sent Coco, Ramón and the animals on to Santa Isabel where they could ask the ranch folk to prepare us a meal. We crossed the arroyo and somewhat wearily climbed the *falda*.

Mindful of the striking differences between the Agua Fria sites, we speculated about this one as we went and arrived to find that it was another new thing quite unlike either of its neighbors up the arroyo. The figures Ramón had spotted were those of two women in solid red, outlined strongly in white, and painted high on the *respaldo*. Each was pierced by a white arrow with a classically drawn head. Below and strung out in a series of little caves and shelters was yet a different collection of paintings. One hollow contained a group of five red rabbits outlined in the white plaster paint. Another contained a doll-like *mono* in red outlined in black and, farthest to the west, was a cave in which we found numerous small bird paintings and a fine large bat ray in orange-red outlined in black. Beside that, there were scattered about on the *respaldo* various deer, a red mountain lion outlined in white,

and a group of large *monos* in the same colors. In a dark nook of one of the shelters I found a memento of Agua Fria, a small black deer which was a virtual replica of the large one which so dominated the other site.

We walked the mile or less to the ranch and, after dinner, packed up and continued our backtrack. At sunset we passed the Boca de San Zacarías, the great wall of *monos* clearly visible in the shadows of the south slope. We camped a short distance west at the foot of a grade that would take us out of the Arroyo de Santa Isabel.

In the morning we had a long and scenic ride, first up the *cuesta*, then across a mesa and through broken tableland until we took our midday break exactly on the pass which crossed the north shoulder of the Pilón de San Matías, the most conspicuous and recognizable mountain in the entire area. We rested there awhile and I climbed a short distance toward the bullet-shaped peak to get a look around. Ahead I could see the *cuesta* which would take us down into the arroyo of San Matías; I could also see a cañada which Coco called San Matiitas, or little San Matías. The name sounded familiar. Checking back, I found that Diguet visited a site he called San Matillita. I had never been able to find anyone who recognized that name and indeed it was obvious that some error had been made in transcribing it. "San" is masculine and "Matillita" feminine. The sierra people are notorious mumblers and swallowing the final "s" is almost universal. The more I thought about it, the more certain I became that this was the answer. Diguet wrote down what he heard without questioning the logic of gender. The rest of his description is simple to verify. "La Cañada de San Matillita, situated near the 27th parallel on the Pacific watershed of the sierra, flows into the great Arroyo de San Adeo." Here we were no more than 5 minutes south of 27 degrees north latitude on the Pacific slope and Coco informed me that the *cañada* joined the Arroyo de San Tadeo a short distance away. Since there is no saint on the calendar named San Adeo it seems that once again Diguet missed the mark in his transcription.

We descended the *cuesta* and arrived in a broad sandy watercourse. Enrique and I climbed to a small cave about three hundred yards downstream hoping to find the paintings which Diguet had seen. It proved to be in very bad condition, eroded and smoke-blackened, but it contained the remains of many paintings. None, however, was unusual in any way. Diguet had described a group of small and nearly abstract works; these were Great Murals, however, worn, stained, and pitted. It was late and we decided to go on. As tempting as it was to try to dog Diguet's footsteps our resolve failed when faced with the immensity of the area we would have to search.

At sunset, as we rode south in the bed of the waterway we came to a curious sight. A basaltic dike had been formed across this area in some past eon and it had partially weathered out of the softer surrounding material. The exposed portion now marched across the valley, in some places standing to heights of thirty feet or more, and looking like some ancient construction wildly out of place in those remote and deserted surroundings.

The next morning found us making our way down the same waterway which had been joined by the Arroyo de San Tadeo. Despite the Diguet site, I was discouraged from riding up to Rancho San Tadeo itself. Coco said it would cost us a day or more and he knew of no paintings; the ranch was *solo* at the moment which eliminated local assistance. To cap it off Diguet himself merely listed a rock shelter, presumably painted, and never described or referred to in any other way.

About a mile and a half below the junction of the two arroyos we came to a beautiful *angostura*, or narrows, in the waterway. The vertical rock on either side closed to form a channel not much over a hundred feet wide. We rode down this corridor admiring the play of light and shadow on the rich red-brown walls.

The southern mouth of this *angostura* was called La Puerta, the door, and Coco had heard that there were paintings nearby. We were not kept waiting; Ramón spotted them through some trees virtually as we arrived. The eastern rockwall, which narrows to form that side of La Puerta, had a large flat face just above the high water marks of the *canón*. This panel was very slightly overhung by a different volcanic agglomerate layer above it. There, adjacent to The Door itself, was a grand assemblage of painted figures, the whole being about sixty feet long. There were many deer. Two in black were painted as if seated on their haunches. There were also ten or twelve *monos* in a row like those at Boca de San Zacarías. Most interesting of all, there appeared to be an immense, heavy-bodied serpent which ran across the top of the entire group.

Joy at this discovery was heavily tempered by its condition. The entire panel, without the exception of a single figure, was in a very eroded, almost washed-off condition. The cause was unusual. Here the actual paint seems to have been worn away by exposure to wind and water. The rock, for a change, did not seem to be the culprit; the face was hard and smooth. The site illustrated a basic observation: a really good survival depends on many factors. In order to descend to us in anything like the condition in which the Painters left them, the art must have begun with that rare combination of good rock and good protection from wind, rain, and flowing water. La Puerta lacked the last two and survives only as another sad and tantalizing reminder of all that has been lost.

A few minutes' ride below La Puerta brought us to a large cave just above the *caja*. Enrique and I hastily dismounted to inspect it. For our pains we received only another lesson. That place had perfect protection against the elements, but its rock was so soft and crumbling that nothing on its surface could have survived.

By noon we were at Rancho El Dátil. This was the home of Juan Zuñiga, the brother of Venancio, and it had once been the principal Boleo ranch in this region. Here the foremen of all the other ranches gathered monthly to be paid, and here, in the first quarter of this century, was the liveliest scene in all the sierras of Baja California.

Rancho El Dátil occupied a rise just east of the confluence of the arroyo and a *cañada* dropping down from the south. Just below it was a broad flat formed by the wash of the two watercourses. Here had been built corrals. They still stood and were in use; a few cultivated patches scattered among thickets of brush and *carrizo* grew in what once must have been wide fields. That flat area, according to old-timers, was the site of the colorful monthly encampment which accompanied payday. *Fayuqueros*, the mounted dry goods salesmen of the pre-automotive age, were present with anything that might appeal to the temporarily monied mountain people. Some of these men brought young women with them, exotic faces for the provincial ranchers, "beautiful señoritas all the way from Guaymas," one old man told me, "and never the same from month to month." Beside their obvious roles, the girls added a lot to the public revels amongst the tents and clearings of that flat. Few wives attended the paydays and yet there was a fiesta every night. "Those young things never sat down, they danced and sang every song."

Late in the afternoon we headed for the *cuesta* over the pass that separated El Dátil from San Juan. We started up the *cañada* south of the house and passed the crumbling remains of a stone and mortar aquaduct which once had brought water from a spring directly to the fields below. Soon we started up a grade and in a few minutes we found ourselves climbing steeply across a bleak and picturesque slide of tumbled basalt block. It was higher and steeper than the slide at El Muerto, but unfortunately without petroglyphs. Two thirds of the way to the top we heard singing above us and soon spotted a young man on a mule which was stepping in a spry fashion down the rock pile. In a few moments we met Jesús Valenzuela, the rancher at San Juan. We stopped to chat briefly and, discovering our mission, he gave us the best possible news. There was a large painted site near his ranch and it was called Los Monos de San Juan. Further, he was sure that the name was old. I, in my turn, was sure that it must be one of Diguet's sites, not merely a listing like San Tadeo, but a large and important center which Diguet had compared to San Borjitas. Señor Valenzuela was on his way to buy supplies and socialize at El Dátil but he said he would return and show us the paintings.

We camped on the mesa and during the night were surprised as a traveller passed on the trail. The undaunted Jesús Valenzuela had completed his visit and was riding home over that awesome mountain trail in the pitch black of a moonless night.

On the morning of the tenth day of the trip we rose early and headed east. In minutes we came to a lookout over the Arroyo de San Juan and had a noble view of the country in which we would be riding for several days. Perhaps eight hundred feet below was a right-angle turn in the arroyo with the tract of level land usually found at such places. All of it had been cleared and plowed and a tidy rock wall divided it from the bed of the watercourse. A man could be seen stacking brush in piles, several of which were blazing and smoking. An animal trail led up the waterway to a cluster of houses and then disappeared as it followed the arroyo around a corner of the hills. In the distance to the east were the highest peaks we had seen, a really formidable wall running north and south.

A leisurely descent brought us to the farm scene below and before long we had completed the ceremonies of a minimum visit and hit the trail again guided by Valenzuela.

The way was simplicity itself. We followed the bed of the arroyo and in a little over half an hour we were dismounting on the east bank and looking across at Los Monos de San Juan. The actual site was slightly reminiscent of Boca de San Zacarías; it was a very high and long *respaldo* with *monos* quite visible from the trail below. The principal differences were the facts that this site was only fifty feet or so above the arroyo and that its paintings were obviously more numerous and in better condition.

We shouldered all our gear, crossed the riverbed and scrambled up a slope. In a moment we stood where Leon Diguet had stood nearly eighty years before. To savor the moment as fully as possible I rummaged in my papers and found a photocopy of Diguet's original report which included a photograph of this site. In a moment we located the place where it was taken and I solemnly stood for a picture on the spot where Diguet's guide had posed.

Los Monos did not disappoint us. It was a rich tapestry of the Painters' art featuring an assemblage of human figures nearly as numerous as those of San Borjitas and to my eye, more varied and interesting. The *respaldo* was about eighty feet high and hung well over the paintings which occupied its lower twenty-five feet and were on a distinct and recessed rock structure. This painted surface in turn was broken into four areas by the natural erosion of the rock. To the left was a large

LOS MONOS DE SAN JUAN

Here in 1894 Leon Diguet made the first known photograph of a Great Mural site. The picture, re-created above, was published in a French scientific journal. For fifty years Diguet's article and its few illustrations were the world's only view of these aboriginal art centers. In 1973 the Diguet photographs were compared to the locations at which they were made. There was no observable change in the condition of the paintings.

plate-like depression filled with about twenty-five *monos*, largely of the red-and-black vertically-divided ilk. That group was dominated by the figure of a gigantic red *león* seemingly suspended over the *monos*. To the right of this grouping and slightly higher was another concave panel nearly double the width of the first. It too had a multitude of human figures, men and women.

Beneath the right end of the latter panel was a shelf-like protruberance overhanging a tiny cave, also heavily painted. Diguet's photo showed this area, including part of the large panel above. To the right of the small cave, and quite separated by a rock formation, was another little painted cave.

En masse, the human figures that make up Los Monos de San Juan are particularly effective. It is one of those places, rare among the Great Murals, where the figures work with each other to create a composition, a work greater than the sum of its parts. El Batequi is the greatest of these places. The Serpent Cave, the Family of Man group at La Palma, and the cavalcade at San Gregorio I are others. Here at San Juan it is less a sense of overall composition but rather one of the neighboring *monos* creating an atmosphere for each other. They are arranged like a multitude attending a momentous event. One behind another, many abreast, they wait out the ages as witnesses to forgotten rites.

This is perhaps the most subtly varied of the great *mono* assemblages. All figures appear, superficially at least, to be closely related. The paints are alike, the drawings oddly similar with shortened legs and elongated bodies that seem expressive of emotion. They bend as if recoiling from unseen dangers, there is a flexibility to their lines scarcely equalled elsewhere. Close inspection shows a great variety of treatment in headdresses, and many are absolutely unique. One black women has a red head with a black spot, recalling a cyclopean eye. Another, a black man, has a beautiful moundlike headdress created by engraving the rock into the pattern of a dandelion gone to seed.

Los Monos is a true gallery of the Painters; it is a place which requires time and concentration to appreciate. In this, I find that it contrasts with San Borjitas where an equally large number of *monos* are disposed in such a random pattern as to make an effective abstract. They are arrayed neither with nor against each other; they cooperate only as a design. The individual stiff, sausage-like figures impart less of beauty, of horror, of human involvement than those of San Juan. The contrast is especially interesting because the two sites are in the same sierra and only a little over twenty miles apart.

In general, the rock of the lower painted areas, the caves, is poorer. The art works there were in relatively bad condition. The paintings on the two major panels were much better, many being entire with little pitting or flaking to destroy line and color. There was, however, a different sort of degradation associated with all these upper paintings. Water seepage, probably, or some other agency had coated their surfaces with a milky-looking film. This coating dulled the drawing and muted the colors. At first I thought it might merely be dirt or dust which had settled on the inclined surface. However, a water-soaked rag could remove none of the deposit; when wet, the colors became more vivid but they shortly dried to their original condition.

Our examination of the condition of the work at Los Monos soon prompted a comparison with the Diguet photo. This was a rare opportunity. To my knowledge Diguet's are by far the earliest photographs of Great Murals, and of them, this one at San Juan is best. The quality of the reproduction was poor, but, according to what I could see, there had been no change in the painted area covered by the photograph. Subsequently I have seen a better print of Diguet's picture and have compared it with mine. The results were the same; there was no appreciable change.

Other parts of the paintings had fared differently. Outside the area covered by the 1894 photo were two large irregular patches of clean rock several square feet in extent. Here the painted surface was unexpectedly flaked away, the ground was littered with painted bits. In answer to our obvious puzzlement, Valenzuela told us a heartbreaking story. Twenty years before, a man from the coast was working at San Juan. He fell out with his employer, was discharged, and left in a drunken condition. The people soon heard shots, "a real *fusilada*," Jesús told us, and feared that someone had met the inebriate and come to harm. Riding out they found to their relief that he had only discharged his .30-30 carbine at Los Monos de San Juan. Our informant showed us that the more localized damage of the right panel had partially destroyed a particularly beautiful and unique deer painted in a strong red and outlined in black.

Enrique and I looked in frustration at the piles of colored tesserae, the residue of the lost art. We recalled the terrible odds against the survival of the Great Murals; these had survived well with the gift of good rock and adequate shelter. Another enemy of the paintings had to be added to our list, the most implacable of all the potentially destructive forces, the only one which has the ability to search and destroy.

We left that magnificent painted place with understandably mixed feelings and rode up the arroyo, each quiet with his own thoughts. All along the way were the impressive remains of a system of waterpipes installed long ago by the Boleo. *Chubascos* had since wrecked the whole enterprise and most of the works were fallen or smashed into litter along that sometimes tumultuous waterway. It was odd to see twenty-foot lengths of six-inch pipe lying about in a place so far from any vestiges of the culture that produced them.

A half-mile ride brought us to a very beautiful *angostura*. Once again high rock walls rose on either side and we fell to looking for additional rock art which Jesús Valenzuela had mentioned before returning to his home. As usual, Ramón first recognized the faint showings and we were soon toiling up a *falda* unusually steep in a land of steep slopes. The paintings were minor after Los Monos but full of interest for us. The first thing that met my eye, for example, was another of the floppy-eared *monos* which we had

first seen at Boca de San Zacarías. This one was pierced by several arrows with carefully drawn feathers. There were male and female *monos* outlined with white plaster but never filled in with color. There was also an unusual black deer.

While Enrique and I admired and photographed that collection, Ramón was off to the east scouting along the base of the same continuing *respaldo*. He returned saying that he had found a curiosity unknown to him before, a human handprint. That was exciting. Handprints are among the oldest and commonest rock painting devices known. They have been found on every inhabited continent, and in just about every place frequented by ancient artists, yet I had not seen or heard of one among the Great Murals. We followed Ramón to the spot. There, about seven feet off the ground, on a broken rock face was a negative hand print, in other words, an image made by placing a hand on the rock and painting around it. Curious, we placed our hands over the image and found that the painter had been smaller than any of us. The original hand must have been about a tenth smaller than that of Ramón, a sturdily built man five feet and nine inches tall.

Resuming our ride we soon came to the narrowest place in all the *angostura* and found it filled with water. However, the depth was not alarming and we rode on past the ruins of a dam and up out of the narrows altogether. That put us in a broad open arroyo and as the sun set we halted briefly at two small caves with insignificant and badly preserved paintings. As it became quite dark we rode into a rancho where Coco planned to spend the night.

As we pulled up we were met by a most friendly man, Ramón Avila, master of San Marcos. He made us welcome and we passed a pleasant evening catching up on sierra gossip.

In the morning we headed east toward Rancho San Pedro. Avila accompanied us for a quarter of a mile and showed us a painted rock face on the north side of the arroyo. There we saw a large woman's figure outlined in an orange-pink and various other smaller figures too poor to record.

For the next two hours or so we rode up a very broad arroyo in which grew large *mezquite* and *bebelama* trees. Ahead, the imposing wall of mountains loomed taller and closer. A map check showed the reason. Some of those peaks were near 6,000 feet, we were at 2,000 feet and they were only four or five miles away.

Just before noon we came to Rancho San Pedro, almost a village, with several houses scattered along the south bank of the watercourse. We approached one designated by Coco and dismounted as the local men, women, children, and dogs came out to participate in the rare event of a visit.

That spot has quite a history. The Jesuits discovered it before 1730 and, noting its potential animal forage, founded a ranch and visiting station called San Pedro y San Pablo. Before long the cattle herds here and at El Valle, a few miles south, were the greatest of all the missions of the peninsula. A stone chapel was supposed to have been built at each place. The ranches remained successful during the decline and closing of Guadalupe Mission, the original Indian population being replaced by the families of the mission soldiers and cowherds, the ancestors of the present sierra folk.

We were invited to coffee and visiting at the home of Toribio Rojas. Then, while Coco and Ramón really got down to a serious visit, and while we waited for Toribio's wife to prepare a *comida*, Enrique and I looked around. The men had pointed to a mound when we asked about a stone chapel. Now we looked it over. Inside was a cleared area of thirteen by thirty-five feet. Its walls were of stone over three feet thick and laid up to a height of nearly five feet. Above that height the walls had been built of adobe block, a section of which survived on the south side. The present moundlike condition outside was caused by the melting away and falling of the adobe. Although the ruin was not especially impressive, we were moved by our encounter with it. Probably built by the German, Father Everard Helen, about 1735, that modest little rectangle was the last tangible remains of the Jesuit dream in a lonely corner of their onetime realm.

During a welcome dinner we queried our host extensively about paintings but the pickings proved to be slim. Three local men were present and they could think of only one site, unimpressive and difficult to reach. The conversation did have an unexpected twist. Toribio's wife turned out to have been born and raised at San Tadeo. She was able to tell me what I had missed by electing not to visit that place. According to her positive recollections, there were perhaps half a dozen groups of paintings in caves and on low

cantiles between the point where we entered the Arroyo de San Tadeo and another point a short distance above the ranch of the same name. She was not so positive as to the kind or quality of paintings, "regular paintings," she said, "*monos*," birds, deer, who knows what all?" All we could do was shrug it off and drop a card into the index for a future trip.

In mid-afternoon we started east again, passed the more prosperous looking ranch of another Rojas brother and soon veered off to the south to climb a tremendous *cuesta*. By dusk we had climbed to Rancho Potrerito, an abandoned Boleo construction at an elevation of about 4,500 feet. It had a spring, and water was still piped to a *pila* and watering trough. Here we passed the night camped within the stone walls of the Boleo corral.

In the morning we set out to investigate possible painted sites. Coco and Enrique went to find the place described by the Rojas brothers. Ramón worked his way over to the *salto*, a seasonal waterfall west of the ranch, and I wound down to look at its base. We were attracted to the latter sites by the combination of water and obvious rock faces that might have been painted. Because it was the first time we had split up over any considerable distance, each party carried half of Enrique's pocket-size two-way radio set. Ramón and I toiled for an hour and a half to our separate conclusions that the steep *cañada* and *salto* had no paintings. Then we joined on the ridge below the ranch and, at the appointed hour, called Enrique.

In a few seconds we had a weak but audible reply. Coco and Enrique had used almost all their time crossing a series of rugged ridges and finding El Barco (The Ship), the rock formation described by Toribio Rojas. They had just arrived and were looking at paintings. Apparently they were small and in rather poor condition but Enrique was enthusiastic nevertheless. "They are different," he told me, "it's a new style and different looking paint. There is a lot of yellow paint here." I was tired already but I didn't want to miss anything. We got directions and started out.

The rock art site at El Barco had turned out to be a rather hard, durable *respaldo* on the lower part of the north face of a conspicuous outcropping. Seen from the valley below the whole structure looked like the prow of a ship, hence the name. The paintings were indeed new to us;

110

still the realistic outlines of animals, they had a new twist. The interior color of the larger figures, all deer, consisted of stripes or checkerboarding. The birds were more conventional but the smaller paintings also included a rare but unmistakable lizard and a deer with antlers immensely large in proportion to its tiny body. The colors were unusual as Enrique had reported. Half were in yellow ochre, heretofore an extremely rare pigment and the rest were done in a magenta cast of red. All were quite worn by exposure, a circumstance owing, as at La Puerta, more to poor protection than to a poor quality of stone.

The rock surface was unusual as well, a hard, smooth-feeling stone which was as pitted as the moon, apparently from gas bubbles in the original melt. Enrique, having had much time to inspect the art, devoted himself to investigating the larger pits which were within reach. Shortly he made a find. One, and then another, of these natural pockets produced accumulations of half-inch button-shaped pieces of the black substance which we had seen exuding from crevices in so many caves. Here the find was especially odd. None of the stuff was present in its natural state; it must have been brought by men.

By climbing up from El Barco we reached the trail which communicated Potrerito with the old mission community of Guadalupe lying over the range to the east. That proved to be an easier way and we returned to camp without repeating the trials of the morning.

The next day we climbed, or I should say more accurately and gratefully, our mules climbed a thousand feet to a 5,500-foot pass. Then we came down the highest and one of the steepest grades in the sierra, the Cuesta de la Palmita. When we arrived at its base the elevation was 3,000 feet. We, and certainly the animals, were so tired that we broke down all saddles and loads for a long midday rest. The exertions of both days so caught up with us that we went to sleep in the shadows of some giant *datilillos*.

Sometime later we were aroused by shouts and the pounding of hooves. In a few moments we found ourselves in the center of a small cattle roundup. A half dozen men were roping steers, tying them by the horns to trees, and then whooping off after others. In a few minutes they had passed from sight leaving us with a number of disgruntled bovines on very short ropes.

Our descent had brought us to the head of a broad arroyo with the appropriate if uninspired name of El Valle, The Valley. Here, as at San Pedro, the Jesuits had cattle ranches and a *visita*. As I looked around I could see why the industry had prospered and, no doubt, why it still endured. The arroyo, as mentioned, was unusually broad; it was also unusually level and it was carpeted with more low-growing herbs than I saw anywhere else in the sierra.

As we began to pack up, the cowboys returned to collect their catch. They also were curious about our strange presence in that unvisited place. The men were not actual residents of El Valle. They were engaged in a seasonal roundup, an affair which drew them annually from the more populous eastern slopes. As a result, though we got little direction for our search of the moment, we received several clues to investigate during a later part of our trip. The cowboys were stopping at Rancho El Güéribo and invited us to join them.

The trail down the arroyo lay along the east side of the broad wash. High mountains ranged around in a great horseshoe open at the south; on the skyline to the southeast was a large natural arch. As I rode along musing about El Valle it occurred to me that the chapel ruins might be worth a visit and that we had not asked anyone about them. Despite my interest in mission literature, I knew of no modern account of anyone's visit to the place. Coco knew little except that it was behind us and across the arroyo. We backtracked and found it with no difficulty.

It was now late in the afternoon, too late for pictures and we spent a scant hour at the site. Nevertheless we saw enough to report that the remains of the *capilla de visita* at El Valle were extensive and, though fallen, were sufficiently undisturbed that they may well give us our best picture of Jesuit works of this type.

The original name of this visiting station was probably La Concepción, and it too must have been built in the 1730's under Everard Helen. We could believe, looking at the ruins, that it had been quite an establishment. The works were more extensive than those surviving at many of the missions themselves, certainly far larger and more complete than those at the mother mission of Gudalupe, less then ten miles to the north. There had been a central plaza one hundred and eight feet square. The church had faced it from the north side and had been of rock and adobe construction with an interior space measuring eighteen by sixty feet. The remains of the walls, now about five feet high, were over three feet thick. They had been built chiefly of large river cobbles weighing from fifty to two hundred pounds. There had once been three windows equally spaced on each side. Facing the square from the west was a smaller building in better repair; it had three rooms and measured overall thirteen by sixty feet and the walls still stood near to full height. We looked it over and judged it to be the priest's house. Facing the square from the east was a curious building ten feet wide and running along the plaza for eighty feet. It was entirely divided into small cubicles; we could only speculate on its many possible uses. Elsewhere there were other piles of stone suggestive of fallen buildings. There was also the ruin of a wall which once must have kept cattle out of the entire chapel compound.

During that evening in camp we had a half dozen visitors and finally succeeded in getting a local painting clue. Accordingly we set out in the morning for a ranch called El Cajón which was located a mile or two downstream. We followed the broad, obvious old mission road to the indicated turn and then went west to the edge of the active watercourse. The ranch was picturesquely situated on a shelf just above the waterway in a winding *angostura* carved from brown bedrock. The rancher greeted us in a friendly fashion and, discovering our purpose, offered to show us the paintings. He led us down to the water, across and up the steep rock of the other side. At a point a little higher than his home opposite were a series of small cave-like depressions.

The paintings on the backwalls and ceilings, both here and in another group a couple of hundred yards south, were chiefly of deer. Also visible were a few small *monos* of the fat striped sort,

a bird and an odd circular design. All were in about as bad condition as such works can be and still remain identifiable. The culprit in their deterioration was a soft, friable rock; the caves were heavily smoked as well.

Resuming our journey we passed to the mouth of the Arroyo del Valle proper and came to its junction with the Arroyo del Rosarito. Here we turned east to visit Rancho Rosarito located a short distance upstream. With that simple maneuver I acquired a new role for several days. Two years before I had come up into the sierra from Mulegé in the company of my old friend Guillermo Villavicencio. At that time I was trying to visit historic and picturesque ranches and Rosarito had been the most remote prize. Of course I had come by an entirely different route and now, rejoining the familiar trail, I found myself in an amusing situation. Winding up a familiar path, I was craning my neck to catch the first glimpse of an orange grove which I knew would appear momentarily. For the next several days we were to be in country which I knew better than even Coco. This resulted in a slight change of my status. I must have puffed up just a little and it was not lost on our legitimate guides. I was welcomed to their ranks with elaborate deferences and frequent mock-solemn questions not unlike the sort of thing I had been known to ask of them.

Rosarito was an old ranch; its origin is not recorded anywhere that I know, but Elias Villavicencio, eighty-eight years old, had lived there all his life and he was sure that his grandfather had lived there as well. At any rate, the place had been a magnificent orange ranch. There were still over two hundred beautiful old trees, some thirty feet tall, which bore heavy crops of excellent Valencias. In the old days the fruit was hauled by burro to Mulegé, La Purísima, or wherever the demand dictated. Today, much of the fruit cannot be sold. Ferries now bring Sonora oranges to the peninsula and land them in the markets for prices that make a three-day burro trip uneconomic.

The ranch people were most attentive. We quickly learned that there were at least three painted sites in the vicinity and one of Don Elias' sons volunteered to guide us.

Our first objective lay in the upper *huerta* of Rancho Rosarito, a second and larger fruit orchard a mile or so up the arroyo from the ranch house. There we were led to a low deep cave on the north side. The place had obviously had long use by the ranch people. Crops had been stored in it for years; the floor was ankle deep in onion skins and stalks. Heavily blackened ceilings showed that it had also been the scene of huge fires. Despite this the ceiling near the mouth at the west end had several good survivals of paintings, one of which has proved to be quite unique. There, in the midst of a group of red and ochre deer, was a large and unmistakable red rattlesnake realistically depicted as if slithering across an open space. Elsewhere in the cave were several large but heavily smoked figures of deer and *monos*. On the west wall near the opening were some more crudely executed figures. One, a *mono* with his body divided into six red-and-ochre segments, was unusual in having a clear indication of genitalia.

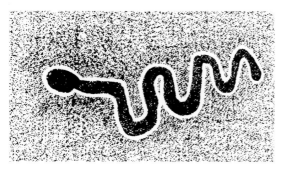

We finished the day with a fruitless trip up the arroyo to Rancho El Potrero. The tenants did not appear to know the country well and they were not able to tell us of any paintings. We returned at dusk to pass the night at Rosarito.

In the morning we left early to visit another promised site. Our path lay due north from the ranch house and involved climbing an extremely steep *falda*. After that we were led on an intricate route through layers of *cantil* and eventually brought to a handsome slit cave which faced west and looked out over the lower end of El Valle. Its elevation was over 3,000 feet and we had climbed a thousand feet from Rosarito.

The contents of the cave were quite different from any of the assemblages which we had encountered to that point. Properly speaking they could not be called Great Murals at all; the largest figures in the cave were less than two feet tall and most were nearer one foot. The subjects were predominantly birds and indeterminant four-legged animals. There were also such ex-

otica as a sunburst and a band of symbols in white which had the look of some unknown written characters. Despite the fact that there were many figures, dozens in fact, and that they were in generally good condition, the place was disappointing. I had a sense that we encountered here a different people, or at least a different inspiration from that which produced the Great Murals. I should emphasize that the scale of the works was not alone responsible for the poor impression. The figures did not seem to have been drawn with any great care; the degree of artistry seemed low.

An afternoon trip up the south wall of the arroyo produced only minor finds. Beside the *cuesta* leading to the mesa were *respaldos* on which had been painted a deer and a couple of *monos* crudely rendered in red. One of the *monos* appeared to be dancing, his knees were bent outward and he too had genitals.

We left Rosarito and rode down its arroyo to pass the night at El Rincón. We continued to the beautiful Rancho Santo Domingo through one of the most scenic of all the sierra's arroyos, a complex watercourse twisting between high walls. The only concern was time; the days simply evaporated. We had now been gone over two weeks and we had traversed only half of the Pacific side of the sierra. Our projection was for a month's trip. At the rate we were going it might take two or three extra weeks and we worried about informing our families and getting extra supplies.

At Santo Domingo the *dueño*, Francisco Aguilar, told us of paintings at Ranchos La Matanza and La Huertita northwest of his ranch. However, he cooled our ardor by telling us further that a visit would take at least three days, and that there was no one about just then who could guide us. Below his ranch we climbed out of the arroyo, now known as Santo Domingo, and crossed the Mesa de la Tinaja. That brought us to an extremely picturesque switchback grade, the

Cuesta del Mezcal. Down it went, serpentining a thousand feet to the bed of the *cañada* below.

By late afternoon we had entered the largest watercourse in the sierra, the Arroyo of Guadalupe itself, midway on its sixty-mile trip to the sea. After all our time in shut-in canyons it seemed very strange to ride up so grand an avenue and it took a while to accustom ourselves to having sand underfoot and arroyo walls which were over half a mile apart. Shortly we came to a huge pool of water against a rock bank at a bend on the south side of the arroyo. I had been there before, it was the Tinaja de la Venada (The Tinaja of the Doe) and there were some tiny and curious paintings on that rock wall. We all walked over for a look after skirting around a body of water seventy by one hundred feet in size, which, in that corner of the world, seemed like a lake.

There were my paintings all right, five dancing men, clearly-painted stick figures about six inches tall. But that was not all, and I learned a lesson which I have had drilled into me by subsequent experiences. On that same rock face were the quite apparent remains of several large *monos* standing abreast. Above was the shadowy form of a painted deer. I had seen the same rock two years before and had examined the dancing men. I had not been remotely aware of the larger painting. The experience has helped me to be more tolerant of people who have lived near paintings for years without being aware of them.

At nightfall we were at Rancho Los Caballos and with less than a two-hour ride in the morning we arrived at Pie de la Cuesta, a ranch belonging to Guillermo Villavicencio Rosas, a man who had guided me on previous occasions. Guillermo was off when we rode in but his wife Nieves waved us into the kitchen for coffee.

We explained our current mission and asked Guillermo's sons and a hired man for information. Señora Villavicencio listened to us and to their inconclusive replies before she broke in. She was raised, she said, up in the Cañada de las Piedras and her brother Loreto told her about paintings when she was young. I knew more or less where the mouth of that *cañada* was and she added that we would find her husband up in that direction. So, about noon, we posted off with several objectives.

First we went to a grove of dates where we heard singing and chopping sounds. There were several men cutting the fruit and we asked them what they might know. One, an older man, proved to be Jeronimo Valenzuela, the father of Jesús who had guided us to Los Monos de San Juan. He knew of some paintings but he deferred to another son, José de Jesús, whose knowledge was more current. The younger man decided that the simplest solution was to take us to the site that they knew. Accordingly we started out. As we did, Guillermo rode up and we had a furious round of embraces, handshakes and introductions. From all the confusion it developed that Guillermo needed help with a small round-up and had counted on our new guide. We quickly solved that problem by trading him Coco and Ramón.

The Cañada de las Piedras is large enough and long enough to be called an arroyo in most parts of Baja California. Only here where it is a tributary to such an immense arroyo could you imagine it getting such secondary billing. It opens into the north side of the arroyo, half way from Pie de la Cuesta to the old *visita* of San Miguel. The body of the *cañada* runs directly north toward the Guadalupe Mission site, a day's ride away. We entered and rode up the wide watercourse for perhaps twenty minutes, then Valenzuela stopped us and pointed up to a *respaldo* atop the usual steep *falda*. We dismounted and climbed up.

The painted site at Boca de la Cañada de las Piedras was once a major ceremonial center. After San Borjitas and San Juan, it is the largest that I have seen in the entire Sierra de Guadalupe. Sadly, it is also in by far the poorest condition. The *respaldo* is very exposed because it is poorly overhung. The rock is also very bad, being soft and badly fractured. The result is a place where the remains of dozens of large *monos* can be discerned only with careful examination. A pocket or recess about twelve feet up and perhaps nine or ten feet in diameter contains the best survivals, a pair of vertically-striped red *monos*. The overall appearance of these figures is very reminiscent of some at San Borjitas (less than fifteen miles away) with the exception that these had their short legs akimbo enclosing sexual organs as if with parentheses.

As close an examination as possible suggested to me that all the figures were artistically related to those of San Borjitas. Remembering this later, I compared photographs of figures at the two sites. One result was interesting; several of the San Borjitas men also may show genitalia, although not so conspicuously. The Great Murals of the Sierra de San Francisco never seem to show male organs, in fact the style of the drawings has the legs placed together in such a way that they could not be indicated. As we shall see later, variant forms are found both north and south of the San Francisco area.

Satisfied at last that we had seen and recorded all that was possible, we returned to Pie de la Cuesta. Guillermo had discovered what Ramón could do in the cowboy line, and he was full of praise.

The next day was long on go and short on paint. We got up early and climbed the steep Cuesta de los Angeles. The experience was nostalgic and a bit amusing as well. Years before, on my first muleback expedition, that had been my first real *cuesta*. I had come over it with a sense of accomplishment and a great respect for mules. Since then I have gone over so many that were greater tests, including La Palmita of recent memory, that I found revisiting Los Angeles a little disappointing. The great challenge had shrunk to the dimensions of just another pass in the rough terrain of Baja California.

We passed through the agricultural valley of Rancho San Martín and continued up to La Vinorama in the same arroyo. Inquiries produced no rock art leads. We rode on to El Tule where we found Alfonso Villavicencio. He remembered me from six years before, invited us in, and proved helpful in answer to our questions. He began by pointing out to us that the rock around the immediate area was very crumbling and would scarcely support painting. He told us that there were paintings at Las Jícamas and La Cuevona, several hours up the arroyo. A young man working for him, Francisco Romero, was invited to tell us about another site called Los Venados in the arroyo of Las Chivas to the south. After much consideration the two decided that Los Venados was the choicest place. We were also fortunate enough to get Romero to guide us as far as the arroyo of El Rincón Grande. This was essential because we were long out of Coco's territory and I certainly was not confident enough of my memories to get us through such broken and utterly waterless country. We pressed Pancho Romero for action and got on the trail in time to pass the night in Las Chivas.

The next day we headed east in the bottom of the good-sized arroyo. In a few minutes a strange scene met our eyes and ears. Far up the steep rocky *falda* to our right there was a clamor of shouting and yelling and we saw a herd of goats racing over that awesome terrain as if their lives depended on it. Tearing along behind and leaping from rock to rock was a boyish figure, the apparent source of all the invective. We all wondered at this but rode on. Within minutes we were at El Ranchito, the tidy ranch of Antonio Osuna. Pancho Romero introduced us and Osuna insisted that we stop for coffee. No sooner had we got seated and launched into our visit than the commotion was heard once more. The goats ran into the ranch and into a corral. After them, flailing away with a stick, ran a lithe young woman of sixteen or seventeen dressed like a boy. Having closed the corral gate, she stalked into the shade of a porch, threw her hat down on a table and massaged her backsides with both hands.

"Two _____ falls!" she said in a loud voice to no one in particular. "I had to chase those _____ _____ goats all over the *falda*. Two falls and two bruises! For two cents I'd beat their backsides bald!"

Antonio took no note of his daughter's outburst. Clearly he was used to her ways, but the rest of us were astonished. I had never run into any temper expressed by a sierra woman, much less profanity and worse; indeed I have heard precious little from men. I learned later that Ramón and Coco were equally surprised. Romero winked at the time of the event and later told us that she was merely a chip off the old block. Apparently Osuna also had a reputation for being socially undisciplined though he was tolerantly regarded as a good but eccentric man. This girl's performance was thrown into particularly bold relief by the behavior of her mother and sister who never raised their voices and rarely their eyes from a succession of chores.

Osuna was stimulated by our interest in Los Venados. As the nearest resident, he had an almost proprietary interest in the cave, and he decided that he should accompany us. We rode an hour up the arroyo bed which became quite reduced as we went. At last Osuna, who was leading, pointed up to a heavy shadow eighty feet or so above the *caja* on the south side. Then he spurred his animal and rode right up the steep *falda*. Not to be put down, we did the same, making it one of the rare occasions when we rode directly into a painted place.

Los Venados could be called a *respaldo*-cave. Basically it consisted of perhaps an eighty-foot run of a routine *respaldo*, or overhung wall. But this recessed surface had further eroded until four deeper pockets were formed. The paintings were concentrated in these pockets. The first moments at this site confirmed a feeling that had been growing on me since we left Los Monos de San Juan. Each subsequent place seemed to have added some element of subject or style or paint that was foreign to the more homogeneous works of the Painters in the Sierra de San Francisco. Here the break was total. Not one work here would have seemed at home in the northern sierra.

The subjects were commonplace enough, large and small deer, *monos*, and a bird or two. There were the omnipresent *pinturitas*, strange little animals, possibly insects, and others too curious or eroded to identify. The most obvious alien element was the means of coloring almost all of the larger figures. They had never been painted in solid colors, they were decorated instead with internal patterns of red or red-and-white stripes. In some, these took the form of crossed stripes or checkerboards, a technique first seen at El Barco. A further strangeness was the frequent use of yellow chalk for the original drawing. This, incidentally, proved to be the only site in which we saw yellow used this way.

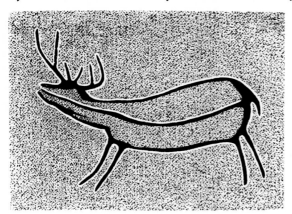

The question of artistry is a difficult one to assess. My first impression of Los Venados was that it was a place where very young artists had practiced. Most of the *monos* were far more primitive than we had been used to seeing. Their proportions and attitudes were most unlifelike,

and they seemed to me to lack even the wooden charm of many San Borjitas figures. The deer, however, had a real style to them. At first I was merely curious, I analyzed them. I grew accustomed to them. In time, by the use of photographs, I have come to fancy them. They have a vitality not found in many of the Great Murals; they also seem to show a strong sense of design due no doubt to my own reaction to crisp stripes and checks. We left the place after an hour and a half of intensive study which left me with an even stronger desire to see what might happen next. It was clear that the Great Murals were evolving as we moved south.

We returned to the Casa Osuna where we sat around and talked at length. There was no rush because we could not go beyond Las Chivas that day. Not a drop of water was to be had between Las Chivas and El Rincón Grande, a full day's ride, and young Señor Romero preferred not to make a dry camp. Speaking of the next day, Osuna reminded us that there were paintings in an arroyo that would lie southeast of our trail. He had only heard of them but had a general idea of their location and offered some directions for finding them. There was no water in the arroyo and the search would require a day at least. Romero would have none of it.

The following day we set out once again and were soon on El Camino Real near the historic mission period ranch of El Cardón, now fallen. We rode by the mouth of the painted arroyo mindful of our loss but also of the immensity of the task that would have faced us. The place displayed range after range of dry hills and our map showed that it was a very long and isolated waterway.

We crossed the arroyo of El Cardón and rode up the Cañada de la Purísima. We took our midday break at the *portezuelo* and then started down the long, long direct arroyo that led to El Rincón Grande and beyond. Pancho Romero took his leave at the *paraje*, assuring us that there was no further need for a guide. Off he went, intent on getting all the way back to El Tule that night.

In late afternoon we came to the broken edge of a picturesque lava flow, a place where the arroyo waters had undermined the basalt and created an abrupt palisade. Scattered along this enticing slate of clean hard rock were a number of petroglyphs. We spotted both animals and fish as we rode along.

We arrived at El Rincón Grande in late afternoon but found that there would be better water and fodder near San José de los Arces. We rode on until dusk and camped near a stream of running water a half mile north of the town.

After we had extended for the night and eaten our dinner, Enrique and I talked over our next steps. My plan from the start had been to get to this place and then turn up the Arroyo de Guajademí and head north toward Mulegé. That would require a new guide; we would not be back in the territory known to Coco until we were several miles north of Mulegé. We had also heard rumors in the sierra about paintings in the environs of San José and nearby Paso Hondo. It would never do to leave without looking into that. The more we talked, the more desirable it seemed to visit the village that night. It would be impossible to anticipate when someone we needed might happen to be in and when he might leave. We took our flashlights and headed along an uncertain path.

At first we had no luck at all. The people who might guide us up Guajademí were all away for a day or more. Just as we were about to leave, a man began to comprehend meaning in my statement that I had ridden through six years before. He asked if I had not ridden with Isaias Mayoral? Yes, I had. Well, Mayoral was visiting in a house down the street. In short order we were talking with a surprised Isaias and he proved to be useful indeed. He knew a painted cave called Loma Alta in the mountains west of Paso Hondo. He could take us there the following day; not only that, but he had access to a truck and could take us to Paso Hondo and back.

That was good news. Our animals certainly could use a day of rest, their first since our day-long hike to El Barco. We went back to camp and passed out.

In mid-morning, Isaias came and honked. We took our hiking necessities and left Coco and Ramón to rest, feed the animals, and arrange for a guide, if possible.

The ride to Paso Hondo was brief. We drove through the town and to a point a mile or so beyond. There was no side road, we simply parked and walked over a ridge, down a gorge of soft crumbling rock and into a little valley containing a ranch. Crossing that, we started up a steep path and labored away in a short-winded silence until we came out on a mesa which sloped up to

mountains on the west. Then for an hour more we hiked up a steeper and steeper grade until we were looking up a final *cañada* at a large and obvious cave. That last stretch was the most trying of all and it was a relief when we got into the shady chamber of Loma Alta and looked around.

"Curiouser and curiouser." Alice's phrase was the first thing that popped into my mind. The Great Murals were changing so rapidly now that they were difficult to recognize. The transformation was perfectly exemplified by a strange checkerboard figure. At first I had little notion as to what it might represent. Then, allowing for the strangeness and the vagueness of the other figures, I realized that it might be a *mono*. Once seen that way, it became more obvious. The head was a block, the body was another. Neck, arms and legs were reduced to simple lines. Nevertheless, this abstract pattern of rectangles stood before me as a man, a man with his arms raised in the classic salute of the Painters.

Another handsome painting defied literal translation altogether. It consisted of a graceful beehive form mounted, as it were, on a short pedestal. The hive was outlined in a pale yellow and filled in with vertical stripes alternately of black and yellow. We dubbed it "the candelabra" with the full realization that it was almost certainly a misnomer. Months later, while studying a photograph of this puzzling work, I stumbled on its true identity. A large red deer had been rather sloppily painted just beneath it. obviously at a later period. In the photograph I found that I could clearly see a painting under the red deer. It was a tall rectangular form divided into black and yellow blocks. The "candelabra" was its head, and it proved to be a *mono* of the nearly abstract school of its more visible pink and black neighbor.

Some other figures were more abstract, some less. A few were no more than deliberate arrangements of lines. Several small animals were so generalized that they might equally well have represented deer, or rabbits, or coyotes.

As at Los Venados, the first impressions were of careless work. I was disappointed that I had come so far and got so tired in order to look at such scrawls. But a little study moderated that judgment. The rock at Loma Alta was very hard, the surfaces showed no sloughing whatever. Paintings like abstract *monos* composed of rec-

LOMA ALTA

This pattern of rectangles and a similar one in yellow and black nearby are the most abstract representations of the human figure yet identified in the Painters' region. Attempts to locate the origin of this style outside the Great Mural area have failed so far. But study inside showed that, as the search moved south, there was a growing emphasis on less realistic outlines and on checkerboard infills. At present, the trail ends at Loma Alta.

118

LOMA ALTA

The fractured and many-faceted rock forming the cave's backwall has an unusually durable surface. Since this expanse is also well-protected it provides an ideal location for the survival of paintings. Works which appear old here may prove to be among the oldest in the Great Mural region, an especially interesting possibility since Loma Alta is very near that region's southern limits.

tangles probably were very old. Since they were somewhat faded in appearance, it was probable that the loss of color was due entirely to the weathering of the paint, a most unusual circumstance in a land where rock is usually the culprit.

A thought came to me at Loma Alta. We knew that fifty miles south in the Loreto region paintings were almost entirely non-representational. Were we seeing a gradual phasing of Great Mural art into the smaller polychrome abstractions that lay south? Obviously more fieldwork was needed.

No sooner had we returned to San José de Los Arces than we literally bumped into Federico Arce Meza from El Rincón Grande, a man with whom my party had passed the night six years before. As soon as we mentioned rock art, he became quite excited. We must return to El Rincón Grande and he would show us many figures painted and engraved on the *cantil* no more than ten minutes' walk from his house. Off we went.

The painted site at El Rincón Grande proved to be rather less exciting than Señora Arce's excellent coffee, which followed. The place was a wall of basalt, a continuation of the one on which we had noticed the petroglyphs on our ride down the arroyo. In various overhung locations there were small *monos*, a couple of nice turtles, a few simplistic fish and some petroglyphs. Of the latter only one caught my eye sufficiently to record. It showed two deer facing each other almost nose to nose. The curves of their necks and forelegs were like two arcs of the same ellipse.

Later, after reviewing all I could learn about painting in this area, I decided that this modest little site is probably Diguet's number 17, "a cliff with paintings near Rancho San Jose, in the Arroyo of Guajadami."

Back at our camp we found all in order and a reasonable arrangement made for the following day. Ramón had news of paintings at a place called Agua Puerca only an hour or so out on our route, and others near a ranch called Jáuja, high in the sierra. There was a man named Esteban Romero visiting in town who was returning to the same region. He would guide us at least to the mountain ranches where presumably we could make other arrangements.

Romero proved in practice to be the poorest guide of that or any trip. He also had the shortest tenure. We had been on the trail no more than

an hour when we were joined by others headed into the sierra. A short while later I asked Romero if we were not near Agua Puerca. He told me that we had passed it. Why had we passed it?

Because, he said, it was not worth the stopping, there was nothing to see. I was not happy at that; we had discussed the purpose of our trip with the man at length. I stopped the caravan and said that we were going back for a look. Romero continued with the other mountaineers. He had decided to go home, he said, and not to be a guide. They rode north as we turned around.

Agua Puerca was definitely worth the stop. The cave was well up the east wall of the canyon and clearly visible from the trail. We crossed the very broad arroyo on our animals, tethered them under trees and climbed up one more familiarly steep *falda*. The cave was large, complex in form, and had been heavily painted but, as so often had happened elsewhere, a large amount of the painted rock had fallen. Despite that, there were some interesting figures, the most arresting of which was a vertically-striped *mono* so similar that it might have been stolen from the gallery at Boca de las Piedras. There were also

birds and a yellow deer. While Enrique and I made photographs, Ramón was looking around the environs. He soon reported a find, a slit cave at a slightly lower level and just to the west. The cave was so low that we literally had to crawl under its shelf-like roof and then lie on our backs to see the work. Once again Ramón had found negative hand prints, this time many of them.

Two, especially notable, formed a pair thumb-to-thumb; one was red, the other white. There were also many *pinturitas* in the finest strokes we were ever to see. These virtual line paintings were of deer and other smaller and often symbolic subjects.

Perhaps the most interesting discovery of all was the fact that cracks in the rock had been stuffed with many four-to-six-inch splints of pitahaya wood. We were puzzled as to the reason. Could the ends have been pounded and used as brushes?

We started up the great arroyo once more. Now we had a problem. It was not likely that we could get lost in that avenue-like wash but it was also not obvious that we would recognize the *cuesta* which would take us to Jáuja, nor that we could follow the right trail even if we got up the proper *cuesta*. Enrique and I kicked it around. Coco was gloomy. He seemed depressed now that we were in country about which he knew nothing. Ramón was cheerful and unconcerned. What was the worst that could happen? We would wind up on a trail to the wrong ranch. Perhaps they would have paintings of their own. Why not have an adventure, we decided. We rode on knowing nothing but using binoculars on every *respaldo* and *cantil* that we passed.

This Guajademí trail is a very ancient one. Padre Francisco María Picolo learned of it shortly after he came to Misión Santa Rosalía de Mulegé, and in 1712 he, some soldiers and Indian guides came up out of Arroyo Mulegé and entered the head of Arroyo Guajademí. They then followed the arroyo to the Pacific. The ultimate result of that exploration was the founding of Misión La Purísima. Guajademí remained the route which connected the two missions. After my long association with El Camino Real I was thrilled to add the experience of another major link. It was obviously an old Indian trail as well and we could expect much art along its way. Finally it was a beautiful avenue into a remote and little-visited corner of the sierra. Come what might, I had a good feeling as we rode north.

As sunset shone in the sky far above our path in the shady depths, we came to a second great turn in the canyon, a place called Agua Honda. Here, we believed, would be the *cuesta* to Jáuja. As we drew near we could see it clearly and we rejoiced to put one uncertainty aside. We camped on the *ancón* exactly at the foot of the *cuesta*. A few hundred feet up the hill to the east was a cave. A mile or less to the south was another, large and inviting. A storekeeper in San José had told us that the former was painted. No one had mentioned the other. We were always in a quandary in these situations. Was the large one ignored because it was known to be unpainted? Or, was the cave near us known to contain paintings simply because it was close to the trail and easy to investigate? It was so late that, for the moment, we chose the near one.

There were paintings, crude and defaced by smoke and erosion. Only one stood out as a type, a huge deer over ten feet long which had been engraved deeply into the soft rock of the cave wall. The incised lines had then received a heavy coat of white paint. As we made our way down again we passed a layer of soft tuff at the foot of the same *respaldo* which contained the cave. In it were a myriad of drillings, holes about half an inch in diameter and two to three inches deep, arranged into lines, loops, rows, crosses, boxes and totally random patterns. There were also deeply carved petroglyphs of fish, vulva symbols, and parallel lines.

Since we had no water for the animals we gave up the idea of taking the time to visit the large cave, and we climbed the *cuesta* for Jáuja. At the top we learned from my altimeter that our climb had been 1,500 feet and I had grateful thoughts about my uncomplaining *mula*. Briefly, to the southeast, we had a magnificent view of the Sierra de la Giganta, dominated by a succession of massive peaks. Then our trail headed off to the northeast across a rolling mesa dotted with blue-gray *palo fierro* and leafless *palo brea*. In less than an hour we arrived at a ranch and stopped for directions. The place was called Tajo Viejo, no one knew of any paintings, and Jáuja was to be found two or three hours farther on the same trail. We rode on. In a half hour or so we came over a rise and dropped down on another ranch with a large water catchment. El Sapo was the name, a woman told us, she knew of no paintings, and Jáuja was farther on. She pointed northeast again. We skirted a deep *cañada* and after two more hours spotted a ranch in the midst of a very large and level tableland. We rode up to it. Jáuja.

The tenant rancher was Juan Mayoral Higuera. With him were two brothers and their families.

AGUA HONDA

Layers of soft tuffs were responsible for the primary erosion that formed many painted caves. As this layer deteriorated, rock above lost support and fell in scallop-shaped vertical masses which left the characteristic voids used by the Painters. As a result the tuff layer is found low in the caves and it was the favorite medium in which to execute carvings, engravings, and drillings. All are common but this is the most elaborate drilling site thus far reported.

122

We were made welcome, we broke down our things and were seated in the kitchen. Juan Mayoral understood our quest with little explanation. Another *Norteamericano*, Eric Ritter, had come up from Mulegé the previous year and he too had wanted to see rock art sites. As for the sites themselves, well, what could he say about them? They had pictures such as the Indians always made, neither more nor less. How large were they? Well, some were larger than others and all were *regular*, not larger or smaller than one might encounter elsewhere. All the Mayorales had an indirect and curiously lilting manner of speech, and as our host went on with his entirely circular discourse on Indian art I felt as if it would mesmerize us all and that we might be turned to stones like those that littered the Mesa de Jáuja. Finally, some coffee was produced. I looked at my watch and found that we had been sitting for almost an hour.

A boy came by with a yoke over his shoulders from which two five gallon tins were suspended. Juan and his brothers rose languidly and found other containers. Come, we were told, it is time to go to the *tinaja*. We trooped off to the west along a well beaten trail. In ten minutes we came to the very head of a *cañada*, a falls where water from the mesa dropped into a gorge that would carry it a thousand feet to the bed of the arroyo below. A steep trail had been worked into the rock south of the falls and we picked our way down a hundred feet to a murky *tinaja* which provided the drinking water for the ranch. The boy began to fill his cans while Juan and a brother motioned us onward. We climbed up to a cave at the base of the seasonal falls and our host pointed to a spot above us on the rough overhang.

The rock was hard and smooth and it had fractured into a maze of separate facets. Two of these were painted in a faded red. The subjects consisted solely of several fish, a bird and a tiny deer. Tears came to my eyes as I stood and looked. Somehow I was not prepared; I was caught off guard by the beauty of the work. The group of fish on the lower rock face seemed to move in water, such was their artistry. From stains that ran down the entire rock face it was clear that after a rain, water would run directly over the fish and they would be seen literally swimming in the stream.

The *tinaja* and its little gorge are oddly named;

"San Pedro Avincolo" seems to show an Italian influence. In any event, I wish that the name commemorated that saint's association with fish rather than with chains.

I finally tore myself away. The cans had all been filled and we filed out. I looked back for a last time at the *salto* and its precious burden. It had a small collection, that gallery, but it was worth every step that brought us there.

Above the falls were a maze of petroglyphs scattered about on large rocks. The subjects were animals and birds. One especially caught my eyes. On a large rounded boulder a series of dainty deer prints had been engraved as if the animal had made them in walking across. All the petroglyphs were heavily patinated and had an old appearance.

Later, a brother took us on a long walk to the east across the stone-paved mesa. He began to point to *metates* and petroglyphs and soon we realized that we were seeing hundreds, which meant that the area contained thousands. There was no apparent end to them; there were even petroglyphs on *metates*. Such legions of grindstones strongly suggested a sizeable crop of some seed to grind. The only candidate appeared to be *palo fierro*, a legume, which does produce a heavy crop of seed-bearing pods.

We saw several broken examples of Baja California's rarest *metate*, those which are formed front, back, and edges into handsome stone dishes of rectangular outline. These were all made of *tezontle*, a relatively easily worked type of scoria or vesicular basalt. Why had all of that type that I had encountered been broken? Could that have been a tradition? Señor Mayoral was amused at the question. He knew nothing of Indian traditions but he had his own answer to the puzzle. Such artifacts were handsome and useful. Whenever the ranch people found one they took it home to use. In time they wore out. End of theory. I will bet that he was right.

It was cold out on that windswept mesa and when I went to bed I pulled the flap over my face and shut out the chill and the stars as well. Sometime in the night a radio came on and waked me. I peeked out. There were the stars but there was no glimmer of dawn. My watch broke the unpleasant news: it was 4 A.M. In a few minutes pots and pans rattled, fires crackled, and there was the singsong of Mayoral speech. Presently people began to pass me going to the corral with buckets for the morning milking. A girl passed, trailing the aroma of coffee.

"Coffee?" I asked.

"Come, I have a cup for you."

I crawled out and got my coat and boots. The wind had died, the stars were snapping and it was beautiful. The coffee was beautiful also but it chilled quickly. Everyone worked away with practiced hands and twenty-gallon washboilers filled with milk. The coffee girl was homely but not in the dark; she sang sweetly about love but of what I could not tell.

"What do you love?" I asked.

"I love to be warm."

In its time the sky lightened and the stars went out. The work at the corral was done and we went in for breakfast. Cheese-making was begun and we who had no part in it feared that we might get stalled again in the slow rhythm of Mayoral ways. Tactful questions were put and by midmorning we actually managed to extricate Juan and get away. Despite our impatience at times, we had been most fortunate to catch these helpful people when we did. In a few weeks the water of the *tajo*, an artificial catchment at a low spot on the mesa, would dry up and then the herd of cattle and the people would leave.

We rode west down a thousand-foot grade and entered a *cañada* just before it opened into the Arroyo de Guajademí. During much of our descent we could see a large *respaldo*-cave on the other side of the *cañada*. The place was called El Zapote after a ranch just downstream. We crossed the *cañada* and pulled our animals up in the shade of some trees near the cave.

The *respaldo* and the cave had once been heavily painted. There were vestiges of pigment everywhere, but not a single painted figure could be discerned. The causes were obviously exposure and a very soft and crumbling sort of volcanic agglomerate. In spite of these negative factors there were some remarkable survivals.

Six figures of deer on the order of six to eight feet long had been engraved into the rock surface exactly in the fashion we had seen at the foot of the *cuesta* near Agua Honda. White, red, and yellow paints had been applied thickly to these recessed outlines and some had survived. All of the figures seemed rather awkward and graceless to me but the technique was fascinating as a variation within the Great Mural Region.

Another feature of the place caught our eyes. In the cave part, at the east end of the *respaldo*, the numerous rock crevices had many of the pitahaya wood splints jammed forcibly into them. These continued up to the astonishing height of at least eighteen feet. Furthermore, a circumstance we had not noticed at Agua Puerca, each of them had burned down until it was flush with the rock. That gave us something to chew on. Were these then tapers? Were they lighted for night vigils or religious services?

Mayoral took us across the *caja* of the great arroyo. We rode for perhaps half an hour and turned west to approach some rich pink rock formations. Passing the first of these we rode up to the middle of the group and dismounted. Our guide called the place Cueva Colorada. He pushed a few branches aside and led us through the rocks to a little natural courtyard in the center. Facing us on the west side was a very low cave and on its bulging roof was a choice piece of art.

Using the same technique that we had just observed at El Zapote, an artist had created a pair of deer facing each other and with their noses in contact. The pose is so identical to the petroglyph described at El Rincón Grande that I am forced to believe that one is the copy of the other. Oddly they do not appear to be from the same hand; the work at Cueva Colorada has much surer lines, better proportion and a sense of style quite missing at El Rincón Grande.

A great deal of the beauty of this work is derived from the artist's use of the rock form on which he did his engraving. The inspiration is reminiscent of Altamira, the famous Spanish Palaeolithic site, where rounded protuberances of the cave ceiling were painted and used to advantage as the forms of bison. Here at Cueva Colorada the effect is subtler. The artist has designed his group not only to fit onto an oval-shaped rock convexity, but he has also contrived his design so that it repeats the elliptic rock form in the lines of the lower front parts of the deer. The result is a very sophisticated, cameo-like sculpture.

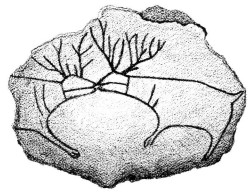

A few other figures, including a fish and some smaller deer, had been rendered in the same fashion but had not survived well in the soft rock. After I had pictures of everything, I lingered by the kissing deer. Once again I was held by a sense of art that transcended mere antiquarian or ethnographic interests; *Ars gratia artis*.

We rode north once more and presently entered a narrows where the once wideset walls of the arroyo closed down on us. In that place was Rancho Guajademí, a place also tended by the Mayorales. We rode in and dropped the saddles and loads to give the animals a rest. There was a good-sized orchard and it needed water. I hated to see large orange trees wilting but Mayoral seemed as unconcerned about this as all else. "In its time," his manner seemed to say. We picked ripe oranges and harvested fresh mint for teas in the nights ahead.

After farewells we parted, north and south. Ours was a steep climb and it brought us to the prize vista of the trip. We quitted the last slope of Guajademí and, at the pass, a few steps put us on the brink of the gigantic amphitheater which is the Arroyo de Mulegé. In front of us was a yawning drop, beyond that a sweeping view of the twenty-five miles to the gulf and the islands beyond.

In truth we had little time to enjoy the scene. It was growing late and the wind was howling. We scarcely wanted to get caught at that nearly 3,000-foot pass but there was not a stopping place on the dizzying *cuesta* we must descend. We moved, and though the entire descent was lovely in the extreme, we did not dawdle over any of

its parts. By dark we were camped just south of Rancho El Potrero, in the broad plain of the Arroyo de Mulegé.

A mile or so southeast of us was a high hill or a small mountain, as you will. In the morning a man from El Potrero told us that it harbored a fine collection of paintings. He was good enough to cart Enrique and me over for a quick look. We first stopped at Rancho Horconcitos, nestled on the east side of the hill, and the rancher joined us for such an early stroll that we got to the painted *respaldo* before it was struck by the rising sun.

Nothing could have better reinforced our sense of having quit Guajademí and, indeed, the sierra itself. Here, all in an identical red, were *pinturitas*, largely of fish and turtles. Although the rock face was crowded with figures, there was no overpainting and all were equally well-preserved. The work did not remind me of anything we had seen nearly so much as it did of numerous *pinturitas* which I had seen around the nearby Bahía de la Concepción. Enrique and I concurred that they were the freshest *appearing* works we had ever seen.

On my list of hints and clues I had several entries for Rancho La Trinidad beginning with Leon Diguet. He had made it number thirteen on his list, "Paintings in a cañada near the Rancho Trinidad, about 12 leagues from Mulegé." When we got back to camp and loaded up, I headed our little caravan due west to investigate the reports. The ride was simplicity itself over the levelest of level ground. The tenant family was at home in the ranch house, and we found them *simpático* in the extreme. The man interested himself in our quest and volunteered to take us for a look at the painted place.

A quarter-mile walk brought us to the mouth of an unusually attractive *cañón*, a perfect miniature of some of the great sierra watercourses. Floor and walls alike were bedrock, a lovely pink stone that shone in the sun and glowed in the shade. Scattered along the narrow corridor were huge blocks of the same material fallen from the vertical walls. It crossed my mind, as we walked along, that this place should be set aside, preserved as a park for all time. It also seemed unlikely that the art could match the surroundings.

We came to a place where the little canyon was choked with house-sized boulders. Our guide took us up to our right out of the *caja* proper and into the remains of a cave whose roof had fallen. There on a single large rock face was the art of La Trinidad. The first impression was that of an aboriginal *graffiti* wall; a disordered array of drawings in several styles, sizes and paints. Certain oddities added to the confusion. Several medium-sized deer were stiffly painted in stark white completely upside down. Here and there were groups of peoples' handprints also in white. Some vandalism, probably recent, had been scrawled across lower parts in charcoal. But the untidy and disorganized effect of the whole belied the charm of the parts. That wall bore some miniature masterpieces and we spent a delightful time sorting them out and enjoying them.

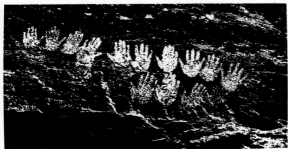

If any one figure or group could be said to dominate, it was a large checkerboard deer high in a central part of the wall. This graceful antlered form, rendered in a beautiful orange-red, was accompanied by three smaller does or fawns created by the same hand. All moved with unhurried purpose from right to left across the canvas. Below and to their left, in the same paint were several extraordinarily graceful fish. One, the largest, appeared to represent a corvina and

was unusual on several counts. Most curious was that, like the San Pedro Avincolo fish, it was not depicted head up and tail down as were nearly all others in the Great Mural area. Second, it was drawn with an internal pattern suspiciously like bones; it was an x-ray vision of a fish. And last, it was transfixed by a nicely fletched arrow, a common enough device with animals or *monos*, but rare indeed with fish.

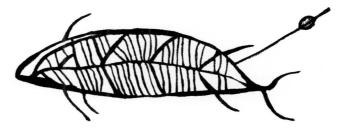

Elsewhere there were scattered a strange skeletal *mono*, and a variety of other small men and animals, mostly quite inartistic, done in red, white and black.

Something beside its beauty influenced me to repeated inspections of the single large figure, the graceful checkerboard deer. It looked familiar but none of us could place it. Later, at home, I found the answer while looking through my photographs. A large deer at Los Venados seems almost to have been struck from the same plate.

During my preoccupation, Enrique, who had a penchant for examining every crevice, came up with evidence that the entire cave had once been painted. By getting down on stomach or knees he had inspected the rock pile which had resulted from the fall of material from other walls and the ceiling. He pointed out parts of other paintings visible in the rubble. I looked back at the surviving wall not sure whether to be elated at its survival or sad at so great a loss.

Across the way was another cave, a real cave, deep and tunnel-like. It was a lovely structure worked into the warm pink rock but it had no paintings; its surface was sloughing off in scales. There and elsewhere in the *cañón* we noticed an interesting phenomenon. Where water had percolated through the rock above and evaporated as it was released, there was a deposit of a pure white solid. It seemed likely that this was the pigment used in the unusually large number of white paintings in the vicinity.

After returning to the ranch we transferred our operation a scant hour away to a spot in the same

126

LA TRINIDAD

This simple panel is one of the most beautiful and affecting of all the Painters' creations. Vermilion paint consorts admirably with the rich rock of the cañón wall; the flaming colors contrast strangely with the calm and grace of the stately checkerboard deer accompanied by two fawns. The theme must have been very familiar to the artist; it was almost certainly he who created the impressive buck at Los Venados illustrated on page 116.

cañón just below Rancho San Patricio. This was not quite as simple as the phrase "same *cañón*" makes it sound. La Trinidad is so choked with fallen rock that there is no passage, and we had to go by a steep roundabout to the east. Nevertheless, by dark we found ourselves back in the same sort of lovely surroundings. The tenant at San Patricio came down to our camp to offer his help. He was a young man and he professed to know several painted sites in the area. For the moment he confirmed what we had heard at La Trinidad. There were paintings almost under our noses. It was dark but we were curious. We all had flashlights and he was willing to guide, so we set off stepping with care to avoid the spines and rocks of an uncertain trail.

The *cañón*, just at that point, made a spectacular hairpin turn which we cut off by climbing a ridge. After crossing the *caja* we climbed up to a low cave. It was a strange sensation, something entirely new, to be poking around a painted cave at night. Our flashlights would scan the rough ceiling and walls and painted figures seemed to leap when struck by the beam. The first thing I found was a small ceiling panel with several dazzlingly white handprints. We soon tired of the novelty and picked our way back to bed.

The morning light conveyed a better picture of the place, but, unlike La Trinidad, the art here really was no match for the beautiful surroundings. Not only were the paintings small and inconsequential but there were also numerous instances of vandalism. In a fairly short time we prepared to leave and reported in at San Patricio.

Our guide of the flashlight tour repeated his story of two other rock art sites. A long discussion showed that they had to be visited on a side trip because no one knew how we could continue directly from the places he would show us. We cooked up a plan. Coco had no interest in going so we left him to be sure that the unused animals ate well, and the rest of us headed west to see what could be seen.

The less said about that day the better. The young man proved to be entirely sincere but possessed of a poor memory or poor judgment. He took us on to an arroyo with the engaging name of Tata Dios (The Arroyo of Grandfather God). He took us to the Arroyo de Los Zalates. Our entire finds for the day included one line of extremely weathered handprints, a nice wall

of petroglyphs, and a small painted panel so eroded that the images literally did not emerge in our photos. We got back to San Patricio late in the day and set out for Rancho San Dieguito on the trail indicated by our guide. We arrived at dark to find that there was another route between the ranches which was only half as long.

Our next known objective was the vicinity of San Sebastián thirty miles away in the upper part of the Arroyo of San José de Magadalena. Our route would bear more west than north and generally would be crossing arroyos rather than running up or down them. Despite the fact that San Borjitas Cave lay almost on our projected path, we had received no information about other potential sites. Our plan had to be very simple. We would cover the ground and get what news we could along the way.

We started up the arroyo of San Dieguito and followed it until high hills turned us west. Skirting these we found an ancient and little-used *cuesta* and crossed a high arm of the sierra. On the other side a gentle and grassy *cañada* led us down to a surprise encounter with a wheel track auto road. We followed that downstream until it joined a larger road. That soon looked familiar to me. Two years before when visiting San Borjitas I had come up this road but I did not remember the spur that we had just descended. A short while later while spending the night at Rancho Las Tinajas, I learned why I had been confused. That spur was a new construction by the Gorosave family intended to bring tourists to the famous painted site. I had thus ridden within a half hour of the cave without realizing it. Since my companions had looked forward to seeing San Borjitas, I was not soon allowed to forget my guiding *gaffe*.

Riding up the Arroyo de San Baltazar we passed Rancho Las Tinajitas and soon quit the arroyo altogether by way of a pass to the north. While descending a *cañada* on the other side I made one of our few independent discoveries. In the deep shadow of a gorge to the east I saw a cave. Though binoculars showed nothing of interest I was determined to investigate. We detoured and made a brisk little climb up a wooded waterway.

The cave was made of good hard rock and displayed several paintings. None, however, could be photographed or reasonably appreciated. So often I have recounted the forces and the odds that oppose the survival of painted rock art. Here was a new hazard. Water had percolated through the massive crown of rock over the cave. It had flowed out of cracks in the hard roof and left a mineral deposit all over ceiling and walls. The paintings were literally buried in insoluble salts, their colors showed to a degree, their outlines less well. In spite of this we could detect a strange limbless figure pierced by arrows and the forms of at least two deer. An hour or so later when we arrived at Rancho Las Cañadas, we learned that the place we had found was called El Salto. The local people apparently did not know that it contained paintings.

From Las Cañadas we proceeded west over a pass to San Isidro. We could get no reports of rock art there, so we rode on toward San Sebastián, stopping for the night a mile or two beyond San Isidro.

The next morning we soon came to Rancho Las Bebelamas. Coco was now back on familiar ground and he remembered talk of paintings. We rode in to ask and encountered two women drawing water from the well. Our questions amused them. Yes, of course, it was well known that they had paintings. Where? One of them pointed to a rock outcropping fifty yards away. We walked around a corral and looked up at a tiny *respaldo*-cave.

On the ceiling was a profusion of little figures in red-brown and black; none was over a foot and a half in height. There were two bicolored *monos*, a deer, a probable crab and several with an uncertain but zoological look. Many rocks had fallen from the ceiling and carried away all or parts of paintings. All those that remained were obscured somewhat by lesser forms of the same water stains which we had seen at El Salto.

Another short ride brought us down into the main arroyo of San Sebastián near Rancho San Javier. Wtihin minutes we saw a series of caves up a *cañada* to our left. Enrique and I were trailing at the time, we yelled ahead that we were stopping, and then turned up the *cañada*. We quickly came to a point below the caves and dismounted. As we did, a man on a white mule came along behind us and saluted us politely. A brief exchange introduced us all and explained our mission. The man was Melchor Villavicencio González and his ranch was San Javier in that same cañada. As for the caves, yes, they were indeed painted. And the good *señor* insisted on

filling the totally unnecessary office of guide to those small nearby places. No matter, we enjoyed his enthusiasm. We scrambled up and had a good time inspecting what were chiefly a varied collection of *pinturitas* which ranged from the most ordinary to some inspired and stylish originals. One of the rock shelters was in itself a handsome curiosity. It appeared to have been formed as an immense bubble in basalt, and rock layers were formed around it as if it were an onion. This whole assemblage was exposed in cross-section and made quite a display on the hillside. The smooth concave facets within exhibited paintings of a striped *mono*, a red *mono*, and a very fine but faded *borrego*. This last was especially interesting because the *borrego*, such a common subject in the San Francisco region, had been conspicuously absent from this sierra.

The cave nearest the main arroyo might well be called "The Cave of the Hands." There were many handprints within and, more unusual, painted depictions of hands. This cave also had a spritely compound figure, a tiny red *mono* with outsize hands and feet superimposed on a fat black-striped deer which looked more like a Klondike watermelon.

To the north, across the broad main arroyo we spotted yet another cave. Señor Villavicencio had gone home so we could not ask him about it. We crossed and hiked up quite a hill. There were paintings inside the cave, the crudest and most childish we were to see on the trip. Daubed on broken rock outcroppings were *monos* and animals painted in unbelievably gaudy shades of mustard yellow and orange-red. At first I suspected a hoax, but close inspection did suggest that the work had some antiquity. In any event, I feel sure that it came from hands other and later than the Painters.

Finally, after all those diversions, we rode on the last mile to San Sebastián. Here we found

SAN JAVIER

This small cave is engraved with hundreds of oval devices virtually identical to others created all over the world during the past twenty thousand years. Anthropologists consider them vulva symbols and speculate over their meaning. It has been suggested that they were created during fertility ceremonies, girls' puberty rites, or as calendrical notations making use of the regularity of the menstrual cycle and its similarity to the lunar month. Whatever the reason, they are the commonest symbols found engraved in the soft rocks of shelters in the Great Mural region.

Guillermo Villavicencio's father, Jesús, who took us in and gave us a hand in unpacking. Later we sat around and discussed rock art. In the course of the conversation he mentioned a Doctor Villalpando from Santa Rosalía who had visited several painted sites in the area of San Sebastián. We paid attention because Jesús Valenzuela had also mentioned this man's name at Los Monos de San Juan. In addition, Tacho Arce had known him casually and remembered that he had visited San Francisco and seen Cueva del Ratón and perhaps others in the San Francisco area. It was now obvious that the doctor had visited many sites and perhaps could contribute to everyone's knowledge of the Great Murals. When I had returned home, Enrique Hambleton was able to get a current address in Mexico City. I wrote and found a willing and helpful informant.

Dr. Cuauhtemoc Villalpando Mexia practiced general medicine in Santa Rosalía for sixteen years during the 1950's and 1960's. Whenever his calls necessitated visits to the sierras, he made it a point to ask about and see paintings and petroglyphs. As a result, he saw not only Cueva del Ratón in the Sierra de San Francisco, but also La Natividad and Cuesta Palmarito. In the closer Sierra de Guadalupe he was able to visit a dozen or so sites. These explorations certainly made him at one time a leading authority on the works and their locations. When Doctor Villalpando read of Gardner's discoveries, he wrote to him and, in an ensuing correspondence, sent color transparencies of some of what he had seen. His knowledge was briefly noted in an article in *Life en Espanol* in 1962. Apparently he never undertook to publish his discoveries, but he deserves a place in the history of the Great Murals.

As Jesús Villavicencio rattled off the names of places Villalpando had visited, he included San Javier. We stopped him to say that we too had visited San Javier. What had we seen at San Javier? We told him. "Oh, below the ranch," he said, "but what of the ones above the ranch? They are more important." What could we say? We explained that we had met Melchor and that he had showed us the works at Boca de San Javier. We said that he had not mentioned a thing about any paintings above. The upshot of the talk was that our host would accompany us in the morning to two places which he knew

well, Las Cruces and the upper San Javier.

So, the next morning bright and early found us going down the arroyo to a place called Pozo Viejo just below Rancho Las Cruces. The rock art site consisted of a very unprotected *respaldo* which had on it a large collection of rather badly weathered art. Over a run of perhaps fifty feet there were handsome small petroglyphs of fish, several badly faded *monos* and deer and an especially good *borrego* with handsome horns. He too, alas, was dimming.

When we had turned around and were backtracking to San Javier it was uncomfortable to think of confronting Don Melchor. Perhaps he had not wanted us tramping through his place. On the other hand, perhaps it was our present guide who was confused; there might be no art above San Javier.

The problem was not to present itself immediately. At the ranch, the *dueño* was out and we were met by his daughter. Guillermo's father told her what we were about and led us on through. In minutes we were in a narrow and steep little *cañada*. We climbed its south bank and scouted around. Señor Villavicencio seemed confused and apologetic. He pushed ahead to check out a high *respaldo* far above us. Enrique and I were amused. We thought the matter had been settled, but to be safe we prospected on.

Hidden by brush, a small but deep cave opened onto the steep slope. Inside not a flake of paint was to be seen, but what a find it was. Every inch of the walls was carved; there were literally hundreds of carved symbols. And they were all exactly the same: vulva symbols. Of course, I had seen these before, there were a few at several San Francisco sites and an area of San Borjitas Cave was devoted to them, but this, this was laughable. I called Enrique. He came in, turned around once, and whistled. "What would you call this?" "The Playboy Cave," I joked. The name stuck.

We could hear our would-be guide thrashing around far above us but, as he gave no word, we continued our own search. The slope became impassable and we went down. In the *caja* I quickly found two caves exactly facing each other. That on the south side was clean of paint. That on the north was the jackpot, or as close as we were to get to it. Inside were a number of large, handsome *monos* in red and black divided vertically. All were in the most lamentable of flaked and washed off condition. We pored over them for a while. Our guide rejoined us and, having found nothing more, decided this must be the art that he remembered. We returned to the *caja*. Just below the cave was an open wall of rock. On it was a shoulder-to-shoulder group of giant *monos* reminiscent of Boca de San Zacarías. They were, if possible, in even worse condition than those within. We started back to the ranch in low spirits from our encounter with such deterioration.

Don Melchor was waiting for us in a jovial mood. Had we had a good tour? How did we like the paintings? His daughter had coffee waiting for us and we rested a while in his pleasant *corredor*. Why had he ignored these interesting places when he first heard about our quest? We will never, never know.

The painted place at San Sebastián itself was so obvious that the people merely pointed to it and Enrique and I set off by ourselves. The goal was a cave which could be seen clearly as a dark spot on the brow of a hill to the west. We soon came to the foot of the hill and labored up several hundred feet to what proved to be a wide, shallow rock shelter rather than a cave. The back wall was formed from two different rocks neither of which had proved ideal for supporting paintings. The upper was a softer material with a surface that crumbled as it weathered. A virile black *borrego* was fading away as small bits of its substance were lost.

The lower rock was much harder, a mosaic of small fractured domains of basalt which wept with ground water and accumulated caliche along every crack. On this surface were a black *aura* and the best survivals in the cave, a row of five small whales. These last were indeed iconoclastic, lined up from left to right in order of increasing size with their tails up and heads down. To my knowledge this breaks all the conventions observed in the depiction of fish, though whales may command special rules.

Enrique and I expended a good deal of further energy and the better part of an hour visiting a much larger cave north of the one just described. It was deep, so deep a flashlight would have been needed to explore its recesses. It was complex with large openings in front and on top as well. It was such a fascinating place in short that it had not attracted a single painting, not even a trace. That illustrated an important point. There are so many such places, often near painted ones, that we are reminded of the probable ritual character of the paintings. It seems almost certain that authority designated the places to paint and that they were not selected simply on the basis of availability.

We returned to headquarters just in time to arrange a move to Los Gatos, a ranch up the valley. We hurried and completed the short hour's ride just before sunset; in fact the proximity of that sunset created an amusing *tableau*. We pulled into the ranch and met the prosperous brothers Villavicencio López who were the owners. We told them what we were about and they told us we must hurry. They had paintings to show us which could scarcely be seen except in late afternoon. We grabbed our cameras and, with the enthusiastic brothers leaping ahead, literally ran up a very steep *falda* and a high one at that. We got to a cave front with about three minutes of sunlight left and hastily snapped pictures of large, handsome deer. Then we trouped at a leisurely pace down the hill and enjoyed an evening of some of the best and most generous hospitality in the sierra. Later when our transparencies were processed all those taken on that mad, lung-bursting jaunt turned out to have been spoiled by strong shadows. It probably was the only time of day when we would have encountered such a problem. *Es la vida.*

For the record this site was north of the ranch

directly up the slope, a long slit cave which faced west. The paintings were on the exterior face and the inner ceiling and they consisted of six deer, four in very good condition. Several other figures were to be found on various parts of the ceiling but they were too deteriorated to analyze.

In the morning we began a more sober study of the Los Gatos area. We started very early with a huge cave on the other side of the arroyo and downstream a quarter of a mile. From a distance it looked as if it would be extremely simple to reach. In practice, its approach, which was no steeper than a hundred others, proved to be guarded by a legion of *garabatillo* shrubs whose long wand-like branches are armed with nasty hooks. We approached this cave at a very dignified pace, a dignity marred by frequest resorts to hands-and-knees progress.

The cave itself was the largest that we investigated on this trip. Its general dimensions were on the order of sixty feet wide, twenty feet high and eighty feet deep. Beside that, it had galleries that ran deeper, but, unlike the deep cave near San Sebastián, this one had been heavily painted in its day. The remains of the figures of about twenty deer could be seen on the east and back walls. In spite of advanced deterioration they displayed an interesting feature. Most of them were in the size range of two to four feet, an oddity since this size is rare in any event and, when it does occur, is found in groups with larger murals.

A third Los Gatos site was visited as we left the area. It was an impressive ceremonial center located in a cave near the mouth of the second *cañada* west of the ranch. The cave was long and rather shallow. The ceiling and back wall were both extremely heavily painted almost entirely with heroic-sized *monos*. Sadly, the entire mural assemblage was in an advanced state of decomposition. It was at the point where a viewer had to puzzle out each figure and try to visualize missing parts.

As we left Los Gatos and headed northwest we were once again on El Camino Real, the route I had travelled six years before. As we made our way up Arroyo San Venancio I was fascinated by the interplay of both familiar and strange elements. I suppose that my attention was selective in the first place and that my memory stored only some of what met the senses. At any rate,

riding along, I had the sensation of watching a familiar film which had been heavily intercut with another which I was seeing for the first time.

We rode up to the top of San Venancio and came to a point where the trail divided. El Camino Real proceeded northwest down a remarkable *cuesta* which we had rediscovered on our previous trip. Modern traffic goes down another longer and poorer grade to Rancho El Rincón to the east. Having done the first already I was inclined to try the other. Coco and Ramón clinched the decision by pointing out that the family at El Rincón, known to both of them, could be helpful if there should be any painting in the area. We stopped for a few moments at the *portezuelo* to savor one of the peninsula's most beautiful views. Before us was the broad arroyo of Santa Agueda, miles wide. Beyond, rose the Sierra de Santa Lucía, a line of rugged, broken hills, and behind that, towering over all, the serene cone of Cerro La Vírgen, trailing its usual wisp of clouds.

Down we went, on a long and tiring descent for the animals. At El Rincón we were unfortunate to miss the *dueño*, as his wife and daughters were not knowledgeable in the matter of paintings. Ramón, however, was very philosophical about this matter as we rode away a couple of hours later. The *dueño*, he pointed out, could hardly have cooked the meal which we had just enjoyed.

Our route lay across the slopes that separated us from El Camino Real. We were heading in a direction now in little demand and we found no real trail for an hour or more. Eventually, however, we had to cross a route that came up the valley from Santa Agueda. When we did, we got our bearings and soon were following the old King's Highway as it made its remarkably direct northwest passage of the broken terrain.

Late in the afternoon I was able to point to the west and show Enrique an important place in my own history. Clearly visible a couple of miles away was the huge tumbled boulder of La Candelaría where I saw my first Great Murals. We toyed briefly with a thought of visiting the shrine but opted instead to save the time for new discoveries.

On my other pursuit of El Camino Real, our party had got sidetracked just here and had gone by error over the *cuesta* of La Candelaría in order to get out of the Arroyo de Santa Agueda. We discovered the mistake after several miles but did not feel that we had time to backtrack and do it over. We had to assume the whereabouts of the road in that short but troublesome stretch. This time we stuck to the more northerly and, I am sure, authentic route which passed over a lower and less trying pass. In the area of the pass we were able to observe a beautiful piece of Boleo road building, a truly impressive and well preserved *cuesta* which led — nowhere. Its construction had been interrupted and there it was spiralling up a steep hillside to an abrupt end. Ramón remarked on its unused condition, "unworn," he called it, and said it was a pity we could not find the wrappings and the sales slip so that it could be returned for credit. For my part, I was happy, when we reached the top of the old *cuesta*, to discover that the King's Highway did just what we had assumed six years before.

That pass essentially put us once again on the plain of San Ignacio. Though we faced a long ride down an arroyo, we would have not a single *cuesta* to traverse in the two days it would take us to get back to our starting point at Rancho La Esperanza.

That night, in order to reach Rancho Santa Cruz, we rode in the dark for the first time. There was no moon, but I discovered that the mules apparently depended on even starlight to a degree. When we passed under canopies of trees they became much more hesitant and had a few small footing problems. Out in the open they seemed to move at much the pace employed during the day.

The family at Santa Cruz was large and lively. They were also relatives of Coco so we had no trouble enlisting their attention and help. The young men had herded cattle around there for years, they were observant, and the mention of paintings brought prompt response. Several places were described which lay along our next day's journey.

Thanks in large part to the unusually good local information, the following day unfolded as one of the most efficient and productive of the trip. We started down the arroyo of Santa Cruz until, in an hour, we came to the ruins of Rancho San Antonio, our first signpost. Continuing for a quarter of a mile we looked along the top of the *falda* south of the trail as we had been instructed.

The directions were perfect, we found our quarry easily on a *respaldo* only a hundred feet off the trail and perhaps fifty above it.

The first view of this site reminded me forcibly of the relationship between geography and the Great Murals. Now that we were back at the north end of the sierra and not over thirty miles from the Sierra de San Francisco, the art was assuming the very familiar look of San Francisco work. Here was a wall with over twenty large *monos* in the pure tradition of the Great Mural heartland. Most followed the conventional red-and-black vertical division pattern and they were ranged across the *respaldo* shoulder-to-shoulder, or actually one superimposed on another, so closely were they spaced.

Having established their routine character it is necessary to add that there was one highly unusual aspect of this *mono* display. Three of them were painted over the heads of the others and exactly inverted, feet up and heads and extended arms down.

As the morning wore on, the simplicity of our ride began to sink in; there were no real ups or downs. We were so comfortable in the warm sun that it was almost possible to doze in the saddle. Less than two hours from San Antonio we came to the second place on our list; a cave near the top of a small hill on the north side of the arroyo. The paintings were small but curious. One was a red figure that looked like a large worm or eel, but it was the other two that really attracted our attention. The first was a miniature red-and-black *mono*, about eighteen inches tall. His right arm was extended into a circular net-like appendage over half the size of the *mono*. The other figure was similar except that it was all red and inverted. Its net was an extension of the left arm. We had received no name for this site except that it was near the Cuesta de Las Tunas.

Another hour brought us to a great bend in the arroyo just south of the historic ranch of San Borjitas. Here, precisely at a right turn of the watercourse, we found ourselves riding toward a high bank containing many caves and sheltered overhangs. We dismounted and within minutes had determined that at least six or seven were heavily painted.

The seven rock shelters gave us two hours of pleasure and frustration. The former was due to the fact that there were many, many works and that among them were several attractive compositions such as a group of small deer frolicking across the wall of a cave. The frustration was for the usual cause, bad rock and deteriorated art. The entire complex of caves and rock shelters was composed of a yellow-beige volcanic agglomerate. This made an attractive background for the works and a very effective color contrast to the predominant black paint of this site. But the rock was also soft and crumbling and not a figure survived without substantial damage due to rock failure.

In the end we shrugged it off. There was obviously no point in being downcast by encounters with irremediable losses. Enrique and I, who had reminded each other so many times that we should rejoice at any survival whatever, were put to practicing what we preached. We studied and photographed every group.

The total material at San Borjitas Norte is very large and a shelter-by-shelter description would be wearing; the salient features lend themselves better to a summary. The site had been painted in at least two different periods. There was a lot of overpainting and quite a little difference in the deterioration of lower and upper layers. While style is a riskier criterion it can be given as an opinion at least that there were two major style periods as well.

Most of the paint was black but there were also a few red figures and a number of black-and-red *monos*. There was also a showing of ochre paint used on the outlines of deer; these were in very poor condition. As mentioned before, there were several definite groups of paintings probably made at one time by one artist. Three such were parades of very small deer, two in black and one in red. Others were pairs or threesomes of larger black animals, probably deer.

When we finally quit the hillside we rode on a short distance to a very fine petroglyph site which Guillermo Villavicencio had noticed on our trip six years before. On a high rock was a group of five deer from the same hand. They were large for petroglyph figures, ranging from one to two feet in length. They were arranged into a vertical design and all faced the same direction. The feature that attracted me was the sense that, in style, they related to the nearby paintings. I believe that this is more true of petroglyphs in the larger San Ignacio area than in any other region I have studied.

Enrique pointed out a second noteworthy fact. The basalt *cantil* and boulder pile on the east side of the arroyo, the formation which bears all these petroglyphs, has been engraved in two widely-separated periods. Most of the figures have a light but definite golden patination. A few, including a *mono* over four feet high, are much older. Those of its vintage are so heavily patinated that they have no contrast in relation to their background. Such works are difficult to detect without the help of side-lighting which betrays their incised lines. That *mono*, incidentally, bore a striking resemblance to the "rectangle" men of far away Loma Alta.

The area proved to be a maze of both petroglyphs and pictographs. At the mouth of a *cañada* across from the old San Borjitas ranch site there was another large batch of engravings and below the ranch, also on the opposite or west side, was a wall of rock with both engravings and paintings. The pursuit of all this was exhausting. It is a temptation, heretical of course, to admit that we tired of the chase.

That was substantially the end of our encounter with the rock art of the Sierra de Guadalupe. Almost but not quite. As we rode down the arroyo at the last fringe of the sierra, I spotted paintings on two exposed rock faces, small and faded but unmistakably part of the incredibly prolific art production which characterized the Painters.

This survey of the Sierra de Guadalupe proved that large representational paintings could be found in numbers in every corner of that large area. It showed that the rock surfaces, on the whole, are less durable than in the San Francisco area and that, as a consequence, the paintings are in poorer condition.

In the Sierra de Guadalupe we saw a much higher percentage of small and apparently casually created works. We observed that the paintings at the north end closely resembled the Great Murals of nearby Sierra de San Francisco and, as they were found farther and farther south, that they varied more and more from San Francisco prototypes. Yet in the south there did not appear to be a major new school of art; the variations seemed continuous and gave the impression that they represented the final echoes of the Great Mural impetus as it faded away far from its source.

It is difficult to evaluate the paintings in the mountains of Guadalupe either as to quantity or quality. A single search, even of a month's duration, could not conclusively show the extent of the phenomenon. Some incidents of our trip and a few subsequent developments illustrate this problem.

Consider our encounter with Melchor Villavicencio at San Javier. He knew our interests and showed us examples of paintings. He forgot others that waited a few minutes' walk away. There you have a classic Baja California dilemma. Melchor Villavicencio is not a rare eccentric. Half the people of the sierras are probably capable of just such paradoxical behavior.

In 1975 I was invited by Fernando González Diaz Lombardo to guide a helicopter expedition which would show paintings to various interested Mexicans. On our itinerary was Los Monos de San Juan. We landed between Rancho San Juan and the painted site, and, in a few minutes, were joined by Jesús Valenzuela who had come out to investigate the commotion. As we walked up the arroyo we passed an obvious rock shelter which we had asked about on our first trip. On that occasion Jesús told us that it contained "nothing of interest." On the second visit I walked over for a look. One small area was painted with reasonably well-preserved and interesting *monos*. The uppermost was inverted, a curiosity which we had noted only at San Antonio and which we could have seen far earlier here. I asked Valenzuela about his first dismissal of the site. His answer was simple and logical. With so huge an assemblage as Los Monos only a few hundred yards away he could not imagine that those few figures would interest us.

A few minutes later, at Los Monos, I found two obvious negative hand paintings which all of us had overlooked on our first visit. It is clear that many factors militate against finding all the paintings or sites in an area during any single venture. Only in the Sierra de San Francisco do I have any confidence in my statistics; there, at least, they are based on a half-dozen extended searches.

Knowing these things the reader must imagine the true status of rock art sites in the Sierra de Guadalupe, a place which has essentially been prospected only once. It seems likely that, for every site discovered, several must remain hidden. Rock painting *aficionados* should be kept busy and satisfied for years to come while combing the vast, broken expanses between San Ignacio and La Purísima.

The Sierra de San Juan

Astride the 28th parallel, which divides the states of Baja California, is the smallest of the painted sierras, the remnants of a single volcano whose flows and bedded ash covered a triangular area twenty miles on a side. Its central peak, the twin spire of the Cerro de San Juan, rises to an elevation of four thousand five hundred feet due north of the Sierra de San Francisco and only twelve miles from the gulf shore. The aboriginal people knew this place; their trails lead to its meager springs from every point of the compass. The missionaries tried building roads over several routes while searching for the best of a bad lot. Far from major settlements and poorly served by any sort of roads today, this rugged, broken place is quiet and deserted. A newcomer to its inner recesses can feel like the first man. It is a shock to stumble onto a labor from mission times or a cave painted by the ancients.

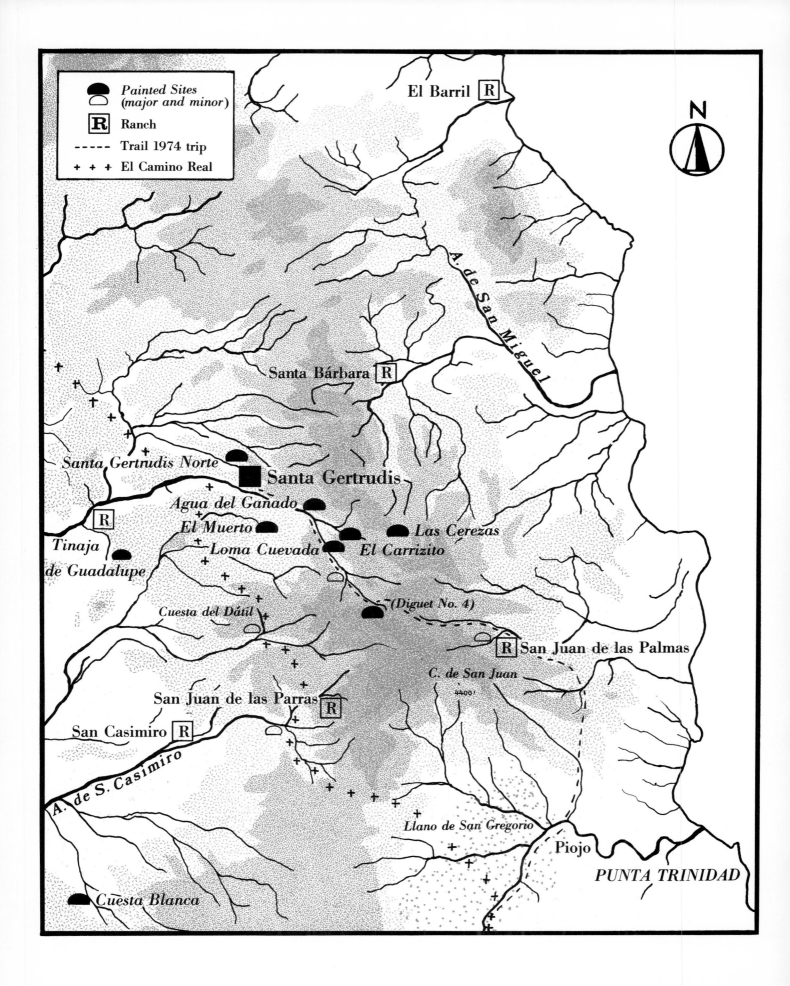

Legend:
- Painted Sites (major and minor)
- **R** Ranch
- - - - - Trail 1974 trip
- + + + El Camino Real

N

El Barril **R**

A. de San Miguel

Santa Bárbara **R**

Santa Gertrudis Norte

Santa Gertrudis

Agua del Gañado

R

El Muerto

Las Cerezas

Tinaja
de Guadalupe

Loma Cuevada *El Carrizito*

Cuesta del Dátil

(Diguet No. 4)

R San Juan de las Palmas

C. de San Juan

4400'

San Juan de las Parras

R

San Casimiro **R**

A. de S. Casimiro

Llano de San Gregorio

Piojo

PUNTA TRINIDAD

Cuesta Blanca

My first encounters with traces of the Painters in the Sierra de San Juan were by pure chance. After the 1967 pursuit of El Camino Real from Loreto to San Diego I was left with much uncertainty about the route of the old road in the rugged San Juan region. Later I returned to investigate and in the course of doing so I stumbled onto a number of rock art sites. They actually displayed little but their very presence held out the tantalizing possibility of more.

After a number of excursions into the Sierra de San Francisco and the one long survey of Guadalupe I was finally able to get back to San Juan. A trip was organized at La Esperanza in the spring of 1974 and, by good fortune, it was combined with the exploration of the Sierra de San Borja described elsewhere.

It was late in March when Tacho, Ramón, Enrique and I rode north. Our route lay along the east or gulf slope of the Sierra de San Francisco and, for the first two days, it was El Camino Real of mission days. However, at the Llano de San Gregorio there was the opportunity to explore a route which deserves a footnote in U.S. history.

In 1849, through ignorance or necessity a number of American gold-seekers came to Baja California and attempted the overland trip to the gold fields. Some survived the ordeal but many did not as they struggled along without guides or adequate animals. Food was scarce but the lack of water was the most crucial element. The diaries of survivors recount excruciating hardships, and local lore dating from times as close as 1853 tells of the roadside burials of hapless 49ers all along the route from the Llano de San Gregorio to Mission San Fernando.

By turning north at Piojo on the southern rim of the Llano de San Gregorio we were able to follow a well-defined trail across that flat expanse and on into the small but rugged Sierra de San Juan which lay between us and Santa Gertrudis. At first this late variant of El Camino Real stayed on the gulf side of the sierra and crossed only low ridges. But at Rancho San Juan de las Palmas the indicated route crossed a high arm of the sierra by a thoroughly steep *cuesta*, which appeared in the bitter accounts of the 49ers.

At San Juan de las Palmas a small group of caves could be seen about a hundred yards above the ranch house. These proved to be painted but the few small artworks were in the final stages of deterioration.

The *cuesta* was climbed slowly to a high pass; just beyond, the trail started down a large brush-choked *cañada*. After an hour's ride our sharp lookout produced results. Just above a very steep watercourse entering the *cañada* from the south were several layers of high *respaldos*. On two of them we could make out prominent paintings.

The upper level in particular was interesting for its typical San Francisco style of art. It displayed a group of larger-than-life *monos* and three *borregos* as well. One of these was unique, in my experience, in that it was divided between a red head and forequarters and entirely black hindquarters. In general the site was disappointing due to its poor condition. We felt deceived because our binoculars had suggested better things. Before long we were familiar with this phenomenon. Apparently the scattered bits of

139

partially disintegrated paintings tend to coalesce in such small, highly magnified images and suggest that they are better works than they prove to be when confronted at close range.

Later, working with a map, it was possible to place the site at the head of the Arroyo Santa Gertrudis drainage. From its location near the pass it could be deduced that it was Diguet's No. 4, "Between Santa Gertrudis and Puerto Trinidad, about the highest point of the *cuesta* of San Juan."

When the *cañada* in which we had been riding opened into a larger waterway, we found a second site on the west wall of the latter. A stiff climb took us to a *respaldo* which showed a sun symbol, rare in the Great Mural region, and a number of very badly decomposed animal forms.

At nightfall we came to as curious a group of caves as may be found on the entire peninsula. In the middle of the arroyo, which by then was very broad, there rose an "island" of beautiful reddish-pink *cantera*, a type of volcanic agglomerate rock. This height was stepped with caves shaped like eyesockets and so numerous that the ensemble looked like a strawberry jar.

A laborious search of the many caves and depressions disclosed that two had been painted. One, higher and more southerly, had three *monos* side by side like a sampler. The first was divided vertically between black and red, the second was black and the third was red. The second painted cave contained a large red-and-black animal which Tacho identified as a *borrega* and it also had a fascinating maze of small figures a foot or two in height. These depicted men, animals and birds but fish were commonest, an unusual occurrence.

In the morning we photographed this "Loma Cuevada" or cave-covered hill, as we facetiously dubbed it. Then we rode for an hour and a half before encountering another painted site at Agua del Ganado, a striking setting. On the east side of the arroyo and towering over it was a grand bluff, very steep and of course made up of many layers. By using binoculars we were able to see paintings on a *respaldo* near the top. By now such evidence was suspect and we were impatient to reach Santa Gertrudis and continue to the Sierra de San Borja. Somewhat reluctantly the bluff was left behind.

In Santa Gertrudis we contacted an old friend of Tacho's, Victor Aguilar Zuñiga, and had a long discussion of the area's Indian past. Victor knew a number of painted sites but his time estimate was discouraging; five or six days would be needed to see them all. In the end we compromised on two days and Victor took us to the three nearest places.

The first morning, he led us on foot from his home up a steep trail to the northeast. A brisk forty-minute walk brought us to a small shallow cave overlooking a minor *cañada* about a mile north of the old mission center. Every inch of the back wall of the shelter had once been painted and repainted. The rock was soft and poor and much of it had deteriorated so as to release its paint. Despite that the place fairly glowed with color and the wall retained the air of a faded tapestry or Persian rug.

Individual figures were extremely difficult to distinguish, but there had clearly been *monos* and deer. The rich colors and the few recognizable drawings were strikingly familiar. The art in this cave reminded me strongly of Cuesta San Pablo I and IV as well as two sites in the Arroyo de la Cuesta Blanca. Significantly all of those are on the extreme north end of the Sierra de San Francisco, that part closest to the San Juan region.

It is very frustrating to report a site such as this. On the one hand it is possible to say that, in its prime, it was a gem, a place magnificently decorated in the pursuit of the Painters' ends. But, it must be added that its enjoyment today is limited to those with a feel for the art and a knowledge of what it can be. No photograph can show its past glories.

Oddly, Victor knew no name for the cave's location, nor for the *cañada* below. When we were able to find no better knowledge among other Santa Gertrudis people, we named the site, for convenience, Santa Gertrudis Norte.

By riding back up the Arroyo de Santa Gertrudis for the space of an hour and a half and leaving it by a *cuesta* to the south, Victor brought us to a high, open cave overlooking the arroyo. The art of this place also was very faded. The walls of the shallow shelter displayed a few deer and rabbits in very pale colors. The most interesting remains were those of a turtle and a well drawn, heavy-bodied fish.

Over a pass, our guide took us into the headwaters of the Arroyo del Muerto, the next drainage system southwest of the Arroyo de Santa Gertru-

dis. Looking down from a hillside over the upper end of the arroyo was a curiously overhung shelter. We approached it from the east along the top of the *falda* and parked our animals in the shade and literally under a mass of paintings.

A soft layer of rock some eight feet high had weathered away to a depth of a few feet, leaving a massive harder layer overhanging. The lower side of the latter is therefore the ceiling of a shelter and it has on it a good number of paintings. There are about a dozen *monos*, and a great turtle in one rather crude painting style easily distinguished by its orange-red paint. A large black bird, an *aura* or hawk, may be of this school as well.

A distinct curiosity of this group of *monos* is the treatment of their legs. All the bodies whose lower parts can be distinguished taper to a point and display no separation whatever into distinct limbs. As an additional oddity, one of them seems to have been first drawn as a complete fish including small fins. The subsequent addition of arms converted the figure to a *mono* not markedly different from the others. This was not simply an overpainting, it was clearly a deliberate change in the identity of a figure. This is a very rare occurrence among the Great Murals.

To the right of the group distinguished by the orange-red paint, there is another sizeable wall-and-ceiling area painted in the colors and style of Santa Gertrudis Norte and the similar sites at Cuesta San Pablo and the Arroyo de la Cuesta Blanca. Deer predominate in these more faded figures but the prize survival is a handsome pair of five-foot red-and-black fish. Their condition is very bad but by good fortune the elegantly crafted tails are quite clear and enough paint remains to reconstruct the remainder.

El Muerto is not, in the larger scheme of the Great Murals, a particularly well-preserved site.

But in the San Juan area, where the rock is apparently very soft, the place is outstanding. Its paintings are in the best condition of any so far reported from this region.

Victor mentioned some other paintings known to his brother, Manuel, who lived at Rancho Santa Barbara east of Santa Gertrudis. We did not at the time feel that we could make such a detour. Instead, we rode to San Borja.

As we returned from that northern excursion some four weeks later our route brought us near the western fringe of the San Juan eminence. We took the occasion to visit a site reported at the Tinaja de Guadalupe near the ranch of the same name.

The entire Guadalupe area shows extensive signs of human habitation. There are numerous caves and many of them have modest midden deposits. There are *metates* in great numbers at these sites and also in open clearings called *rancherías* which are found on nearly every level piece of ground. Near the center of all these artifacts is a high hill called the Pilón de Guadalupe which has a regular conical form that can be distinguished from great distances. A small watercourse runs from the east side of this *pilón* around to the south and on its south side is a large cave shelter.

Reports had described extensive painting in the cave. Our visit disclosed a sad development very parallel to that which we had observed at the painted cave at La Trinidad in the Arroyo de Mulegé. A large part of the roof had recently fallen and most of the paintings fell with it. Five faded *monos* and a small deer survived on other less-painted surfaces.

In the fall of 1974 I returned with my friend, William Price, and we prevailed on Victor and Manuel Aguilar Zuñiga to take us into the Santa Barbara region east of Santa Gertrudis.

The trail led out of the arroyo and onto a mesa, then for an hour's ride it parallelled the arroyo until we came to a point just above the great bluff on which we had left the uninvestigated paintings in the spring. The trail then turned northeast and started down the impressively steep Arroyo de Santa Barbara which leads to the gulf coast. Far below in the *caja* we came to a fork in the trail. The left branch led down to the ranch; we took it and spent the night with Miguel's family in an extremely beautiful setting replete with palms, red rock canyons and a sweeping view of foothills and the blue gulf.

In the morning we returned to the fork, ascended heights to the south, and spent the following two days investigating a series of small painted sites near the peninsular divide which separates Santa Barbara from the Pacific-bound drainage of the Arroyo de Santa Gertrudis. The character of the geology in that place and the patterns in which it had eroded produced a rather odd pattern to our travels and the locations of the painted sites. *Cañadas* leading toward the gulf cut the spine of the sierra in an alternate pattern with *cañadas* leading toward the Pacific. The first painted site was on the Pacific drainage near the head of the Cañada de las Cerezas.

Las Cerezas consisted of a *respaldo* and cave combination about a hundred feet long. The *respaldo*, at the east end, had been painted with large, well-defined red-and-black *monos* and deer. Enough survived to show that the work was good. In addition a number of small figures persisted in better condition. They included *monos* and notably an angular black bird and a conspicuous group of three red birds.

The cave at the west end had once had numerous paintings but the rock was so deteriorated and heavily smoked that not much could be made out.

An hour's ride to the southeast put us in a *cañada* called La Joya which drained to the gulf. On the east side was a large open cave near the trail. In spite of its high ceiling, which must have been sixteen or eighteen feet off the ground, the entire interior was smoked to a deep black relieved only by patches where the deteriorating rock surface was cleaning itself. These smoked caves are common in the sierras of the mid-peninsula. For want of a better term, Tacho, Ramón, Enrique Hambleton and I had fallen into the habit of calling them "kitchens," the implicit idea being that these were places used selectively for cooking. It had also occurred to us that, during cold weather, these places might have had night fires to warm occupants while they slept. Bill Price and I discussed all this while examining the big smoked cave at La Joya. He considered the explanations that I have just outlined and immediately offered an objection which had already bothered me. Cook fires are rarely large enough to substantially smoke even a low cave roof. Fires to warm people are usually kept small and are fed often. Price offered another suggestion. The people of this region appear to have practiced cremation of their dead for a very long time. Human burials are virtually unknown. Might these smoked caves be crematories? The idea has merit. There is a large supply of dry wood in most arroyos and *cañadas*. A cave would conserve the heat of a fire so that it would better dessicate and burn a cadaver and calcine the bones. Such pyres would indeed smoke the interiors of even large caves. Repeated use would produce the dense blackening seen at many sites.

Above the large cave and ranged up the hillside were a number of smaller caves and shelters eroded in a complicated pattern from dark red volcanic rock. Several had been decorated with fairly crude figures all rendered in red paint. We saw a *borrego* and possibly a *berrendo* in bad condition. In better shape were a four-foot turtle, unusually large for this subject, and a bird. A group of small *monos*, painted in a low hollow were the most artistic remains.

Only a couple of hundred yards away in some narrows of the *cañada* was a large *tinaja* and good water. This could easily explain the extensive aboriginal activity in the neighborhood.

At the distance of a five minutes' walk to the west from the *tinaja* there is a pass which leads to an abrupt drop into a *cañada* of the Arroyo de Santa Gertrudis. Manuel returned to Santa Barbara but Victor took us down a very poor trail into that *cañada*. After a rough and twisting ride, we got out of its steepest and narrowest part and entered a long regular waterway heading northwest, the Cañada del Carrizito. As we rode down, a large cave appeared in our view high on the south slope of the canyon. Victor knew nothing of it so it was given the binocular test. Several faded paintings were readily visible; we broke down our packs, stripped off saddles, and started up the high slope.

This cave in the Cañada del Carrizito is about eighty feet long and twenty high and was once heavily decorated over much of its rather large inner surface. The left third of its length is a real cave perhaps thirty-five feet deep, the middle third is an alcove raised off the ground so that a climb is necessary for a close view of its works. The right side is a pure *respaldo*, a fairly flat wall protected only by an upper overhang. The entire volume bears a remarkable resemblance to the cave at La Candelaria in the Sierra de San Francisco, but this is a smaller mirror image replica.

In the true cave at the left is a large black *borrego*, very faded. All other paintings in this section are reduced to vestiges except those all or partly worked on hard inclusive rocks. On two such surfaces there are entire birds and rabbits. In the central part of the shelter a sizeable piece of basalt exposed as part of the generally soft surface bears an astonishing collection of small painted figures. Rabbits, birds, deer, turtle and a couple of rotund *monos* leap with startling color and clarity from this better-favored surface. And all around it the pale, soft agglomerate has shed its painted burden without a trace.

High on the center and right part of the back

wall were the figures of deer that we had seen from afar. Once again the field glasses had played tricks on us and, at close range, the paintings looked like wraiths, the last flickers of a legend almost lost.

At the point where the Cañada del Carrizito intersected the main arroyo, a familiar sight was in evidence. Directly ahead of us as we emerged was the tall bluff composed of layer after layer of *respaldos*, the same *pilón* whose paintings we had spurned in our haste of six months before. Now we stopped for a full investigation.

After a thorough survey it was decided to attack the southeast side of the bluff and we began what proved to be a stiff climb. In thirty minutes, however, I had arrived at the highest layer and found the paintings noted previously. All proved to be very faded though most of the figures could be made out. The principal subject was man, large red and red-and-black *monos* predominated. There were also two or three large red birds. The prize of this collection, as at El Carrizito, was a single inclusive rock which stood well out from a wall and bore on its hard smooth surface a number of neatly executed red-and-black *monos* less than a foot tall. This beautiful work had suffered an inexplicable act of vandalism. Someone had used a pointed object, perhaps a sharp stone, to pound the face area of the central *mono*, the only one with a headdress. This site was so high and so remote that it would seem safe from any wanton act. Of course it is entirely possible that the damage is almost as old as the work and represented personal or tribal rivalry.

On the level of the *respaldo* below, Victor prospected about and shortly found more art, a pair of crudely realized red-and-black deer and other faded deer and *monos*. As we climbed down we worked along the edge of a tiny *cañada* heading east. Victor and I both spotted paintings on its other wall. After the long climb down, we immediately began the ascent of the opposite slope. After a wearying climb we stood in front of three *monos*. Two were very tall and red-and-black, one of them representing a woman. The other was small and black. All were crude and childish in proportion and technique, as artistically negligible as anything we were to see in the area.

The return to these high paintings at Agua del Ganado ended the survey of the Sierra de San

Juan. The area initially had had much promise and it proved in fact to contain numbers of Great Mural sites. Some of its art must have once been fascinating and very beautiful; remnants at Santa Gertrudis Norte and Arroyo del Muerto attest strongly to that. But something important is missing in all that is known of the Painters' work in this region. There is little sense that art has survived. This feeling is a common experience at place after place in the four-sierra range of the Great Murals. More sites than not show vestiges only and dash the hopes of the most patient and realistic searchers. But no other region within those sierras has failed, as has San Juan thus far, to provide a single real survival, a single place where the art lives and breathes and the hunter experiences the joy of knowing it for its own sake. Yet these San Juan paintings and their locations are worth knowing. They add a critical dimension to our understanding, they are the northern frontier of the San Francisco style. No time was lost in their pursuit and the job needs to be finished. But so far at least there is an almost tangible void.

Perhaps the next cave will break the spell.

The Sierra de San Borja

From the Bahía de los Angeles on the north to the hamlet of El Arco on the south and dominating the whole lower end of Baja California's northern state is a range of mountains and foothills which resembles a geologic sampler. The underpinnings are granite interspersed with pockets of metamorphic rock. Overlying are volcanic flows millions of years congealed. It is not unusual to see a pile of granite boulders weathering from its parent mass while still wearing an outlandish cap of lava. Despite its mixed parentage the range as a whole is more unified in form than most of its peninsular neighbors and presents a continuous wall toward the gulf and a gentler decline of long, arroyo-cut slopes leading to the west. There was a time, a generation or two ago, when a score of families lived at widely set locations in every corner of the sierra. Drought and economic changes have swept the heights. Lore and guides are in lamentably short supply.

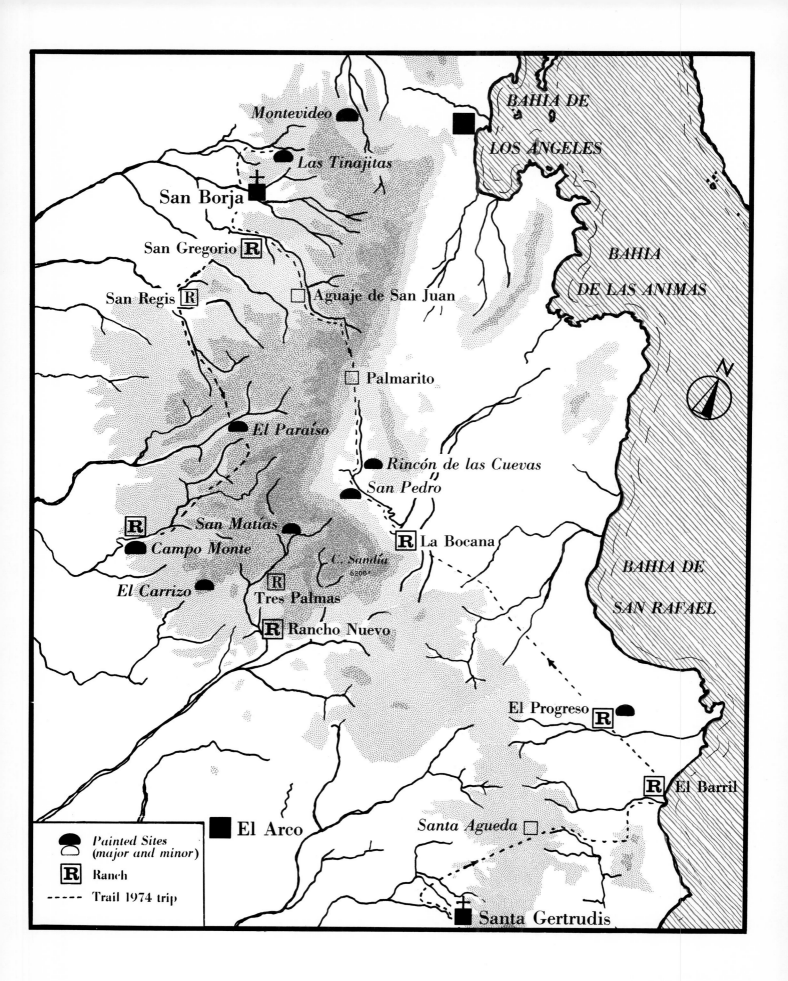

BAHIA DE
LOS ÁNGELES

BAHIA
DE LAS ANIMAS

BAHIA DE
SAN RAFAEL

Montevideo

Las Tinajitas

San Borja

San Gregorio R

San Regis R

Aguaje de San Juan

Palmarito

El Paraíso

Rincón de las Cuevas
San Pedro

R

San Matías

Campo Monte

R La Bocana

C. Sandía
6206'

El Carrizo

R

Tres Palmas

R Rancho Nuevo

El Progreso R

R El Barril

El Arco

Santa Agueda

Painted Sites
(major and minor)

R Ranch

Trail 1974 trip

Santa Gertrudis

Explorations of the Sierra de San Francisco and the long expedition through the Sierra de Guadalupe had raised some tantalizing suggestions. The art of San Francisco had proved to be very homogeneous with only a scattering of eccentric works. The art of the adjacent northern end of the Guadalupe region had turned out to be very similar but differences had grown as the inventory was carried farther south. This suggested the possibility that the San Francisco mountains were the homeland of the Great Mural phenomenon, and that it had spread through movements of its parent culture or by the acculturation of neighbors. If that had indeed been the case, it seemed likely that there would have been a corresponding spread into the adjacent mountains lying to the north. That last frontier would be the Sierra de San Borja, a challenging row of peaks clearly visible from the uplands of San Francisco.

History offered no encouragement for the pursuit of the Great Murals north of Santa Gertrudis. In fact there were flat statements dating as far back as Clavijero that the large paintings were to be found between the 27th and 28th parallels. Diguet listed a site north of Calmallí but neglected to specify whether it represented petroglyphs or paintings, a vagueness which suggested that he may have reported hearsay. The paintings which had been documented from the northerly region in general were on a smaller scale and of another school altogether, characterized by polychromed groupings of abstract symbols. Only a few rumors suggested that the tradition of large realistic paintings extended in that direction.

In the fall of 1973, after the month-long exploration of the Sierra de Guadalupe, I planned a spring venture to include San Borja if any solid clues could be found. Tacho Arce was asked to make inquiries of all his extensive acquaintances.

When the spring came, a surprise was waiting at La Esperanza. There was Manuel Flores, a member of a large family of *vaqueros* working as tenant ranchers in the Sierra de San Borja. Years before I had treated Manuel when he was ill in a remote place. When he heard that we were looking for paintings he got a ride down to tell Tacho what he knew. Our meeting was a fortunate accident.

Manuel Flores, with his brother Ignacio, had a ranch at Campo Monte northwest of El Arco. All around them they had found paintings, large paintings, of *monos*, deer, *borrego*, and so forth. If we could visit his ranch he would show us everything.

Our plans fell nicely together. We were set at the time to embark on a survey of the Sierra de San Juan, an exploration described earlier in these pages. That ended at Santa Gertrudis in the company of our guide for that region, Victor Aguilar Zuñiga. Victor did not know the Sierra de San Borja himself. However, he and Tacho both knew the several Villavicencio brothers living in the general area of El Barril on the gulf coast. All agreed that they were the authorities on San Borja. Their father was born at El Paraíso in the heart of the sierra and they had all run cattle in the region for years. In the end Victor agreed to guide us across the little-known stretch from Santa Gertrudis to the Villavicencios' ranches.

The trip to El Barril required two days. There was no appreciable rock art along the way but on the afternoon of the first day we entered a valley called Santa Agueda where there were innumerable other Indian remains.

According to Victor the place had been a ranch of the Santa Gertrudis mission and the idea was supported by several old stone corrals. That it had also been an earlier seasonal Indian encampment was even more obvious. There was a large *tinaja* and, in its environs, dozens of rock circles and literally hundreds of *metates* and *manos* scattered over the level ground. Also the place was thickly grown with the giant yucca, called *datilillo*, the fruit and seeds of which were important Indian dietary items.

We were disappointed at El Barril, a place apparently without rock art. A resident, José Rosas Villavicencio, who guided Erle Stanley Gardner to the great painted complex in the Sierra de San Francisco, proved to know far less about San Borja. The best he could do was to suggest that we visit two of his brothers at Rancho Progreso less than ten miles to the west. These men, Higinio and Lorenzo Villavicencio, were able to show three painted sites in the Progreso area, sites which were quite different from anything farther south.

The plain around Progreso was dotted with piles of huge granite boulders, some as much as twenty feet in diameter. With stones of such dimensions the voids between could be equal to small caves. Two of the rock art sites actually consisted of paintings on the bottoms of such great boulders, bottoms exposed because the rocks leaned or rested irregularly on others. The paintings in these poorly-protected rock shelters were relatively small, eight to twenty-four inches, and depicted fish, turtle, deer and perhaps rabbits in red paint.

The third site, and the most impressive, consisted of a pair of small interconnected caves weathered from *in situ* granite that formed the base of a sizeable hill. One of these contained a group of figures in the same colors and dimensions but suggestive of a different art tradition.

In sum, the art in the Progreso region seemed to bear out the tradition which placed the Great Murals to the south. However, we were determined to press on and we were encouraged by at least two factors. The most obvious was Manuel Flores' description of six-foot high paintings in the San Borja foothills far to the west, but even locally there was an indication that the small red paintings might not be the whole story. Progreso was in low, level country and experience had shown conclusively that in other regions at least the giant figures were found in more mountainous settings.

Despite his years of cattle herding in the San Borja uplands, Higinio could not remember a single painted site. As an intelligent man he was embarrassed to admit it, but he had simply never had any interest in the matter and had never paid attention to whatever gossip reported such findings.

We headed northwest on a wheel-track auto road and in a day's ride came to the mouth of Arroyo San Pedro, the largest watercourse on the eastern slope of the sierra. Here at a ranch appropriately called La Bocana we found the tenant rancher, Ignacio Murillo. "Galo," as he is universally called, was delighted to see Tacho. The two were childhood friends and had not met for forty years. They had of course kept up on each other through the inevitable peninsular grapevine and indeed Galo even knew something of what we were about. As Tacho had imagined, Galo was willing to guide us and after a day of preparation we were headed up the arroyo over the clear showings of the eastern alternate route of El Camino Real.

Galo was honest in his report on paintings. He personally knew of only one site in the entire San Pedro region, but he enthusiastically endorsed the method that we had developed. He promised to take us to each inhabited ranch to ask for local information.

Two hours out of La Bocana we came to the spring and the ruins of historic Rancho San Pedro. We also came to the abandoned stamp mill which an American had used for years in a small gold mining activity. The water, which would be our last for a day's ride, made us suspicious that paintings might be near. However, the immediate neighborhood consisted of hills formed from a soft fractured metamorphic rock. These were shot with quartz veins which must have been the source of gold. Enrique had noticed some higher hills of granite a half mile or so to the west and he was determined to explore. As he started up a rough *cañada* I followed his progress with my field glasses. A few minutes after he entered the steep-sided watercourse between the high hills, he turned and raised both arms aloft to mimic a *mono*. That was a thoroughly exciting gesture in a place so far north. I hurried to join him.

In that *cañada* Enrique had found a site which yielded, in a run of no more than a hundred yards, five Great Mural figures and a number of smaller ones. There were three deer about one and a half times as large as life and two *monos* about four feet tall. One of the latter broke with all previously noted tradition by having the arms extended downward.

The paint was exclusively red, but in shades ranging from rust to maroon. None of the figures was solitary; they were arranged in groups of three to five. Each such grouping was painted on a separate nearly vertical granite surface. All were unusually exposed to the elements as compared to most of the Great Mural sites to the south.

After the briefest inspection, I offered my companion hearty congratulations because he had established concretely the existence of large naturalistic paintings substantially north of the 28th parallel.

The next day Galo showed us his site, significantly called Rincón de las Cuevas, the recess of the caves. Only three hours' ride north of San Pedro we were directed up a *cañada* to the northeast of the main wash of the arroyo. According to Galo this box canyon had long been used as a place for cattle roundups and the caves had often served the *vaqueros* as shelters.

The terrain here was different. In the decidedly mixed geology of the Sierra de San Borja, we were now at the eroded edge of an ancient volcanic formation about 2,000 feet above sea level. The caves were small examples of those typical in the entirely volcanic San Francisco mountains, and in the first cave we found an array of paintings which might have come directly from San Francisco. There were the remains of carefully and beautifully painted representations of deer, rabbits and men. Remains, only remains. Fires apparently of rather recent origin had been built against the painted walls and they had caused the surface rock to expand and flake away in sheets. Above, the paintings were badly smoked. On the floor near the back wall and partially obscured by the fallen debris, we found a maze of those enigmatic cup-like pits which we had encountered at a few other random sites.

We poured over the polychromed patches of paint and tried to interpret them. We photographed the small areas that were reasonably intact. Later, when our trip was done, we were to feel the sense of loss even more strongly. All the other San Borja Great Mural sites were to present a distinctly parochial aspect. Style, paints and the types of sites would define a Red-on-Granite school of painting of which our recent find at San Pedro was typical. But that little cave at Rincón de las Cuevas demonstrated with finality that the familiar tradition of the Great Mural heartland extended well into the Sierra de San Borja. And, for the moment at least, it is the only evidence.

Our journey continued with a spectacular crossing of the 4,400-foot pass between Arroyo San Pedro and the Arroyo of San Gregorio which leads to San Borja. From the pass we had a sweeping view of the gulf dotted with islands as large as the sixty-mile-long Angel de la Guarda to the north and ranging down through assorted shapes and sizes to mere rocky pinnacles. A panorama of bays was apparent also; we could see the *bahías* of Los Angeles, Las Animas, and San Rafael. After that it was a wrench to turn west and plunge into the narrow confines of another *cañada*. We arrived at the Aguaje of San Juan in the gloom of evening and camped among the ruins of a ranch and visiting station of the San Borja Mission. During this ride we saw no promising caves or *respaldos* and indeed saw only a single work of rock art, a badly-faded white painting on a vertical basalt surface. The form resembled a string of beads or a section of intestines.

At Rancho San Gregorio the *dueno*, Armando Villavicencio, assured us that there were no paintings in that region. He did, however, know of some a few miles north of San Borja. We immediately asked him to guide us and, to save time, Enrique and I went with him in his truck while Tacho, Ramón and Galo brought our caravan to San Borja itself.

The place to which Armando drove was at an elevation of about 2,100 feet on the south side of Arroyo Grande, a set of bluffs around the mouth of a small, open *cañada* called Las Tinajitas. These bluffs were literally honeycombed with tiny caves; the formation looked for all the world like a miniature of our Loma Cuevada in the arroyo of Santa Gertrudis. For two hours Armando, Enrique and I poked through an enchanting maze of over twenty painted caves decorated with hundreds of abstract forms in an unusually broad palette of colors. White, ochre and orange were common as well as the more usual reds and black.

None of this work was familiar from our long pursuit of the Great Murals. It seemed instead to be allied with paintings of almost entirely symbolic character found throughout the region to the north as far as Cataviñá near the southern flanks of the Sierra de San Pedro Mártir.

We returned to San Borja and passed the night. Early the following morning I noticed that the high hill just east of the village was crowned with *cantilería* very reminiscent of that which we had seen at Las Tinajitas on the previous day. I got out my binoculars and was able to discover numerous caves and shelters too shaded to see into effectively. The local people were no help; not a soul seemed to have made the climb. Off I went. Twenty minutes of stiff hiking brought me to the level of the shelters at the base of the *cantil*. I made my way along for a hundred yards or more and examined half a dozen promising places. Not a vestige of painting or drawing was to be seen.

Meanwhile, the other members of our group had no luck in finding people who knew of paintings. We also went to San Ignacito to no avail and then headed south to traverse the western drainage of the sierra. At Rancho Santa Ana we stopped to query Amado Villavicencio who had

CAMPO MONTE II and CAMPO MONTE I

The Great Murals in the Sierra de San Borja consist almost entirely of paintings in various shades of red applied to the sides of huge granite boulders. This is a notable departure from the usual practice of painting polychromed works on the walls of caves. A further break with the predominant tradition can be seen in the downthrust arms of the three linked human figures, Los Tres Reyes, or The Three Kings at Campo Monte II. Both sites display gunfire damage.

lived in the region all his life. When he likewise could offer no help, we continued south over high hills.

The character of the country changed dramatically. From volcanic scapes covered with *cardón* and *cirios* we had passed into a region of metamorphic rock like that of San Pedro on the other side of the sierra. Here too were many signs of gold-seeking; little shafts and tiny mills for reducing ore. The plant cover changed as well; we now rode among the heaviest stands of the elephant tree, *copalquín*, that I had ever seen. These trees with their contorted forms and swollen trunks and branches were bizarre enough at best, but all those in this region were heavily infected with dodder, a parasite consisting solely of orange hairlike strands. The scenes through which we rode had a nightmarish quality; ragged hills bristling with grotesque leafless trees, each of which sprouted a tangled head of flaming hair.

We came to Rancho San Miguel and found it abandoned, its large *huerta* had died off to a few hardy olives, and the substantial adobe *casa* was beginning to tumble. In a way, San Miguel characterized the problems that we and any others would have doing research in the Sierra de San Borja. Most of the ranches were abandoned, most of the knowledgeable old-timers were dead or scattered. Rather sadly we turned east to go up the arroyo to San Regis which, like San Miguel, had been an agricultural center since the early days of the San Borja mission.

San Regis presented a more cheerful picture. Part of the large *huerta* was being tended and a sizeable vineyard was leafing out strongly. Two widely-spaced *casas* were occupied, albeit each by only a single old man.

We had come specifically to see one of these men. Back at San Borja we had been told about Antonio Rios, the caretaker at San Regis. Rios was reputed to be the last pureblooded Cochimí Indian in that quarter of the peninsula; he was also supposed to know the western slopes of the sierra better than anyone else available.

We found Rios clearing irrigation ditches. He was a quiet, shy little man in his sixties, wiry of build with skin like tanned leather. We outlined our quest and asked for his help. Without committing himself he laid his hoe aside and suggested that we sit down and have coffee.

We sat under a shady *mezquite* in front of Antonio Rios' tiny house and told him what we had done and where we had gone. He knew Galo Murillo from some distant year and apparently liked him. He warmed to Tacho and Galo's obvious good humor, he even contributed a few stories. Gradually he began to tell us what he knew about Indian remains. In the end he agreed to guide us from San Regis to Manuel Flores' ranch at Campo Monte and to take us to the only painted site he knew in the intervening country.

In the days that followed we got better acquainted with the gentle Indian but we were disappointed in our expectations. His family descended from neophytes of the San Borja and San Ignacio missions but at San Regis, they had been isolated from other Indians so long that Antonio for instance, had never learned a word of Cochimí. And as we rode along, it was obvious that the ancient trails, rock circles, *metates* and, eventually, paintings, though familiar, were as alien to him as they were to Tacho, Galo or Ramón.

We crossed from Arroyo San Regis to one called Catarina. Antonio told us that these two joined to the west near a ranch called El Cardonal. Also near that ranch he knew of a painted rock. His description sounded familiar: two deer painted in red on the side of a granite boulder. Since there was an auto road to Cardonal we decided to return by car and save the nearly two days that the detour would have cost.

On the *cuesta* that led out of Arroyo Catarina another abrupt change in plant life was evident. The giant agave, or *mezcal*, had been rare or absent from the terrain we had covered. Suddenly it became one of the commonest plants of the slopes and mesas. That observation recalled Dr. Homer Aschmann's hypothesis that the Indians of San Borja mission had used them as food during famine periods until they were gone for up to two days' travel in all directions from the population center. Our encounter in this lonely region seemed to bear out the idea. Other observations were thrust upon us. The *cardón* obviously favored southern exposures while *cirio* preferred northern. Riding south, we descended from mesa to arroyo by way of *cuestas* surrounded by *cardón* and climbed out through equally thick stands of *cirio*.

From Catarina the trail crossed the Mesa of Corral Blanco and descended the Cuesta of San Bartolo into El Paraíso, the largest arroyo in the sierra. The drop from mesa to arroyo floor was over 1,300 feet, to a place of trees, water, and huge blocks of granite. Antonio Rios led the way past the abandoned ranch of San Bartolo to a sandy flat near a pool thick with rushes. He pointed across the pool to a vertical face of granite that towered above. It was his painted site, a place he had called Los Venados (the deer). It was a simple but impressive scene. The granite formed a large clean canvas and on it was the painted representation of a single large deer in a maroon shade. The animal showed very clearly even in the late afternoon shadow, only the head was badly faded.

We crossed the watercourse and clambered up to the painted area. Essentially, we had seen it all. Once there had been a second figure to the right of the great deer but the same flow of water which had so faded its head had virtually obliterated the other figure. Only a pair of legs showed where it had been. That was the extent of Antonio Rios' contribution to rock art knowledge, a single great deer in a totally remote place. It was symbolic of the difficulties and the grudging rewards in that vast sierra.

Just north of the campsite and several hundred feet up the steepest sort of *falda* was a marvelous row of *cantilería*, or columnar basalt. In the morning Enrique explored it and found a small shelter containing crudely-painted works. One very badly worn *mono* appeared to be a duplicate of the odd arms-down figure we had seen at the first site in Arroyo San Pedro. As nearly as I could determine from so faded an image, it had bowed legs and male genitalia like some *monos* we had seen in the Sierra de Guadalupe.

We left the arroyo of El Paraíso by way of the Cuesta de las Cruces which climbed to a mesa whose elevation was 3,000 feet. As we broke on-

to the mesa we startled a large deer which fled across very broken ground in a series of heroic leaps. One posture was frozen in my mind as I watched the succession of bounds; at the top of each flight the forelegs were back and the hindlegs brought forward in a startling recreation of the painting in the arroyo behind us. It is obvious that the ancient painters were observant and knew their animals. By extension it seems probable that many other paintings of animals which appear to portray awkward or unlikely movements are equally based on models from life.

A long day took us south to Campo Monte, a region of unrelieved granite outcroppings. By good fortune the Flores brothers were at home and, within a few minutes of our arrival, the paintings were being pointed out. Manuel Flores had certainly not exaggerated. From his doorstep two actual paintings could be seen and four others readily indicated. We hurried for an inspection. The first group was opposite the ranch and south perhaps a hundred yards. On a single granite boulder were life-sized deer, a *borrego*, a turtle, as well as smaller *monos*, birds, and fish including a manta ray. There was a great deal of overpainting, the first we had seen in the entire San Borja area.

The second site visited was across the arroyo and hence facing east. This one commanded a large stretch of the arroyo from its position high on a point that forced a bend in the waterway. This group was dominated by one very large *mono*. To the right three others, smaller and nearly identical in shape, stood side by side, with their arms in the unusual downward position that seemed to be limited to the Sierra de San

Borja. Manuel Flores called the latter figures with linked arms, "Los Tres Reyes," The Three Kings. These striking *monos* were accompanied by paintings of small deer and birds which seemed to move as a herd about them.

The other sites had distinctly lesser offerings. One consisted of a pair of large *monos* with a tiny *mono* like a child at its feet. Another showed three giant *monos* so faded as to have lost all individual features. A third was no more than a single large deer, almost a replica of the survivor at San Bartolo as nearly as could be told from its disintegrated image. The last was curious. As we walked back to the ranch we saw a small, clear painting that might have come from Arroyo Grande. It consisted of purely abstract designs and looked entirely out of place in the company of the naturalism that looked down from the other rocks.

were numbers, quality, and condition. In all of these matters Campo Monte vastly outshone not only any individual Great Mural site that we had seen in the Sierra de San Borja, but all the others combined.

The painting locations were instructive. Each group was on a rock face visible from and facing the bed of the arroyo. It seemed almost certain that they were placed so as to be exposed to the view of people using the *caja* of the arroyo as an avenue. To test this hypothesis, we walked up and down the two hundred yards in which the paintings were located and found that they occupied all the best places in terms of the size and conspicuousness of the available rock surfaces.

We left the Campo Monte area with one last find. Not more than two miles from the principal concentration of paintings, Ramón spotted a handsome *borrego* above a small wash near the trail. It too was red-on-granite, apparently the common currency for painting over a very large area.

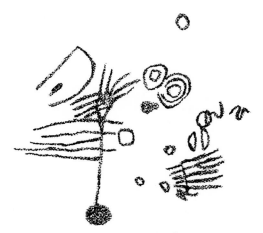

In a sense there were no other surprises. All the paintings were in red and all were on vertical faces of granite. The significant elements

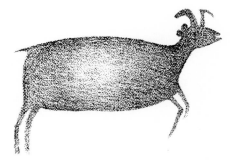

That ended our three-week exploration of the Sierra de San Borja. The balance of a month-long trip produced the finds at Arroyo Cuesta Blanca

EL PROGRESO and MONTEVIDEO

The Great Murals are not an island of primitive art on an otherwise barren peninsula. The smaller and strikingly different works of other cultures are found in adjacent but not overlapping territories. The small, quasi-realistic works at El Progreso, at top, are representative of those found on low ground along the gulf coast. The fanciful, multicolored, abstract style seen at Montevideo seems to stretch north of San Borja over as great, if not as densely painted, a range as that of the Great Murals.

and El Brinco, which are reported under the appropriate heading of The Sierra de San Francisco. However, the San Borja story was not quite ended. In the fall of 1974 I returned with a list of all the clues and suggestions picked up in the spring but not acted on. My companion was William Price, once my student and long-time friend with a university degree in anthropology.

Around the village of San Borja I had heard many references to paintings in the Arroyo Montevideo just off the road to Bahía de Los Angeles. Antero Díaz at the Bahía gave us precise instructions. A comparison showed that his directions exactly matched others I had received years before from Dr. Reid Moran at the San Diego Natural History Museum and from William Weber Johnson, the author of the Time-Life book on Baja California. When we came to the actual site further coincidences were apparent. The paintings were immediately recognizable as those published in Mexico by Ing. Ernesto Raúl López as located at "Volcancito." In short, it was apparent that these must be some of the peninsula's best known works of rock art.

The site consisted of a fifty-foot cliff of solid volcanic rock lined with small caves and shallow depressions. These were characterized by generally smooth interior rock surfaces. Many were painted and the school of art was identical, or at least closely related, to that of the nearby Arroyo Grande. The figures on the whole were somewhat larger and the work more skillful. It was the largest and finest display of the abstract, symbolic type of aboriginal painting that had as yet been reported from Baja California.

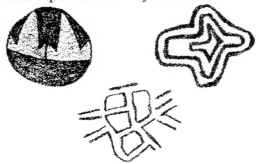

The Montevideo figures contrasted strongly with the typical Great Murals. Beside the obviously different subject matter, these figures were smaller, displayed a wider range of colors, and were more precisely worked. The last of these traits was probably due in part to their smaller size and the unusually smooth surfaces on which they were painted.

Despite the almost universally abstract character of the Montevideo designs, two natural forms stood out. One was a stiff long-bodied *mono* about forty inches tall, similar to those at San Pedro or Campo Monte except that it was divided vertically into red and black zones in the San Francisco fashion. Another realistic work almost certainly represented a flowering plant. This beautiful painting added to the petroglyph from Cuesta Blanca and the identical leaf paintings at San Gregorito and El Parral to form the very short list of plant depictions encountered during my explorations.

William Price and I next drove to El Arco and entered the sierra from the south via Calmallí and Rancho Nuevo. At the latter place Jesús Aguilar, whom I knew from the search for El Camino Real, was able to provide animals and we rode north to Tres Palmas, the ranch of Francisco Romero who had guided me before. Our goals were paintings at San Sebastián and San Matías reported by the Flores brothers and other cowboys that I had quizzed. Romero proved familiar only with the San Matías work. He certainly knew the San Sebastián area intimately from cattle roundups but he had never heard of paintings and hesitated to undertake a blind hunt over an area of several square miles. Accordingly we went to San Matías.

As we approached, the region had a thoroughly familiar look. The arroyo wound through an increasingly high and narrow channel between walls of *in situ* granite blocks. The way was littered with boulders derived from the same source. All of this was reminiscent of both San Pedro and Campo Monte. We rode for hours past rock faces which it seemed must be painted, but continual surveillance produced no results.

Finally we turned north into the Cañada de San Matías and before long the waterway became too boulder-choked for mule travel. We unsaddled the animals, tied them, and proceeded on foot. Within ten minutes Romero was able to show us what he described as "El Rey de San

Matías." He pointed to some obvious paintings in a shallow depression high on the west side of the *cañada*. With extreme difficulty William and I made our way up and into the shelter. There were only two painted figures, a five-foot *mono* in red in extremely faded condition, and another of similar size, El Rey, which was sharp and bright. The principal features of El Rey, like its location, were familiar from previous San Borja experiences. The red-on-granite style of *mono* showed in the elongated, formless body and the short arms. Less usual was the elaborate representation of hair or a headdress and the large number of apparent arrows with which the body fairly bristled.

Below, Francisco Romero had found some other paintings and we descended. Under an immense fallen and fractured slab of granite were about two dozen small red paintings, mostly of deer. They had apparently been done when the slab was in a more vertical position. Some subsequent movement had left the works visible only in a narrow slit or from peek-through crevices beneath the slab. As a result of the changed position the art was almost impossible to photograph but it also was superbly protected from the elements and in generally good condition.

A search of the area produced only one other *mono* farther up the *cañada*, a figure about forty inches tall and badly worn away. Surprisingly, its hands and scrotal sac remained clearly delineated.

During our return to Tres Palmas Romero told of knowing some similar rock art near Rancho La Huerta, a half-day ride to the west. We extended our tour accordingly and shortly after noon of the following day arrived at that ranch. In fact, the actual site was over another *cuesta* to the west and nearer the abandoned Rancho El Carrizo to which we made our way.

The paintings were in two locations a little over a quarter of a mile apart. The first was on the familiar sort of exposed granite face just south

of the trail. Two large figures were in evidence, a *borrego* with marvelous horns and a deer heavily antlered, both in poor condition but clearly visible.

The second was immediately south of the orchard at the abandoned ranch. There, literally within a pile of granite boulders, were small *monos* and a two-foot fish, all in the usual red.

That ended for the moment the search for ancient art in the Sierra de San Borja. The small number of sites discovered in the four weeks which were devoted to the area is not indicative of the potential. As compared to similar studies in other sierras my efforts were hampered by a distinct lack of good local information. The area which offered suitable rock for this Red-on-Granite school is vast and it is also poorly known and poorly watered. Despite these obstacles, dozens of additional sites will eventually be located. In the meantime the few reported here demonstrate the broad distribution of large naturalistic paintings north of the 28th parallel and offer considerable insight to their special character. Some useful generalizations may now be made about the Great Murals from this new area.

The works are executed in shades of red on granitic rock. The surfaces chosen are either on large freestanding boulders or weathered blocks of material *in situ*. While large, the painted figures are smaller on the average than those in other Great Mural areas. Human figures especially tend to be around life-size or less. Subject matter in general is limited to deer, *borrego*, and humans.

The style of the paintings is conspicuously homogeneous and discernibly different from works elsewhere in the Great Mural area. Wholly apart from the similarity of their paint and rock surfaces these Red-on-Granite works compel one to think of a regional "school." For example, elsewhere among the Great Murals man has rather natural proportions and invariably upraised arms. In the Red-on-Granite realm of the Sierra de San Borja man is represented less realistically. He is a stiff figure with long torso and short limbs, the arms occasionally thrust down and out instead of up and out.

Sites are small and generally consist of only a few figures. Overpainting, practically a hallmark of the sites to the south, is extremely rare in the Sierra de San Borja.

SAN MATIAS

Man in the southern Sierra de San Borja seems to have left a record of long effort and desultory success. Indian remains are scarce, abandoned mining camps abound and ponderous stone corrals mark deserted cattle ranches. Today, the area is quiet and days of searching for ancient art produced little more than this figure called El Rey, *the King of San Matías by the few local people. Gold is where you find it.*

The condition of all the Red-on-Granite works is remarkably similar. The paint has adhered unusually well to the granite; the hard but finely checked surface provides an excellent basis for an enduring mechanical bond. Offsetting this positive survival factor is the element of exposure. Most of these Red-on-Granite works are on the vertical faces of rounded boulders. Such faces are washed by every rain of any consequence even if the paintings are on the rolled-under surfaces at the bases of the boulders. This situation contrasts strongly with most of the surviving Great Murals to the south which are in rock shelters well protected from rain. The result of this exposure in the Sierra de San Borja is a rather uniform fading coupled with occasional vertical streaks of greater damage attributable to specific flows of water. Nevertheless it is important to reemphasize that there is a striking sameness to the condition of all the Red-on-Granite sites so far discovered. This, taken with their stylistic homogeneity, leads to a preliminary opinion that they were created by the members of a single cultural group during a relatively brief period of time.

This exploration extended beyond the Red-on-Granite area and apparently established the general location of an interface between two cultures with markedly different rock paintings. The abstract works around the village of San Borja seem to derive from a common culture and relate to similar sites stretching for a long distance to the north. The Red-on-Granite works may be distinguishable from the Great Murals to the south, but their affinities clearly incline in that direction rather than toward the polychromed abstractions which make up the art in the region to the north.

Who Were the Painters?

The meager archaeology of the mid-peninsula suggests an occupancy of many thousands of years. San Dieguito Man left his tell-tale artifacts on his way to the Cape. La Jollan and Amargosan-like tools suggest their passing as well. Early splinters of Yuman folk followed at some undetermined time and added to the growing assemblage of human leavings. Europeans found the area peopled by a single far-flung and loosely organized group. These first historic people were still creating from stone and contributing to the archaeological record, but they had no bent for painting. Somewhere during the latter part of this long human occupancy a culture with organized, even institutionalized artists invaded this ground or evolved from its occupants. They painted as few on this globe have done, decorating hundreds of sites with thousands of huge figures. They left no other obvious clues to distinguish them in the parade of peoples. Who were the Painters?

The concept of the Painters as a cultural entity is based solely on spectacular artworks confined to a limited mountain region. The greatest problem in knowing more about them lies in making the short but difficult step from paintings on cave walls to the array of other remains buried or lying about below.

In the Painters' region there is a widespread abundance of artifacts. Trails, hunting blinds, rock circles, firepits, smoked caves, cleared areas on level ground, *metates, manos*, bows and arrows, cores, flakes, projectile points, choppers, scrapers, and other stone implements, seashells, worked bone and shell, woven and braided fibers, firesticks and hearths, and other miscellaneous by-products of human toil are found throughout the painted area, many of them in and around the painted caves. With adequate archaeological research it seems certain that this great pool of material could be stratified both as to time and cultural levels, but the process has barely begun.

Among the scant studies of the peninsula's prehistory the work of Dr. William C. Massey seems most related. In the 1940's Massey made surface collections of artifacts and excavated cursorily at a few sites just south of the Great Mural area. He dubbed his aggregate finds "the Comondú cultural complex" after the major town in the area. The term was descriptive of the work of a postulated group of Native Americans whose long occupancy had produced a poorly differentiated succession of artifacts. He assumed that the Cochimí encountered in the area in historic times represented the last phase of this culture.

The Jesuits, however, found the Great Mural area occupied by Cochimí and a legend widespread among them which related that they were not the Painters nor even their direct descendants. Thus, from the outset, we seem to be denied the simplest assumption of the Painters' identity.

Several Jesuit missionaries left ethnographic writings descriptive of the people living in the Great Mural area in historic times. These works are full of references to cultural traits, crafts, rites, costume and even art; matters which tempt us to all sorts of speculation about possible ties to the rock paintings. Perfect examples are provided in reports penned by Sigismundo Taraval in 1732 while he was stationed at San Ignacio. He remarked that the *guamas*, the shaman of the Cochimí, piled their heads so high with all sorts of objects as to make ludicrous figures of themselves. Elsewhere he notes that the same medicine men had the people placate or moderate the sun by raising their arms to it.

It would be exceedingly simple to accept these firsthand accounts as explanations of two features found in the Great Murals. Many *monos* certainly have headdresses which could be silhouettes of manifold objects worked into a head of hair. All *monos* in two sierras have raised arms, and it is tempting to conclude that they were paintings of just such obeisances to the sun as Taraval described.

But available facts do not permit such conclusions. The only secure link between these peoples is their occupation in different times of the same terrain. Despite the probable lapse of centuries, the Painters faced an environment much like that of the later Cochimí. When we study the economy of the latter we learn about the Painters in the process. In visiting the shores for marine food, the Cochimí must have trod their predecessors' trails. And, when they collected the seeds of the same trees, what was more natural than to kneel at the same grindstones which their elders had left at hand? The great pool of artifacts in the region may show no radical layering of styles or techniques precisely because of the continuity or commonality of the peoples involved. The choice of the name Painters is frankly designed to circumvent controversy. Whether archaeology eventually shows that they were indeed an alien group intrusive from the north or merely an earlier phase of Cochimí culture, the name serves equally well to designate the people from whom the Great Murals sprang.

If the succession of midpeninsular peoples cannot yet be accurately distinguished, they can as a group be compared through their artifacts with others in the greater continental area. The total remains to which the Painters clearly contributed can be sifted for factors conspicuously present or absent.

The missing elements in the Great Mural region are perhaps the more striking. From the cumulative record we know that the Painters lacked a number of rather fundamental cultural attainments which were widespread in the greater Southwest. For example, they did not have permanent buildings. They practiced no form of agriculture. They made no pottery. They did not have the domestic dog.

The artifact assemblage as a whole is that of a hunting and gathering people more primitive in terms of durable remains than most other Southwest groups. Other than the paintings themselves the artifacts are poor-to-commonplace in terms of design or craft. But long-lived remains do not tell the whole story. Palaeolithic people in an environment like this created a great deal more than is suggested by their meager durable remains. Such cultures concentrated on the production of light, portable and hence ephemeral artifacts. Products crafted of wood, hide and fibers almost certainly were more evolved and differentiated than those of the stone array.

Movement was the key to life for people inhabiting the central desert of Baja California in any time. No area could support man in any numbers through the year, not even the seashore.

Along the coasts there were very few permanent springs and most of those who used marine food sources must have done so in short forays, especially after rains had filled temporary water catchments.

Elsewhere human life depended on seasonally available fruit, seeds, stems and roots. Missionary accounts and our own observation suggest that hunting was an activity which required a great deal of time and energy. It probably was not economic purely in terms of food but rather was partially ritualized as well as providing the useful by-products of meat, leather, gut, bone and decorative items.

Peoples' lives were passed in making seasonal rounds. In the summer and fall they occupied the foothills and margins of the plains where cactus produced copious fruit. Later they moved to the washes where seed-bearing trees ripened their pods. In late winter they were probably forced to the intermediate mesas to gather giant agaves whose hearts they roasted as a staple of diet.

At some time during these annual rounds the sierra upland figured as either a pass from plain to plain or as a focus of interest in itself. Most of the hunting must have taken place on the mesas and there too were the thickest accumulations of edible agaves. Several trails cross each of the midpeninsular sierras and in the heights they branch to enter mesas and *cañadas*. Along their ways are found strategically-placed circular walls of stones which the sierra people of today call hunting blinds. These trails also pass numerous smoke-blackened caves and shelters, *tinajas*, and the rings of rocks on the ground which have often been called "sleeping circles." Everywhere along the trails there are stone artifacts and seashells in such numbers as to suggest long usage.

But, if a succession of cultures occupied the sierras, only one left convincing proof that it did so for reasons other than simple economic necessity. The Painters made these places holy ground. They came to practice the higher human pursuits of magic, ritual, and symbolism. And, though they may never have thought of it in such a way at all, they left us with a vast museum of naively beautiful art.

The galleries of the Great Murals are so hushed and deserted today that it requires a real effort to imagine the activity that must have accompanied their making. The quiet and serenity of these sunlit gorges tempt us to suppose that they have always been that way and that the art works in their profusion were as much a part of creation as the warm-toned rock or the rustling palms. But the feeling passes. The paintings exercise a different fascination; there is a sense of our own kind calling out. In our minds we populate the place and imagine the scene as it might have been during the busy ceremony of decorating these walls.

THE PAINTERS AT WORK

The season was probably fall. The summer rains would have filled the *tinajas* to provide water in every corner of the sierras. For a few weeks the *pitahaya* crop could have provided the abundance of food which would have allowed a few helpers to feed themselves and the artists with ease. Temperatures at that time were moderate and the caves, especially with fires, would have provided better night shelters than most of the stops on the rounds of the Painters' lives.

When a group met to enact the painting ritual their needs extended beyond food, water, paint and brushes. As we stand today and admire the murals in the larger shelters we are acutely aware that considerable constructions must have been needed as well. Some of the figures have been rendered at heights over thirty feet above the shelter floors; this implies the use of tremendous ladders or scaffolds.

Interested people who know these places from photographs only have suggested other means by which artists might have reached such high places. A common thought is that the floor level of the shelters might once have been higher. Another solution has been proposed: these people, known to be skilled makers of cordage, let themselves down from the top in slings and worked while suspended. Inspection of the sites destroys both hypotheses at a glance. The painted shelters were not formed by a gradual wearing down of the floor in any instance but rather by the collapsing of sheets of material off the walls. In addition, much evidence involving style and preservation indicates that the highest works are usually the newest, not the oldest. The suspension idea is equally unfeasible. All the painted walls are topped by rock masses which extend up and out for great distances from the paint-

ings.

The construction of ladders or scaffolds would have been a difficult project, but the materials and technology were available. Most of the shelters containing high figures are found in or near palm-lined arroyos. The trunks of the palms range up to more than fifty feet in length. In addition the entire area is liberally supplied with *cardón*, the giant cactus whose skeleton consists of a bundle of straight wands of a light but fairly strong fibrous wood. Hunting produced hides from which thongs could have been cut. With these materials, as well as the previously mentioned cordage, it is not hard to envision constructions to facilitate painting. One possibility could have consisted of *cardón* stakes leaned each two or three feet against the desired wall and then converted to a continuous or broad ladder by having more *cardón* wands bound across them to form rungs. This mesh could have been made as wide as desired and to heights of twenty feet or more. To climb higher the Painters could have used palm trunks for vertical members.

With ladders another problem presented itself. Try to visualize an artist attempting to draw a freehand picture of man or animal ten feet high and with natural proportions. Imagine that he had to stand on a ladder which placed him very close to the wall so that he could not step back or lean back to see his entire sketch. Such obstacles clearly were not beyond the Painters' ingenuity. The problem was solved by long practice, by frequent descents of the ladder for inspection, or perhaps by constant communication with an accomplice standing at a vantage point below.

However speculative our view of these preparations, we are on firm ground as we approach the actual creation of the art. There is ample evidence to indicate that many, if not all, of the artists started by sketching the figures in chalk. Many painted figures retain vestiges of chalk outlines, and in at least a few cases sketching and painting is clearly the sequence of events. At El Brinco V, in a closely-spaced group of four nicely delineated little rabbits, two have been painted black and two more, with identical outlines, remain only sketched in white chalk. The same site has an unpainted chalk sketch of a medium-sized human figure with an elaborate headdress.

The visible remains of chalk outlines are easily confused with painted outlines. Many Great Mural works are finished with fine bands carefully painted in white, black, pink or orange. Weathering sometimes reduces these painted outlines to the superficial appearance of chalking. A close inspection, however, will readily show the difference; the painted work, even when eroded, retains flakes of solid paint too thick and regular to result from even a heavy chalking. The right end of the grand cavalcade at El Batequi (see page 38) appears on careful examination to show both sorts of outlining.

Examples of the chalks used by the Painters may very well exist to this day. Three men in the Sierra de Guadalupe and one in that of San Francisco have given me similar plausible accounts of finding chalks. Each found a small ball or stick of white or brightly-colored chalk-like substance which he tried on rock and found capable of making a good colored line. Each identified the stuff as man-made, evidently a powdered rock loosely cemented with some binder.

Paintings that retain no vestige of chalking or outlining may very well have been done with charcoal, an effective but short-lived sketching material.

Once an artist had his figures chalked on the wall, it is quite clear that he had several choices as to the precise technique of filling in the color. These differences may have had to do with the paint substances available or more likely they were dictated by the custom of his time. In any event it seems that his intention was to achieve as colorful or vivid an effect as possible.

As these works have eroded each sort has come to exhibit its own pattern of disintegration. Some of what evidently were once remains of solid color have faded away very evenly and retain the look of a wash of color until they are finally eroded to extinction. These appear to have been applied originally as a slurry which produced a thick, even coat of paint with good adherence to the rock.

Some eroded works display streaks of color. The simplest are probably no more than the deterioration of areas that were once chalked solid. These are betrayed at times by a scratched as well as colored surface. The strokes show quite clearly and are usually parallel. Another variety of streaked surface seems to result from the erosion of paint applied rather sparingly with a fairly dry brush. A few heavy strokes were probably used to get paint on the area where it was then worked around to cover. Erosion has apparently removed a good deal of the latter working and left a pattern of the heavier brush strokes. By and large the streaked works of either type appear to be among the latest of the Great Murals.

Painted outlines give much evidence of having been done with great care. At many sites there are figures in which white or occasionally pink outlines have survived better than any of the larger colored areas. On close examination these outlines prove to be composed of a heavy layer of paint probably applied as a thick slurry. In addition, the excellent survival of white paint in general suggests another factor. The Painters may well have learned some of the properties of lime and made it in simple pile-of-rock kilns. They were not lacking for materials. The arroyos are littered with dry wood and there are small pockets of limestone scattered all over the Great Mural region.

At any rate, some of the surviving white paint has a remarkably plaster-like character and there are several instances where it literally survives intact on a heavily-eroded surface and bridges over small voids in the honeycombed rock beneath. At a number of sites, including El Carrizo and Santa Isabel in the Sierra de Guadalupe, there are figures whose white-painted outlines survive virtually entire, while only the barest vestiges of the interior paint can be detected.

The longevity of all the paints and hence the works as a whole may be purely accidental. It is hard to reconcile the idea that the Painters intended their works to endure with their almost universal willingness to paint over the art of their own forefathers.

In summary, all the different painting techniques seem to have been employed toward a common goal. The Painters obviously intended to create groups of large human and animal figures impressively displayed and rendered boldly in the most brilliant available colors. A high percentage are remote and inaccessible and yet seem designed to be seen from great distances and, in fact, dominate considerable areas. This is particularly true of human figures. Animal representations may be placed so low, or on walls parallel to sight lines, that they are difficult to perceive at any distance. But *monos*, especially in large groups, are painted higher or on surfaces well exposed to even distant observers.

Rock paintings of men and animals is a world-wide phenomenon associated with palaeolithic man. The works of many ages and many different places could be described accurately in the same general terms. A few specifics are needed to characterize and distinguish the Painters' work.

The term "Great Murals" is an arbitrary one designed to recognize three characteristics of these works: their size, locations and medium. The typical site in the Great Mural region is a cave or rock shelter which displays art in the form of figures which are life-sized or greater and worked on the walls or wall-ceilings in the medium of paint. Another consistent feature is not suggested by the name Great Murals: the vast majority of the painted figures represent men or animals delineated in the clear terms of a formal realism. An analysis of these works demonstrates forcefully that their production was not casual or the product of individual inspirations or self-expression. On the contrary, they betray the presence of a remarkably rigid code. For example, each creature has a characteristic and invariable aspect. Men are seen head-on with arms extended upward in a gesture suggestive of the classic "I surrender" pose of our culture. Deer, mountain sheep, antelope, rabbits, mountain lion, coyote and wild cat are shown in an active profile as if running or leaping. Fish and turtle are depicted in dorsal view. Birds appear as if seen from below while in flight with the peculiarity of having their heads turned in profile, probably in order to display the beak.

In spite of their obviously representational character, the "naturalism" of the Great Murals was actually subject to a number of formal and arbitrary usages. Man is presented in a generally head-on view and the upraised arms and flat view of the extended hands are natural enough. But the feet are turned outward and then rotated spatially so that they alone appear as if seen from above, that is, as a flat foot with toes extended. This display of the feet and toes is a form of twisted perspective created in the minds of artists and not possible in reality. It shows that these figures are ideagraphs of men and not in any sense sketches. In addition, there are features which could be depicted readily in the generally realistic outline but are regularly and conspicuously missing. These include ears and genitalia.

Woman is distinguished from man only by the addition of rather long pointed breasts which are presented as in double profile and hence appear to issue from each arm-pit. This convention is quite analogous to the treatment of the similarly oriented feet.

Sexual distinctions in animals seem to be limited to those portrayable by the presence or absence or differences in horns or antlers. Some paintings seem to suggest pregnancy. However, the observable spread of body types in each species ranges from thin to heavy; it is impossible to say which ones might have been intended to represent pregnancy.

Twisted perspective is not the strangest facet of the Painters' "reality." Only the outlines or silhouettes of their figures have any observable relation to the men or beasts depicted. All of the anatomical features which should appear *within* the diagnostic outline are missing. Human figures never display eyes, noses or mouths, for example. The animals portrayed in profile, or with head only in profile, such as birds, do have mouths and noses, or their equivalent, but never eyes. All of this obviously follows a rule: only the outline drawing is representational; all that lies within is some sort of conventional abstraction.

In the majority of the painted figures the characteristic and formalized outline is simply filled with a layer of paint undifferentiated in hue or density. However, an additional large minority of figures are bicolored and the areas of the two colors form a wide variety of conventionalized patterns. Some of these are so relatively rare that only the perusal of dozens or hundreds of sites proves that they have precedents.

It is in this area of the infill patterns that we see the greatest distinction between the works of the Painters in the several sierras. San Borja, the most northerly, exhibits Great Murals almost exclusively infilled with a plain red wash.

San Francisco follows suit but adds solid black and the very common red-and-black bicolored figures. Men, fish, birds, and turtles painted in two colors are divided vertically; other animals normally are red with black bellies and inner legs. In the Sierra de San Francisco there are also figures which are striped, but this is a statistically rare pattern of infill.

In the Sierra de Guadalupe we find all these and more. As we view them ever farther south, there is an increasing incidence of checkerboard infills. *Monos* are very likely to be filled in with vertical lines so regular as to make them look like the segmented trunks of *cardón* or *viznaga* cactus.

Throughout the range of the Great Murals and at virtually every site there are to be found numerous small figures in sizes from under a foot to two feet in extent. While these do not meet the arbitrary size criterion assigned to Great Murals, the techniques and subject matter are so similar as to suggest simultaneous creation. These small figures are usually placed low in any total display.

This simple review of the Great Murals' obvious characteristics falls far short of answering many of the questions they raise. We cannot cite any evidence which explains why the figures have realistic outlines and fanciful internal details. Or why each sort of creature seems frozen into the mode of a particular attitude. We cannot explain the presence or absence of arrows or spears in different figures or different sites. Without archaeological research and a great deal more study of the figures not much can be said about their origin, development, or decline. Such enlightenment will follow when human priorities will it.

But these paintings are the only present message from the Painters and that message is not so cryptic that it cannot be read at all. The elements of tradition and discipline are strikingly evident. The very fact that so many conventions were observed over a considerable period of time argues that these people knew how to practice and accept authority. The painted record also betrays a degree of tribal organization which supported a class of artists, probably not full-time but certainly for some significant periods. This support apparently extended beyond the mere feeding of a materially non-productive group. It included making long trips to provide special colored rocks and then the great deal of labor needed to grind them into suitable pigments. Other large outlays of labor were required to collect materials and erect scaffoldings.

The fact that similar but not identical paintings are found over large areas bespeaks a high degree of rather specific communication. The mechanisms are still obscure; we do not know if the Painters' conventions were transmitted by word of mouth, by means of sketches, or by visits between groups who actually viewed each other's art. But whatever the mode, complex communications took place and the resulting work has a codified relatedness reminiscent of that seen in centuries of Russian icons or millenia of Chinese brush paintings.

Much of what we see and feel in the lofty aspirations and esthetic accomplishments of the Painters' art seems at odds with the poverty of their other material remains. No doubt this is due in part to our own technical bias. Western man has always tended to evaluate other cultures on the basis of their material achievements. The Great Murals perhaps remind us that man at his simplest is a complex proposition.

DATING THE PAINTERS

On the fourth of July of 1054 A.D., as reckoned by the Julian calendar, a brilliant object appeared in the heavens in the constellation Taurus. It was visible in broad daylight for twenty-three days and at night for over six hundred more. The event was reported by Chinese astronomers of the Sung Dynasty in a record called the *Sung-Shih*. That record, by a fortuitous chain of circumstances, may be instrumental in dating the epoch of the Great Murals.

During the '20s and '30s of this century, the American astronomer, Edwin Powell Hubble, conducted his renowned studies of celestial nebulae. During this research he proposed that the great Crab Nebula had had its origin about 900 years previously in a supernova explosion. He noted the coincidence in time and location suggested by the *Sung-Shih*. Further studies and calculations by others strengthened this theory. It is now well accepted that the Chinese saw and recorded the birth of the Crab Nebula.

Another American astronomer, William C. Miller of the Mt. Wilson and Palomar Observatories, has calculated that just before the dawn of July 5, 1054, there was a spectacular conjunction of the brilliant supernova and the crescent moon. The event was visible only in Western North America. In 1955, this work was published by Miller in a paper calling attention to the fact that at least two examples of Indian rock art in northern Arizona apparently have recorded the remarkable astronomical occurrence. Miller advanced a number of circumstantial but compelling arguments. The paintings did appear to show just such an occurrence in graphic detail, the use of crescent symbols in any other way was rare or absent in the area, and archaeologists showed that both sites had been occupied during that time.

Subsequently, John C. Brandt, a third American astronomer, and his co-workers have extended Miller's research, confirming his calculations and adding several examples to the list of painted representations of the event.

In the fall of 1971, I noticed a rather small painting on the roof of a slit cave in the Arroyo del Parral of the Sierra de San Francisco. It showed a circle, with rays like a conventional sun symbol, quite close to a larger moon-like object (see page 30). I was immediately struck by its uniqueness. Even at that rather early date in my investigations I was aware of the rarity of abstract symbols of any sort in the Great Mural heartland. Knowing the Painters' propensity for depicting real objects such as men, animals, arrows and spears, I at first assumed that the painting represented the sun and the moon or, even more likely because of their relative sizes, Jupiter or Venus and the Moon.

Later, on reading a newspaper account of Dr. Brandt's work, I was impressed by the similarity of the art he described to that which I had seen. All the pieces seemed to fit. Here too, in my region, such symbols were rare, in fact, rarer than in most of those places where the other supposed supernova paintings were made. If the Painters had been inclined to depict ordinary celestial events, surely there would have been other pictures of the sun, moon, and stars. All my searches have turned up no such works, even

the simple circle is virtually unknown among the Great Murals. It is tempting to conclude along with Miller, Brandt and others that only the sudden apparition of a body so brilliant that it shone by day, and one that may well have first been seen in the company of the moon, moved them to the unusual act of picturing the event. When I sent Dr. Brandt a photograph of the painting in El Parral his response encouraged the supposition. "The painting to my eyes very clearly resembles the other representations of the supernova."

If we accept, for the moment, the hypothesis that the figure in El Parral really represents an event observed in 1054 A.D., then this small painting takes on extreme significance and deserves a close examination.

The work is quite faded and deteriorated. At first glance it would be tempting to judge it as relatively old, at least in comparison to the strikingly well-preserved deer (page 30) painted nearby on the same surface. There is other evidence, however. This cave has a classic formation; its roof was once a hard layer of rock in intimate contact with a soft layer below. That soft layer has weathered away almost entirely to a depth of fifteen feet or so, hence the cave. However, the roof of the cave still has some rather extensive flakes of the softer rock adhering to it. All of the "moon" and part of the "supernova" are painted on this softer relief from the harder and flatter true ceiling material. These parts of the work have suffered the deterioration. At times in the history of the painting, water has percolated through the roof (or passed through cracks) and has been held by these flakes of more porous material. Here it evaporated leaving a deposit of its dissolved solids. This residue, called caliche, also affected the color of paint on this surface. Fortunately the remainder of the supernova is on the harder, unstained part of the ceiling. Here it is in excellent condition and we see its true color, a rather brownish-red as opposed to the rose-pink of the stained area.

Once we understand some of the factors which have affected this painting, it can be compared to others within the same shelter and perhaps, by a shakier extrapolation, with paintings at other sites. Many such comparisons suggest no evidence that the work is either remarkably older or newer than the average of the Great Murals.

There are more conventional dating methods

available; both nuclear and chemical techniques are now in use to fix the ages of archaeological specimens. Unfortunately neither applies readily to the problem. Carbon 14 methods, "radiocarbon dating," want significant quantities of carbon of organic origin for isotopic analysis. The paintings prove to contain very little. The black pigment which survives so well at some sites is apparently a complex of metallic oxides. Where carbon is the pigment, collecting the several grams required for analysis would strip square yards of paintings.

Another potentially applicable dating technique involves quantitative measurements of amino acids which undergo time-related changes. Dr. Jeffrey Bada made such a study on paint from a Great Mural site. The results were frustrating from the dating standpoint at least; the amino acid content of the paint was too low to allow any age determination.

Dr. Meighan is responsible for the sole reported radiocarbon determination from the Great Mural area. During his 1962 visit to Gardner Cave he gathered many artifacts, a collection to which I have referred. Among these was a wooden peg which was submitted to C^{14} study. The age of the wood proved to be 530 plus or minus 80 years. But how are we to interpret this with reference to the paintings? The peg was taken from below the floor surface of a heavily-painted cave. No paint or debris connected specifically with paintings was associated in any way with the peg. Meighan points out that the artifact assemblage as a whole is quite homogeneous and fits well with Massey's Comondú cultural complex. In his opinion the radiocarbon date places this assemblage in time and shows a period when the cave was occupied. In the absence of other significantly different artifacts, we must conclude either that the people of the peg painted the walls, or that the painters left no other artifacts, or at least none that are distinguishable. Dr. Meighan, being positive, practical, and scarcely preferring the romance of uncertainty to the security of data, chooses to place paint and painters in the Comondú complex and the time in the period 530 ± 80 years before 1962. Meighan then indulges in a bit of unexplained conjecture when he chooses to regard his C^{14} finding as the probable end of the painting period and to place its beginning at 500 years before that.

Perhaps the easiest date which we can fix for the paintings is the latest time at which the art could have been practiced. There is much evidence in the writings of the pioneer Jesuits. Nearly all we know of the natives aboriginal condition is from Jesuit accounts. These same Jesuits included some intrepid travellers and explorers, men who got out and knew the Cochimí living in the field as well as those who occupied missions. From the first years of contact there survive a few documents by eyewitnesses which deal in some depth with ethnography. None of these mentions rock painting as a contemporary activity.

Fathers Consag, Barco, Link and Ducrue have left us extensive reports on the historic Cochimí. They lived and worked at missions which were surrounded by many kinds of rock art sites, yet they refer to no current practices in that medium. It will be recalled that two Jesuits, Joseph Rothea and Francisco Escalante, actually visited Great Mural sites and became interested enough to write reports of their observations which were quoted in full earlier in this work. Both made inquiries among their native charges concerning the origin of the rock paintings and both reported folkloric accounts of a giant people from the north who painted in the sierras. Each seems to accept the Indians' legend at least as a reasonable indication of age because neither makes any comment to indicate disagreement. Additionally, each betrays a private opinion that the works were old. Since these eyewitness accounts document the earliest examinations of Great Murals of which we have any known record, it is worth examining their pertinent parts:

Rothea:
"The *durability* of these colors seemed notable to me; being there on the exposed rock in the inclemencies of sun and water where they are no doubt struck by rain, strong wind or water that filters through these same rocks from the hill above, with all this, *after much time*, they remain highly visible."

Joseph Mariano Rothea is a remarkable figure in the history of the San Ignacio area. He worked unusually closely with the chiefs of the various *rancherías* that comprised his mission. Under his direction were built several stone chapels at *visitas*, the visiting stations at satellite ranches. He also supervised the construction of the great dike, La Muralla, in the wash of Arroyo San Ignacio. He planned and partially built the great church of that mission. In the course of these labors he came to know the environs, the climate and the people as few others have. For example, he discovered, no doubt with native guidance, the sources of such stones as *cantera* and *tezontle* needed for the walls, vaults, and tower of his church. Significantly, his *tezontle* quarry lies on a mesa in the Sierra de San Francisco. The clearly-marked mission trail to that area passes within sight of rock art concentrated in the Arroyo del Parral. When this man comments on durability it is clear that he felt that the quality had been tested. Even without his subsequent and unequivocal time reference, "after much time," it is clear that Rothea was referring to something he assumed to be remarkable for its age.

Escalante:
(as quoted by Miguel del Barco): "These paintings are well preserved, clear and perceivable."

Once again the author's intent is clear. One does not flatly refer to something as well-preserved unless he assumes that it is also old.

As further evidence, if the reader will bother to re-read the quotes just given and compare them to the photographs in this book, he will find, over two hundred years after the descriptions were penned, that they apply to many works in their present state with perfect aptness. It should also be recalled that a comparison of Diguet's photo of Los Monos de San Juan with the actual site some eighty years later showed no apparent change. These observations can certainly be used as arguments for the antiquity of the Great Murals.

But even if we can satisfy ourselves with the validity of their opinions, the Jesuit chroniclers could scarcely provide absolute dates. We can only guess at the age that would have so impressed them and elicited such remarks. To be on secure ground all we can do is fix the latest possible date for any of the Great Murals at a time shortly before the missionaries came. This puts their creation back about four hundred years if we allow any time for them to have acquired the appearance of age.

A footnote can be added to this conclusion

that all rock art was created prior to the coming of the Europeans. In many other parts of the world including Cambodia, Australia, South Africa, and the American Southwest, various forms of rock art were being practiced at the time of contact with western culture. In each of these places depictions of European people or their animals, garb, or implements soon followed. Among the Great Murals not one such example can be found. This does nothing to strengthen any belief that the painting tradition was active into the mission period.

Here rests, at present, the case for absolute dates. New data are needed, new techniques may be required. It is clear that one of our most pressing questions hangs in the air unanswered.

As a final note on dating it should be inserted in the record that the Great Murals exhibit a characteristic which allows anyone to fix the relative ages of many of the painted figures.

Overpainting is almost synonymous with the Great Murals. Each generation of the ancients, unmindful of our interests, buried much of what had been painted before, but that act of overpainting is a curse that may prove in another application to be a blessing. Overpainting is obviously sequential, that is, the work on top is newest and so on back to the one which is painted on bare rock or at least is the earliest distinguishable work.

During my preoccupation with the Great Murals, I have been asked no question more frequently than that of their age. As a result, I offer here as much as I know or can reasonably speculate. This opinion, and that is all that it is, is influenced by the evidence already cited and by whatever insight can be gained from living with these works for a long time. I believe that the Great Mural period was about a thousand years in length and that it extended from roughly 500 A.D. to 1500 A.D. This would seem to me to agree very well with such disparate pieces of evidence as Dr. Meighan's wooden peg, the apparent age differences of first and last layers at El Batequi, the supernova, and our general knowledge of climate and the rise and fall of other cultures in the Greater Southwest. It is to be hoped that the matter will not end here. New evidence surely will be found and new minds to weigh it.

Glossary

In some cases the words or usages in this text are peculiar to parts of Baja California and are not found in a standard Spanish-English dictionary.

ancón, a bank or shelf of level ground just above the wash of a watercourse

angostura, a narrows; a narrow part of an arroyo

aura, the common bald vulture

bahía, a bay on ocean or gulf

berrendo, the pronghorn antelope (Antilocapra americana)

borrego, the bighorn sheep or mountain sheep (Ovis canadensis)

brinco, a leap or jump; a place which forces one to jump

caja, the bed or wash of a watercourse

cañada, a watercourse tributary to an arroyo

cañón, an impressively steep-walled narrow watercourse; gorge

cantera, a volcanic agglomerate stone easily worked with hand tools

cantil, a high rock palisade; usually the broken edge of a flow of volcanic stone

cantilería, an impressive array of *cantil; cantil en masse*

cardón, the giant cactus (Pachycereus pringlei); vertical, usually branched and grows to over 50 feet in height

cirio, a columnar plant (Idria columnaris); usually a single unbranched stalk to 40 or more feet

comida, food in general; the midday meal

cuesta, a steep trail up the slope of an arroyo or mountainside

cueva, a cave or large rock shelter

cuevona, an unusually large cave, the largest cave in a region

datilillo, a giant yucca (Yucca valida), similar to the Joshua tree

dueño, owner; proprietor; landlord; master

falda, the slope of a hill; literally, a skirt

huerta, an orchard; a vegetable garden

león, the mountain lion or puma (Felis concolor)

mano, a hand grindstone worked on the surface of a *metate*

metate, a mortar, a grindstone; usually hollowed to mate with the surface of a *mano*

mezcal, any of several native agaves

mezquite, a common arroyo tree (Prosopis juliflora)

mono, a caricature, a drawing of a human figure

paraje, a stopping place; usually has the necessities for passing the night

pilón, pylon; sugar loaf; shaped like a pylon or sugar loaf

pinturita, a small or miniature painting

portezuelo, a high pass between hills

pueblito, a hamlet, a tiny pueblo

ranchería, a settlement of Indians who lived and moved together seasonally; the headquarters of such a group

respaldo, an overhung rock face

salto, a waterfall; the site of a seasonal falls

tezontle, a basaltic rock made light by inclusive gas bubbles

tinaja, a natural water catchment

vaquero, a cowboy

visita, a visiting station; a place outside a mission visited periodically by a priest to hold services

zalate, the native fig tree (Ficus palmeri) which grows to great proportions in the southern half of Baja California

Bibliography

Aschmann, Homer
    1959 *The Central Desert of Baja California: Demography and Ecology*. Ibero-Americana, No. 42. Berkeley and Los Angeles. 1967 Reprint of preceding. Riverside.

Aschmann, Homer, Ed.
    1966 *The Natural and Human History of Baja California*. Baja California Travels Series, No. 7. Dawson's Book Shop, Los Angeles.

Barco, Miguel del
    1973 [Adiciones y Correcciones a la Noticia de Miguel Venegas] Edited by Miguel

León-Portilla and published under the title: *Historia Natural y Crónica de la Antigua California*. Universidad Nacional Autónoma de México, México 1973.

Brandt, John C. and Maran, Stephen P. et al
"Possible Rock Art Records of the Crab Nebula Supernova in the Western United States." In: *Archaeoastronomy in Pre-Columbian America*, edited by A. F. Aveni, University of Texas Press, Austin, Texas (in preparation).

Clavijero, Francisco Javier
1852 *Historia de la Antigua o Baja California*. Juan Navarro, Mexico. (Originally published in Italian in 1789; available in English:
1937 *The History of [Lower] California*, translated by Sara E. Lake and A. A. Gray. Stanford University Press. pp. 84-85. Reprinted 1971, Riverside, Manessier.

Dahlgren, Barbro, and Javier Romero
1951 "La Prehistoria Baja California; Redescubrimiento de Pinturas Rupestres." *Cuadernos Americanos*, 58: 162-176.

Dahlgren de Jordán, Barbro
1954 "Las Pinturas Rupestres de la Baja California." *Artes de México*, 3: 22-28.

Diguet, Léon
1895 "Note sur la Pictographie de la Basse-Californie." *Anthropologie*, 6: 160-175.
1899 "Rapport sur une Mission Scientifique dans la Basse-Californie." *Nouvelle Archives des Missions Scientifiques*, 9: 1-53.
1912 *Baja California: Reseña Geográfica y Estadística*. Mexico City.

Gardner, Erle Stanley
1962a "A Legendary Treasure Left by a Long Lost Tribe." *Life*, 53 (3): 57-64.
1962b *The Hidden Heart of Baja*. New York, Morrow.
1967 *Off the Beaten Track in Baja*. New York, Morrow.

Grant, Campbell
1974 *Rock Art of Baja California* (with: "Notes on the Pictographs of Baja California" by Léon Diguet [1895] translated by Roxanne Lapidus). Dawson's Book Shop, Los Angeles, California.

López, Ernesto Raúl
1970 "Nuevos Hallazgos de Pinturas Rupestres en Baja California." *Calafía*, 1 (2): 19-25. Translation in Pacific Coast Archaeological Society *Quarterly*, 8 (1): 10-14.

Massey, William C.
1947 Brief Report on Archaeological Investigations in Baja California. *Southwestern Journal of Anthropology*, Vol. 3, No. 4, pp. 344-59. Albuquerque.
1949 Tribes and Languages of Baja California. *Southwestern Journal of Anthropology*, Vol. 5, No. 3, pp. 272-307. Albuquerque.
1961a The Cultural Distinction of Aboriginal Baja California. In *Homenaje a Pablo Martínez del Rio*, pp. 411-22. Mexico.

Meighan, Clement W.
1966 "Prehistoric Rock Painting in Baja California." *American Antiquity*, 31 (3): 372-392.
1969 *Indian Art and History, the Testimony of Prehispanic Rock Paintings in Baja California*. Los Angeles, Dawson's Book Shop. Baja California Travels Series 13.

Miller, William C.
1955 "Two Prehistoric Drawings of Possible Astronomical Significance." Astronomical Society of the Pacific, San Francisco, California. Leaflet No. 314 — July, 1955.

Mugazábal, Juan Bautista (?)
1946 In: Bayle, Constantino, *Misión de la Baja California*. Madrid: Editorial Catolica.

Ten Kate, Herman
1883 "Quelques Observations Ethnographiques recueillies dans la Presqu'ile Californienne et en Sonora." *Revue d'Ethnographie*, 11: 321-326.

Acknowledgements

Most of the people who assisted in the pursuit of the Great Murals have become part of the story on these pages, but a few must be added or singled out for especially heartfelt thanks.

Enrique Hambleton accompanied me on three of the last and longest explorations. He assisted and backed me up in many ways, his presence providing invaluable companionship and insurance against the innumerable and unforeseeable problems that arise in remote parts. I am also indebted to him for the photographs which appear on pages 2, 47, and 155 (upper) and assistance in perusing and translating documents in Spanish.

Marie Christine Meynet Forester devoted herself to translating long passages of the writings of Leon Diguet with great care so that several questions could be answered which were complicated by that explorer's colloquial and imprecisely written French.

Dr. Ray F. Weiss and Dr. Jeffrey Bada of Scripps Institution of Oceanography devoted time and their invaluable skills to the analysis of certain materials pertinent to this study.

Ristin Crosby Decker, my elder daughter, contributed the carefully restored facsimile of the painted ceiling at El Batequi which appears on pp. 10-11. This painstaking reconstruction was made from many photographs and her own observations during a visit to the site.

Joanne Crosby, my wife, apart from her contributions to the art of this book, typed the entire manuscript and managed our family and affairs during my necessarily extended absences. The whole project should be considered a cooperative effort.

Index

A FINAL NOTE:

LEON DIGUET AMONG THE GREAT MURALS

Diguet closed his 1895 publication, "Notes on the Pictographs of Baja California," with "a list of localities where one can observe specimens. ..." There followed a list numbered to thirty of which the first eighteen fell in or near the Great Mural area.

1. Cave of el Zalate near the 29°, about fifteen leagues from Calamahi, [Calmallí] near the road from Calamahi to San Borga [San Borja].
2. Cave of el Carmen, between Calamahi [Calmallí] and Santa Gertrudis.
3. Santa Gertrudis, a cave in a cañada opening into the arroyo, across from the mission.
4. Between Santa Gertrudis and puerto Trinidad, near the highest point of the cuesta de San Juan.
5. Cave, a few leagues away from the rancho of San Pablo, near the 28°.
6. Rock shelter one league from the rancho of San Pablo, on the way to Calamahi [Calmallí].
7. The sierra of San Francisco, the rock shelters of Palmarito and of Cuesta blanca and of cueva del Raton, at the height of the sierra and near the rancho of San Francisco.
8. Cañada del Muerto, near the 27°: petroglyphs and cliff with paintings.
9. San Juan in the arroyo of San Pedro.
10. San Matillita, [San Matiitas], cañada opening into the arroyo of San Adeo [San Tadeo].
11. San Adeo [San Tadeo], rock shelter near the rancho.
12. Petroglyphs in the arroyo of las Piedras Pintas, near Mulege.
13. Paintings in a cañada, near the rancho de Trinidad, about ten leagues from Mulege.
14. Paintings in the sierra of Guadalupe, near the ranchos of Guadalupe, San Isabel [Santa Isabel] and of el Pozo.
15. San Borgita [San Borjitas], near the rancho de San Baltazar, 10 leagues from Mulege.
16. Arroyo de Guajadami a few deer painted in the caves and one stone covered with petroglyphs.
17. A cliff with paintings near the rancho of San Jose, in the arroyo de Guajadami.
18. Paintings in a cañada, near the rancho of la Purissima Vieja.

In the past few years this list has been referred to frequently as a gradual awareness of Baja California rock art diffused among scholars and *aficionados*. But those who have used the work have called it vague and inaccurate and some have despaired of finding most of the sites thus listed. Actually, with some fieldwork and by making a few cautious assumptions most of it can be interpreted.

Inconsistency is perhaps the severest obstacle. Some sites are pinpointed (like #4), others are unspecific to the extent of many miles (like #2). Some specify whether paintings or petroglyphs were to be found, others do not. Most refer to single sites but in two cases (#7 and #14), three sites are grouped which are actually miles apart. Finally, the list in general seems to start in the north and work south but there is obvious confusion of this plan in #5, 6, 7, as well as in #14 and 15. In these cases there is either a reversal or a severe doubling back.

The most probable reason for this inconsistent report was that Diguet did not visit all sites himself. He certainly employed guides and when he found that they were reliable and led him to good examples of rock art, he probably asked them about other sites. This could account for odd groupings like #7 and 14.

On the positive side, most of the place names used by Diguet demonstrably survive in the areas involved. Allowing for a few spelling errors by Diguet and making the probable corrections, (in brackets in the list above) only two out of the thirty place names used in #1-18 remain stubbornly obscure. These are the Caves of El Zalate and El Carmen in items #1 and 2. The former of these may be truly lost. A cave with a huge, spreading zalate tree issuing from its mouth would be notable. But these trees are also fairly shortlived. For this reason the name has appeared, mostly ephemerally, in many parts of southern Baja California. El Carmen may simply require more research; little effort has been made to tap the memories of appropriate people.

Locating the remaining placenames does not locate all the art. Items like #5 will always be open to question because of vagueness. Nevertheless, most of the remainder are feasible. The present work describes the probable sites and art for #4, 7, 8, 9, 13, 14, 15, 16 and 17. In addition it gives probable locations for #10, and 11. #12 is well-known.

There may always be a bit of mystery about the travels of Leon Diguet but, by referring to the above and reading his articles and noting what he considered important enough to describe, photograph and draw, we must conclude that we know most of the Great Murals which he was able to contact.